MORE WAY'S TO A MAN'S HEART

Compiled by the Helpful '8'

Edited by
GILLIAN BURR
Assisted by Susan Stone

VALLENTINE, MITCHELL

First published in Great Britain by
VALLENTINE, MITCHELL & CO. LTD.
Gainsborough House, Gainsborough Road,
London E11 1RS

First Edition 1976
Second Edition 1980
Third Edition 1992

ISBN 0 85303 256 4

*Cover photograph: Carol Cutner
China and cutlery by Chinacraft
Drawings: Michael Enfield*

*Printed in Great Britain by
Hartnolls Limited, Bodmin, Cornwall*

Dear Cooks,

Well, here it is, we have finally completed our second book. We hope it will be as successful as the first. The popularity of that book was due to your fabulous recipes, and the refugees helped by Central British Fund are more than grateful for its success. All the royalties from this second book will again be donated to the Central British Fund.

We would like to thank — Betty Ashe, Anne Aubrey, Lesley Bennett, Gillian Burr, Gloria Brown, Charlotte Davis, Faith Duke, Janet Dwek, Jo Garetto, Sheilah Goodman, Valerie Green, Valerie Halpern, Phyllis Kilstock, Renata Knobil, Dianna Marks, Wendy Max, Caroline Posnansky, Valerie Ross, Carol Stone, Linda Stone, Susan Stone, Karoll Solomons, Mavis Sotnick, Yaffa Wagner, Bondi Zimmerman and all our other numerous friends who have helped to make this book possible.

The Helpful '8' Committee.

This book is dedicated to the memory
of our dear friend, the late
Diane Zimmerman

Contents

DRY MEASURE

	1	oz	30	gms
	2	oz	50	gms
	3	oz	80	gms
	3½	oz	100	gms
(¼ lb)	4	oz	100	gms
	5	oz	150	gms
	6	oz	175	gms
	7	oz	200	gms
(½ lb)	8	oz	225	gms
(¼ kilo)	8¾	oz	250	gms
	9	oz	250	gms
	10	oz	275	gms
	11	oz	300	gms
	12	oz	350	gms
	13	oz	375	gms
	14	oz	400	gms
	15	oz	425	gms
(1 lb)	16	oz	450	gms
(½ kilo)	17½	oz	500	gms
	1½	lbs	700	gms

LIQUID MEASURE

1 tablespoon	1 tablespoon
2 tablespoon	2 tablespoon (½ DL)
3 tablespoon	3 tablespoon
4 tablespoon	4 tablespoon
5 tablespoon	1 decilitre
6 tablespoon	1¼ decilitre
8 tablespoon (¼ pint)	1½ decilitre
¼ pint — generous	2 decilitre
½ pint — scant	¼ litre (2½ DL)
½ pint	3 decilitre
¾ pint	½ litre — scant
¾ pint — generous	½ litre
1 pint	½ litre — generous
1¼ pints	¾ litre
1½ pints	1 litre — scant
1¾ pints	1 litre
2 pints	1 litre — generous
2½ pints	1¼ litres
3 pints	1½ litres
3½ pints	2 litres
4 pints	2¼ litres
4¼ pints	2½ litres
5 pints	3 litres

OVEN TEMPERATURE GUIDE

Gas No.	Fahrenheit	Centigrade	Description
¼	250	120	
½	275	140	Very Cool
¾	288	145	
1	300	150	
2	325	160	Cool or Slow
3	350	180	
4	360	185	Moderate
5	375	190	
6	400	200	Moderately Hot
7	425	220	
8	450	230	Hot
9	475	240	Very Hot

2 level tablespoons of flour = 1 oz.
A British pint = 20 fl. ozs.
A British cup = 10 fl. ozs.

1 level tablespoon of sugar = 1 oz.
An American pint = 16 fl. ozs.
An American cup = 8 fl. ozs.

When making American recipes always use American measuring spoons.

All gas temperatures given are prior to conversion to Natural Gas.

Please note that Kosher Gelatine or vegetarian substitute may be used by the Orthodox Jewish housewife. All packet instructions must be carefully followed. This also applies to the following items:— cheese, margarine and biscuits.

Dips & Starters

Ideas for cocktails:--

For slimmers use a slice of cucumber instead of crackers.

Fill celery sticks with cottage cheese.

Place a slice of hardboiled egg on buttered ritz biscuits then put ½ teaspoon of black lumpfish (mock) caviar in centre of each egg yolk.

Dip whole small mushrooms in egg and breadcrumbs, fry till golden -- serve with sauce tartar for starter.

Cut prunes lengthways to remove stones, fill with cream cheese and sprinkle with paprika.

Split part cooked courgettes in half lengthways, remove seeds and fill cavity with chopped liver, sprinkle with breadcrumbs and heat in moderate oven. Serve with sprig of parsley.

An attractive cocktail display can be made by putting squares of cheese followed by a pineapple chunk and a maraschino cherry on a cocktail stick and then sticking it into a grapefruit or orange which has had a slice cut from the bottom to enable it to balance.

Add a tablespoon of mayonnaise to a tin of mashed tuna fish, sardines or liver sausage and place on toast or crackers.

Mash a small tin of salmon or tuna, add beaten egg, seasonings, chopped onion and matzo meal, roll into small balls, coat with matzo meal or chopped nuts and deep fry. Serve immediately.

For speedier bar-tending: when filling an ice-cube tray, drop a quarter-slice of lemon in each section.

Accompaniments To Cocktails

AUBERGINE DIP
(Armenian Recipe)

Nadia Kalindjian

Serves 8   Preparation 45 mins.   Cook 30 mins.   Advance   Freezable

2 Large aubergines
½ cup tahina (available at most health
stores or delicatessens)
Juice of 3-4 lemons
1 crushed clove garlic

1 finely chopped small onion
Salt and pepper
Paprika pepper
1 tablespoon chopped parsley
3-4 tablespoons olive oil

Grill the aubergines until very soft inside. When cool peel them. Put all ingredients into electric blender for a few moments until everything is well blended into a paste. Pour into a serving dish and decorate the top with chopped parsley and red pepper. Serve with fresh french bread or toast.

AVOCADO DIP

Betty Dill

Serves 8   Preparation 10 mins.

2 avocados

Well seasoned French dressing

Mash 1½ avocados until smooth. Season with french dressing. Chop remaining ½ avocado and stir into the mixture.

GUACOMOLE AVOCADO

Debbie Smith

Serves 12   Preparation 15 mins.

4 avocados
1 teaspoon salt
2 tablespoons lemon juice
½ teaspoon Worcester sauce

1 medium tomato
1 small onion
$\frac{1}{8}$ teaspoon tabasco

Mash avocados well with fork. Chop onion very finely also the tomato. Add all other ingredients and stir well. Serve with crackers and dip chips.

LIPTAUR CHEESE

Susan Stone

Serves 8   Preparation 15 mins.   Advance

¼ lb. cream cheese (100 grms)
1 chopped spring onion
2 teaspoons paprika

2 teaspoons caraway seeds
A little milk (optional)

Mix all ingredients together except milk. Only add milk if mixture is too dry. Leave to chill. N.B. stale grated cheddar or any dry cheese can be used instead of cream cheese. A little more milk will be needed in this case.

NUTTY CHEESE DIP

Faith Duke

Serves 12   Preparation 5 mins.

8 oz. butter (225 grms)
6 oz. finely grated cheddar cheese (175 grms)
4 tablespoons smooth peanut butter
4 oz. salted peanuts (100 grms)

¼ pint double cream (2 dl)
Salt and pepper
A little milk if necessary

Beat butter until creamy, beat in cheese and peanut butter. Stir in peanuts. Whip cream until slightly thickened, add salt and pepper. If necessary add a little milk if too stiff. Chill until needed.

ONION DIP

Valerie Green

Serves 8   Preparation 5 mins.   Resting time 30 mins.

½ lb cream cheese (200 grms)
1 carton creamed smetana
Salt, pepper

½ packet dried onion soup mix
6 chopped spring onions
Paprika

Blend cream cheese with ⅔ smetana until smooth add onion soup mix and onions and seasonings to taste. Leave to rest and if needed add rest of smetana. Decorate with paprika and serve with carrots and crisps.

PINEAPPLE & COTTAGE CHEESE DIP

Faith Duke

Serves 12   Preparation 15 mins.

1 lb. cottage cheese (450 grms)
½ lb coarsely chopped pineapple (225 grms)

A little whipped cream.
A little cointreau

Combine pineapple with a little whipped cream. Sieve the cottage cheese. Combine both mixtures and add a little cointreau to taste.

RED CURRANT DIP

Rusty Sotnick

Serves 8   Preparation 15 mins.

3 tablespoons red-currant jelly
¼ pt. whipped cream (2dl).
8 ozs. cottage cheese (225 grms)

4 teaspoons white horseradish sauce
Salt and pepper

Melt jelly over low heat. Add remaining ingredients.

9

AVOCADO CANAPES

Betty Dill

Makes 32   Preparation 10 mins.

1 avocado pear	Garlic Salt
4 slices of bread	Pepper

Make small oblong croûtons. Mash the avocado with garlic salt and pepper to taste, and serve on croûtons.

CHEESE CRESCENTS

Jane Manuel

Makes 36   Preparation 10 mins.   Gas No. 8 (450°)   Cook 15 mins.   Advance   Freezable

12 ozs. puff pastry (350 grms)	½ crushed garlic
6 ozs. cooking cheese (175 grms)	1 level teapoon chopped parsley
8 ozs. grated cheese (225 grms)	Salt & Black pepper
1 large egg – little of egg mixed	Sesame seeds
with 1 tablespoon of oil	1 tablespoon chopped onion

Blend cheeses, add egg and seasonings. Cut pastry into 2″ rounds. Put 1 tbls. of fillings onto each round and press into crescents and seal. Place on ungreased trays and cover with foil and refrigerate until needed. Remove foil. Brush with egg and oil and sprinkle with sesame seeds. Serve hot. Can be frozen raw or kept in refrigerator for 2 days.

CHEESE NUTS

Joan Stiebel

Makes 20 approx.   Preparation 10 mins.   Gas No. 8 (450°)   Cook 10 mins.   Advance

5 ozs. flour (150 grms)	Salt
4 ozs. butter (100 grms)	Cayenne pepper
3 ozs. grated cheese (80 grms)	

Mix flour, cheese, cayenne and salt. Knead in butter. Shape into small balls and press with thumb. Bake in middle of oven.

HOT CHEESE PUFFS

Charlotte Davis

Makes 15   Prepartion 20 mins.   Cook 10 mins.

1 oz. butter (30 grms)	2½ ozs. plain flour (65 grms)
2 eggs beaten	Salt and pepper
¼ pint water (2 dl)	Cayenne pepper
2 ozs. grated cheddar cheese (50 grms)	Oil for deep frying

Melt butter in water and bring to the boil. Remove saucepan from heat. Add flour all at once and beat with wooden spoon until smooth and mixture leaves side of pan. Allow to cool slightly then beat in eggs gradually. Add cheese and season well. Heat oil and drop in teaspoons of mixture. Fry until golden, drain and serve.

CREAM CHEESE PUFFS   Nurit Raphael

Makes 40 approx.   Preparation 30 mins.   Gas No. 5 (375°)   Cook 10 mins

3 packets of Philadelphia cream cheese (large)   Pepper and salt
3 egg yolks   Little paprika   paprika
A dash of onion salt

Cut round pieces of medium thick white toast bread, put into medium hot oven to toast lightly. Mix cheese and egg yolks and seasoning, put thickly on little toasts. Top with paprika. Bake in medium hot oven for about 10 minutes until lightly browned.

"BITE-SIZE" PARTY PIZZAS   Sandy Prevezer

Makes 60 approx. Preparation 30 mins. Gas No. 3 (350°) Cook 10 mins. Advance Freezable NB: If freezing, undercook and then pop them in oven to heat and brown before serving with cocktails

Pastry Dough   1 tin Campbells tomato spaghetti sauce
12 ozs. S.R. flour (350 grms)   Pinch of oregano
1 teaspoon salt   3 ozs. grated cheddar cheese (80 grms)
2 ozs. butter (50 grms)   ¼ lb. black olives (100 grms)
2 ozs. grated cheddar cheese (50 grms)   1 tin anchovies
½ pt. milk to mix (3 dl.)   1 oz. grated parmesan cheese (25 grms)

For the pastry dough: Rub butter into flour and salt. Add 2 ozs. (50 grms) grated cheese then milk and mix to a smooth dough. Roll out and stamp out tiny rounds. Place rounds on baking sheets. On each round put a little tomato sauce and oregano then a tiny pinch from the 3 ozs (80 grms) cheddar cheese. Decorate with a tiny piece of anchovy and olive. Sprinkle with parmesan. Bake 10 minutes or until nicely brown.

Starters

ARTICHOKE AND MUSHROOM STARTER   Ruth Starr

Serves 4   Preparation 5 mins.   Cook 3 mins.

1 tin of artichoke hearts   Breadcrumbs
About 8 large flat mushrooms   1 or 2 eggs, well beaten

Dip artichoke hearts and mushrooms in egg and then into breadcrumbs. Lower into shallow hot fat. Gently fry until brown (about three minutes). Drain on kitchen paper. Serve with tartare sauce.

11

STUFFED ARTICHOKES
Italian Style

Diana Marks

Serves 4   Preparation 15 mins.   Cook 1 hour.

4 artichokes
1½ cups breadcrumbs
¾ cup parmesan cheese
3 tablespoons chopped parsley
2 cloves minced garlic

½ cup minced onion
½ teaspoon salt
¼ teaspoon pepper
4 tablespoons vegetable oil

Wash and drain artichokes. Cut 1 inch off tops and open up. Mix all ingredients except oil. Fill artichokes with mixture in each leaf. Put in large saucepan. Fill with water half way only. Pour 1 tablespoon of oil over each. Bring to the boil and simmer covered, adding water if necessary. Cook for 1 hour or until tender.

ASPARAGUS PATÉ

Hilary Brass

Serves 4   Preparation 10 mins.

4 hardboiled eggs
1 tin asparagus
Small carton double cream

Salt and pepper
Lemon juice to taste

Liquidise eggs and asparagus. Add double cream slowly. Season. Add lemon juice. Serve in ramekins accompanied by herb bread.

AUBERGINE PATÉ

Stella Majeran

Serves 4 Preparation 10 mins. Gas No. 5 (375^{0}) Cook 10-15 mins. Refrigeration 2 hrs. Advance Freezable

2 large aubergines
1 large spanish onion

Salt and pepper
Olive oil
Vinegar

Bake aubergines in oven until skins are wrinkled. Remove skins, mash up aubergines. Add finely chopped spanish onion, salt, pepper, oil and vinegar. Refrigerate for minimum two hours before serving.

AVOCADO COCKTAIL (1)

Berta Lazarus

Serves 4   Preparation 10 mins.

2 Avocado pears
Tinned mandarins or
2 segmented fresh grapefruit

Lettuce leaves
Vinaigrette sauce

Arrange slices of avocado with either fresh grapefruit segments or tinned mandarins on a lettuce leaf. Dress with vinaigrette sauce.

AVOCADO COCKTAIL (2)
Esther Taub

Serves 4-6   Preparation 20 mins.   Refrigeration 1 hour

1 large avocado
½ melon
½ cucumber
Lemon juice

1 teaspoon dried mint
½ cup vinaigrette dressing

Dice everything. Sprinkle with lemon juice and dried mint. Toss in vinaigrette. Serve well chilled in long-stemmed glasses.

AVOCADO A LA 'JAPONAISE'
Fernand Buris

Serves 12   Preparation 20 mins.   Refrigeration 3 hours

6 avocados
1 large tin pink salmon
½ pint double cream (3 dl)
2 sherry glasses white rum

1 small tin red pimento for garnish
Sweet powdered paprika
Salt and pepper to taste

Halve avocados and scoop out flesh reserving shells. Place all ingredients in a large bowl and finely mash until creamy. Fill shells – garnish with pimento. Chill.

AVOCADO MOUSSE
Valerie Selby

Serves 10   Prepartion 15 mins.   Refrigeration 3 hours

6 avocados
Juice of ½ lemon
1 pint sour cream (½ litre)

1 oz. gelatine (30 grms)
2 tablespoons vegetable stock

Liquidize avocado pears and lemon juice – fold in cream, add gelatine that has been dissolved in stock. Put in refrigerator.

AVOCADO-FILLED ORANGES
Ann Millett

Serves 8   Preparation 40 mins.

4 medium oranges
1 small clove of crushed garlic
Dash of tobasco sauce

2 avocados
½ level teaspoon dried mustard

Choose oranges that will fit chosen glasses and cut them in halves. Slightly less than ¼" from the peel, using a grapefruit knife, ease out as much flesh as possible; retaining juice in a bowl. Divide flesh between orange shells. To juice of oranges add garlic, tobasco and mustard. Peel avocados, discard stones. Dice flesh and marinade in juice of orange, turning occasionally for about half an hour. Pile avocados into orange shells. Moisten with a little juice before serving.

13

AVOCADO SYVALA
Nicholas Posnansky

Serves 4-6   Preparation 20 mins.

2 avocado pears	1 tablespoon olive oil
1 finely chopped onion	Salt and pepper
1 (eating) apple	4 tablespoons mayonnaise
2 sticks celery	2 tablespoons tomato ketchup
1½ ozs. smoked salmon (45 grms)	Dash of worcestershire sauce (optional)
Juice ½ lemon	

Peel and mash the avocados. Peel and chop apple, finely chop celery and also smoked salmon. Mix these ingredients together. Add the lemon juice and olive oil, salt and pepper to make into a mousse. Mix the mayonnaise with the tomato ketchup. If slightly too thick add 1 tablespoon of milk. Mix sauce with the avocado mixture. Serve on a bed of lettuce and decorate with a piece of smoked salmon. N.B. The worcestershire sauce is added into the sauce only if taste is for spicy things.

STUFFED AVOCADO
Mrs. R.D. Lunzer

Serves 6   Preparation 10 mins.

3 large ripe avocados	Paprika
1 carton soured cream	Lemon juice
White pepper	1 large smoked trout

Wash, halve and stone avocados. Brush cut surfaces with lemon juice. Place in individual dishes. Bone and skin trout. Place in blender with soured cream. Blend until completely smooth. Season to taste with pepper. Add paprika sufficient to give slight pink colouring. Pile filling into cavities of avocados.

AVOCADO, TOMATO & ONION APPETIZER
Jo Garretto

Serves 4   Preparation 30 mins.

4-6 large slices spanish onion	1-2 tablespoons chopped parsley
2 large ripe avocados	Finely chopped fresh herbs
6 firm ripe tomatoes	Basil, tarragon or chives
	Vinaigrette dressing

Take onion rings apart. Soak them in iced water for 15 minutes: drain thoroughly. Peel avocados and cut into rings across the width slipping each ring off the stone as you slice it. Toss avocado rings in vinaigrette to prevent discolouring. Arrange in deep serving dish. Slice tomatoes — add to avocados, together with onion rings. Sprinkle with chopped parsley and fresh tarragon, basil or chives. Add remainder of vinaigrette. Serve very cold.

CREAMED CAMEMBERT

Faith Duke

Serves 6   Preparation 20 mins.   Refrigeration 14 hours   Advance

1 whole camembert
Dry white wine

$\frac{1}{3}$ cup unsalted butter
Fine toast crumbs

Scrape off the skin of the cheese carefully. Stand the cheese in a bowl and cover with white wine and leave for 12 hours. Drain, wipe dry then cream it with the butter. Re-shape and coat on all sides with very fine toast crumbs. Chill well before serving. Serve with French bread and red wine.

COD APPETIZER

Marc Sofizade

Serves 6   Preparation 30 mins.   Cook 15 mins.   Cooling time 1 hour

2 cod fillets
1 egg
2 tablespoons chopped parsley
1 clove crushed garlic

Flour
Cooking oil
White pepper
Salt
1 fresh lemon

Cut the fillets in pieces (approx 4″ wide). Soak each piece in beaten egg then dip in flour (which has been seasoned with salt and white pepper). Fry each piece in oil until golden on both sides. Leave fish aside until cool. Meantime, crush garlic and place in deep dish with chopped parsley and add 1 cup warm water. When fish is cold, dip each piece of fish into the warm water and place on serving dish. Serve on a bed of lettuce garnished with remainder of chopped parsley and slices of fresh lemon

CREOLE LES ACHARDS

Faith Duke

Serves 6   Preparation 30 mins.   Marinate 3 days.

3 teaspoons salt to 1 pint water
1 medium finely chopped onion
1 pinch saffron
¼ teaspoon salt   } to ¼ pint olive
¼ teaspoon pepper   oil (2 dl.)
¼ teaspoon chilli pepper

Raw carrots, french beans,
Onions, cauliflower, cabbage,
Peppers, coconut, celery,
Palm hearts, etc.

Cut each vegetable into bite size pieces and soak separately in salted water for 24 hours. Drain and place in mounds on a shallow dish. Add the onion, saffron, salt and peppers to the oil and bring to the boil. Pour over the raw vegetables and marinate for 48 hours.

COURGETTE SOUFFLÉ

Carol Chinn

Serves 12   Preparation 30 mins.   Cook 45 mins.   Gas No. 4 (350°)

3 lbs. courgettes (1 kilo. 350 grms)
6 whole eggs and 6 extra whites
5 ozs. gruyere cheese (150 grms)
2 x 2 pint soufflé dishes   (1 litre)
or 2 x 2½ pint soufflé dishes   (1¼ litre)

Bechamel made from 3 ozs.(80 grms) butter
6 tablespoons flour
¾ pint warmed milk (½ litre)
Seasoned well with pepper
Do not add salt till after cheese

Wash courgettes. Slice widthways. Salt slightly and leave in colander to drain. Cook in heavy saucepan with 3 ladles of water till courgettes are soft and water evaporated. Sieve or liquidise and stir resulting purée into Bechamel. Add cheese and well beaten yolks. Leave to cool before folding in stiffly beaten whites. Pour mixture into buttered soufflé dishes (N.B. dishes should be filled about ¾ full). Stand in baking tin filled with water. Sprinkle top with grated cheese and cook in centre of pre-heated oven.

CRUDITÉS

Karol Solomons

Serves 10-12   Preparation 30 mins.

6 small carrots
1 cucumber
4 hard boiled eggs
6 firm tomatoes

1 head celery
1 red cabbage cut into wedges
2 avocados

Any fresh vegetable can be used — the more unusual the better. Clean and slice all ingredients. A large basket is needed, and the vegetables arranged so that they are all sticking out. This makes a lovely easy starter in the centre of the table with two long French breads at either side and if a special party, also serve chicken liver pate and everyone can help themselves. There should be one or two different dressings on the table (see Sauces).

EGG & MEAT SAVOURY

Bernice Burr

Serves 8   Preparation 30 mins.   Refrigeration 3 hours   Advance

1 pint meat stock using calves foot (½ litre)
8 eggs

½ lb. chopped liver or liver sausage
(225 grms.)

Make your favourite stock using calves foot so that the jelly will set firmly. This can be made, cooled and fat removed in advance. Poach eggs in water — whites should be firm and yolk soft. When eggs are cooked, carefully put them into a shallow dish of cold water and leave until required. To assemble, use eight individual dishes. Put a spoonful of liver mixture as base — place drained eggs on liver, then mask egg with carefully melted stock. Decorate as desired either in or on top of set jelly using tomato, green or red pepper, parsley, dill, cucumber etc. Put in fridge so that jelly re-sets. Could be used as a supper dish.

EGG MOUSSE WITH TOMATO SAUCE
Valerie Selby

Serves 12   Preparation 30 mins.   Refrigeration 12 hours

Mousse:
1 pint cream (½ litre)
18 hard boiled eggs
Juice of ½ lemon
Salt & pepper
1 pint Heinz mayonnaise (½ litre)
6 chopped gherkins
3 pint ring mould rinsed in cold water (1½ litre)

Tomato Sauce:
2 tins tomatoes
1 crushed clove of garlic
1 tablespoon oil
10 drops tobasco
Salt & pepper

Mix all mousse ingredients together in a large bowl. Liquidize in three lots. Pour into mould as each lot is done. Smooth top and put into fridge overnight. Liquidize all sauce ingredients together and chill. Unmould mousse. Decorate with watercress. Serve sauce separately.

EGGS IN RED DRESSES
Sigrid Harris

Serves 4   Preparation 30 mins.

2 hard boiled eggs. 4 Tomatoes
1 small packet of Philadelphia Cheese

Chopped parsley
Salt

Wash tomatoes, cut off the tops and carefully remove the insides. Lightly salt. Cut the eggs horizontally, to enable the cut egg to sit in the tomato, loosen the yolks and mash them with the cream cheese into a smooth paste. Put this mixture into a piping bag. Sit each egg white in a tomato – let the edge of the egg stand out a bit – and squeeze the cream cheese mixture into them. Decorate with chopped parsley.

FAINTING OLD MAN
Renee Elkabir

Serves 6   Preparation 45 mins.   Gas No. 4 (360⁰)   Cook 1 hour   Advance   Freezable

2 tomatoes
2 long slim aubergines
2 green peppers
¾ lb minced meat (325 grms)
1 beaten egg

1 tablespoon chopped parsley
1 finely chopped clove of garlic
1 teaspoon mint sauce
Breadcrumbs

Cut aubergines in to sections about ¾″ thick. Cut green peppers according to their sections either into 3 or 4 parts. Hollow a bit from the middle of the aubergines and cut this into little bits and mix with the meat for stuffing. Add chopped garlic, mint sauce and half the beaten egg and stuff all your vegetables about a teaspoon in each. Dip them in the beaten egg and the bread-crumbs. Fry all the stuffed vegetables in corn oil meat side first. Arrange vegetables on a deep tray.
Sauce to cover. 1½ cups of stock, ½ cup of lemon juice, salt and pepper. Boil all this together, pour over vegetables, cover with foil and bake. Serve hot or cold.

GRAVLAX (Swedish)

Phyllis Horal

Serves 4   **Preparation 20 mins.**   **Refrigeration 2 days**

1 lb. salmon trout or mackerel (450 grms.)
4 tablespoons chopped dill
2 tablespoons sugar
2 tablespoons coarse salt
1 teaspoon white pepper

Sauce:
2 tablespoons mild mustard
1 teaspoon mustard powder
2 tablespoons vinegar
Sugar to taste
Dill

Scrape fish and dry thoroughly rub in mixed dry ingredients. Place marinade in a shallow dish and place fish in it. Baste. Put weighted dish on top. Leave in fridge for 48 hours. Cut across (obliquely) in thin slices. Serve with mustard sauce.

DANISH HERRING

Sophie Parker

Serves 12   **Preparation 30 mins**   **Soak 12 hours**   **Advance**

1 cup of chopped onion
1 cup of chopped peeled apple
1 cup of vinegar
Just less than 1 cup of sugar
$\frac{1}{3}$ cup of oil

1 small tin tomato purée
1 teaspoon of mustard
Pinch of pepper
6 salt herrings

Soak salt herrings for 12 hours (changing water). Put sugar in bowl and work in purée, add mustard, oil, vinegar, pepper. Add onion and apple. Cut herrings into small pieces and stir into mixture. Can be stored in jars or bowl in fridge.

SOUSED HERRINGS

Nieves Bello

Serves 12   **Preparation 30 mins.**   **Gas No. 5 (375⁰)**   **Cook 4 hours**   **Advance**

12 fresh herrings
2 sliced onions
6 fluid ozs. malt vinegar (2 dls.)
4 fluid ozs. water (1½ dls.)

6 tablespoons demerera sugar
16 whole black peppers
2 bay leaves

Bone and clean herrings, remove heads, sprinkle with salt and pepper and close up again. Arrange fish on top of sliced onions in ovenproof dish; just large enough to hold them in one layer. Put rest of ingredients into dish and bake in oven No.5 (375⁰) for 20 minutes. Then turn down to No. 2 (325⁰) for 3½ hours, or until liquid is nearly evaporated. Flavour is even better if cooked day before needed then re-heated. Turn fish over twice during cooking. Equally good hot or cold.

KIPPER PASTE
Jewels Leader-Cramer

Serves 10   **Preparation 30 mins.**   **Refrigeration 6 hours**

4 ozs. butter (100 grms) plus
5 ozs. butter (150 grms) cut into bits and
  softened
2 pair kippers (about 2 lb) (900 grms)
3 teaspoons anchovy paste (100 grms)

¼ teaspoon ground clove
¼ teaspoon ground mace
$\frac{1}{8}$ teaspoon cayenne pepper
1½ pints water (1 litre)

Clarify the 4 ozs. of butter by melting slowly over a low heat in a small saucepan. Skim off surface foam and let the butter rest off heat for a minute or two. Then spoon the clean butter into a small cup and discard the milky solids at the bottom of pan. Bring water to the boil in a large shallow pan. Add the kippers. Simmer uncovered until flesh flakes easily. Drain the kippers and remove the skin from the backbone but do not bother to remove tiny bones. Place the fish in electric blender and blend at high speed for five seconds. Add anchovy paste, cloves, mace, cayenne pepper and 5 ozs (150 grms) butter. Blend at high speed, stopping the motor now and again to scrape down and mix with rubber spatula until paste is soft and creamy. Spoon the paste into serving dish 2½" deep — filling dish ¼" from the top. Seal by pouring the cooled clarified butter over the paste. Refrigerate for at least six hours until firm. Refrigerated and tightly covered, the paste can keep for ten days.

MARINATED KIPPERS
Mirelle Dessau

Serves 4   **Preparation 20 mins.**   **Marinate 12 hours**   **Advance**

1 packet of kipper fillets
1 large spanish onion

An oil and vinegar French
dressing with 3 parts vinegar to
1 part oil.

Skin the kipper fillets. Lay onion rings in pyrex dish, place kipper fillets on top and pour dressing over. Marinate at least overnight.

KIPPER MOUSSE
Valerie Ross

Serves 6   **Preparation 35 mins.**   **Refrigeration 2 hours**   **Advance**   **Freezable**

10 ozs. packet of kipper fillets (275 grms)
½ pint single cream (3 dl).
Sauce
1 oz. butter (30 grms)
1 oz. flour (30 grms)
½ pint milk (3 dl)
2 egg yolks

2 whisked egg whites
½ oz. gelatine (15 grms)
Juice of ½ lemon
2 tablespoons water
Salt and pepper

Cook kippers as instructed and remove skin. Mix with a little cream. Pound fillets to paste with remaining cream. Melt butter in pan stir in flour off the heat. Cook for one minute, remove and blend in milk. Return to the heat and bring to the boil stirring all the time. Remove and season. Beat in egg yolks. Dissolve gelatine in the lemon juice and water, and stir in the white sauce. Leave to cool and fold in creamed kipper mixture. Whisk egg whites until almost stiff and fold into mixture. Put in 7" mould. Garnish when set.

STICKY CHOPS
Karol Solomons

Serves 6	Preparation 15 mins.	Gas No. 3(350°)	Cook 1-1½ hours

8 small lamb chops
2 tablespoons tomato ketchup
2 tablespoons Worcestershire sauce
1 tablespoon H.P. sauce
Dash of red wine vinegar
Dash of Tabasco

1 teaspoon salt
1 teaspoon dried mustard
1 teaspoon black pepper
1 teaspoon ground ginger
1 clove garlic
Brown sugar
Lemon juice

Mix all dry ingredients — except sugar. Arrange chops on flat dish and cover with all dry ingredients. Pour over half the sauce mixture — sprinkle with brown sugar and lemon juice. Put in oven. Baste every ¼ hour. After half hour pour away excess fat and pour over the rest of sauce. Cook until sticky.

CHICKEN LIVER PATÉ (1)
Sheilah Goodman

Serves 4	Preparation 20 mins.	Advance	Freezable

½ lb. chicken livers (225 grms)
½ lb. margarine (225 grms)

4 tablespoons brandy
Black pepper and salt

Sauté liver very gently in margarine. Liquidize with brandy. Add seasoning.

CHICKEN LIVER PATÉ (2)
Karol Solomons

Serves 6	Preparation 30 mins.	Advance

1 lb. chicken livers (450 grms)
1 small onion
2 hard boiled eggs

Chicken fat
Salt and pepper

Heavily salt liver. Grill liver on both sides until burnt. Pop into boiling water for two minutes. Cut off edges. Mince finely with raw onions and eggs. Add salt and pepper with enough soft chicken fat to make very smooth.

LIVER PATÉ

A Liver Lover

Serves 6   Preparation 30 mins.   Gas No. 2 (325°)   Cook 1 hour   Refrigeration 1 day

1 lb. liver (450 grms).
1 large onion
1 chicken cube
1 level tablespoon flour
1 egg

Salt and pepper to taste
Pinch of mace, cinnamon, clove,
Bay leaf
1 tablespoon brandy
2 tablespoons oil (optional)
¼ lb. margarine (100 grms)

Sauté onion in oil and 2 ozs. (50 grms) of the margarine until soft. Add liver. Cook gently for five minutes. Dissolve cube in ½ pint boiled water. Melt remainder of margarine, add flour, simmer for a minute. Add hot stock. Whisk briskly until smooth and thick. Take off heat. Drop in egg, whisk again until smooth. Put liver, onions, sauce and seasonings — except bay leaf — into the blender. Liquidize. Turn into greased loaf tin or any other ovenproof dish. Smooth level. Lay bayleaf on top. Cover very tightly with foil. Stand baking dish in a tin 1" deep with hot water and cook. When cool, refrigerate.

CHOPPED LIVER ROLL

Phyllis Millet

Serves 8   Preparation 20 mins.   Gas No 2 (320°)   Cook 20 mins

1 lb. chopped liver (450 grms)
½ lb. puff pastry (225 grms)

White of egg

Make a fat sausage shape with the chopped liver. Roll out pastry and stand liver in centre. Wrap pastry around, seal and brush with beaten egg white. Cook and serve hot or cold with tomato sauce.

COARSE PATÉ

Betty Dill

Serves 10   Preparation 30 mins.   Gas No 3 (350°)   Cook 1½ hours   Advance   Freezable

½ lb. minced veal (225 grms)
½ lb. calves liver (225 grms)
½ lb. sausage meat (225 grms)
¼ lb. smoked beef (100 grms)

1 clove garlic
2 tablespoons white wine or sherry
2 tablespoons brandy

Mince liver with fatty parts of beef. Add garlic. Mix all ingredients together. Put in loaf tin and cover with rest of smoked beef. Stand in larger tin half-filled with water and put in oven.

SMOKED MACKEREL PATÉ

Avril Kleeman

Serves 8   Preparation 30 mins.   Advance

2 slices white bread
1 smoked mackerel
4 oz. cream cheese (100 grms)

Salt and pepper
A little milk
Juice of 1 lemon

Remove crusts from bread and soak it in some milk. Put mackerel, cheese, lemon juice and bread in the liquidizer with sufficient milk to make a smooth paté. Season to taste. Serve in small pots accompanied by hot toast.

MOZZARELLA IN CAROZZA

Susan Stone

Serves 4   Preparation 15 mins.   Cook 15 mins

8 slices of bread (without crusts)   Beaten egg
4 slices mozzarella cheese   Breadcrumbs
8 anchovy fillets

Make four sandwiches with a slice of cheese and two fillets of anchovy to each sandwich. Cut across diagonally to make eight triangles. Pass through beaten egg then breadcrumbs. Leave to dry. Fry in oil until brown and crisp. Serve with a good tomato sauce.

MUSHROOM SOUFFLÉ

Mrs. E. Gessler

Serves 6-8   Preparation 15 mins.   Gas No 1 (300°)   Cook ¾-1 hour

2½ oz. butter (70 grms)   4 eggs
2½ ozs. flour (70 grms)   8 oz. mushrooms (230 grms)
12½ fluid oz. milk (3¾ dl.)   Salt

Melt butter. Add flour. Add milk. Cook over low heat till smooth. Put mixture in mixer. Add salt. Beat in one egg yolk at a time. Add very finely cut mushrooms. Put in large bowl. Beat egg whites very stiffly and fold into mixture. Put in buttered soufflé dish. Sprinkle with breadcrumbs and bake in oven.

ONION TART

Zena Clayton

Serves 8-10   Preparation 15 mins.   Gas No 5 (375°)   Cook ¾ hour   Advance

2 lb. spanish onions (900 grms)   1 packet vegetarian puff pastry
2 eggs   Seasoning
Cooking oil

Peel and slice onions finely. Fry in oil until lightly browned. Drain. Beat eggs with seasoning and mix with onions. Line pie dish with thinly rolled out pastry and pour egg/onion mixture into it. Bake for ½ hour or until well browned. Serve hot or cold.

SALMON NUT COCKTAIL

Sandra Connelly

Serves 4   Preparation 10 mins.

4 oz. cooked fresh salmon (100 grms)   6 radishes
Small crisp apple   Shredded lettuce
¼ cucumber   Mayonnaise
2 ozs. hazel nuts (50 grms)   Ketchup
1 lemon

Flake salmon and dice apple, cucumber, radishes and nuts. Mix together. Add enough ketchup to mayonnaise to get a pleasant pink colour. Bind all ingredients together. Arrange lettuce in long stemmed glasses. Pile mixture on top. Decorate with slices of lemon.

SMOKED SALMON BALLS
Suzanne Rose

Serves 4   **Preparation 20 mins.**   **Refrigeration 1 hour**

8 oz. smoked salmon (225 grms)
2 oz. unsalted butter (50 grms)

Lemon juice
Split almonds

Pureé salmon, butter and a good squeeze of lemon juice in liquidizer. Form into four balls with wet hands. Chill. Decorate a la hedgehog with split almonds.

SHIRA'S DISH
Masha Greenbaum

Serves 12   **Preparation 20 mins.**   **Gas No 5 (375⁰)**   **Cook 50 mins.**   **Advance**   **Freezable**

6 matzos
4 or 5 eggs
2 tablespoons oil

12 ozs. liver (350 grms)
Salt, pepper
Cinnamon

Break up matzos, soak in boiling water, drain. Beat eggs separately, add seasonings, add matzos (reserve a little yolk). Prepare liver as for chopped liver without onion, add seasoning. Place oil in large Pyrex dish. Spread half matzo mixture over bottom of dish. Add all liver. Spread remaining matzo over top. Brush with egg yolk. Bake. N.B. Very good for Passover. Can also be made with filling of minced chicken or mixed vegetables.

SOLE DUGLÈRE
Jacky Bennett

Serves 6   **Preparation 20 mins.**   **Cook 1 min.**

8 fillets lemon sole
Water
6 tomatoes
Tomato ketchup
Salad cream

Lemon juice
Drop of tabasco or Worcestershire sauce
Salt and pepper

Place fish in flat pan. Barely cover with cold water and season. Bring to boil and simmer for one minute. Put on a plate to drain and cool. Trim off any nasty pieces. Skin and chop tomatoes. Mix together required amount of ketchup, salad cream, lemon juice and Tabasco or Worcestershire sauce. Add chopped tomatoes. Place fish in a flat au gratin dish. Cover with sauce. Sprinkle with chopped parsley.

TARAMOSALATA
Tina Greenspan

Serves 6   **Preparation 20 mins.**

3 ozs. crustless bread (80 grms)
8 ozs. smoked cods roe (225 grms)
1 small clove garlic

¼ pint olive oil
Juice of ½ lemon
Black pepper
Black olives

Soak bread for a few minutes. When soft squeeze out as much as possible. Blend bread, roe and garlic together. Add half the oil a little at a time. Add lemon juice and remaining oil. Season to taste with black pepper. Garnish with black olives and serve with hot toast or french bread.

TOMATE FARCIE
Gillian Burr

Serves 12　　　**Preparation 30 mins.**　　　**Gas No 4 (360⁰)**　　　**Cook 10-15 mins.**

24 large tomatoes
1 cup cooked rice
½ lb. mushrooms (225 grms)
½ cup frozen peas

1 large finely chopped onion
A little oil
Salt and pepper
Worcestershire sauce

Slice top off tomatoes. Scoop out flesh of tomatoes, sieve and set aside. Fry onion slowly until soft. Add mushrooms, tomato pulp and peas. Season to taste and add rice. Stuff tomatoes with mixture and replace tops. Place tomatoes in ovenproof dish.

STUFFED TOMATOES (1)
Mrs. V. Knobil

Serves 4　　**Preparation 20 mins.**　　**Gas No 5 (375⁰)**　　**Cook 15 mins**　　**Advance**

4 large firm tomatoes
2 tablespoons breadcrumbs
2 tablespoons coarsely grated cheese
Chopped parsley

1 beaten egg
Butter
2 ozs. chopped mushrooms (50 grms).

Remove the stalks and cut the top off each tomato. Remove the centres and mix with the breadcrumbs, cheese, mushrooms and parsley, and sufficient egg to bind and fill the tomato cases. Replace the tops – dot with butter and bake. Serve on toast or with spaghetti.

STUFFED TOMATOES (2)
Linda Stone

Serves 6　　**Preparation 20 mins.**

6 large tomatoes
6 lettuce leaves
1 cup sauce tartare

1 cup flaked cooked fish or tuna fish
Chopped parsley

Cut off tops of tomatoes. Remove seeds. Turn upside down on kitchen paper to drain. Mix tartare sauce with chosen fish. Fill tomatoes. Sprinkle with parsley. Serve on bed of lettuce leaves.

STUFFED TOMATOES PROVENÇAL
Diana Marks

Serves 8　　**Preparation 20 mins.**　　**Gas No 3 (350⁰)**　　**Cook 20 mins.**　　**Advance**

8 large tomatoes
Breadcrumbs
Chopped onions (lightly fried)
Crushed garlic

Chopped parsley
Mixed herbs
Salt and black pepper

Slice off tops of tomatoes. Take out centres with grapefruit knife and sieve. Remove green stalk. Add all ingredients and bind to smooth consistency. Stuff tomatoes and put in oven. Prick slightly. These can be made early and reheated.

TROUT MOUSSE

Madelaine Cope-Thompson

Serves 10-12   **Preparation 15 mins.**   **Refrigeration 2 hours.**   **Advance**

8 smoked trout
1½ pots sour cream
1 tablespoon of salad cream

1 tablespoon of horseradish sauce (white)
Worcestershire sauce to flavour

Fillet smoked trout then mince it. Mix all ingredients together. Put mixture in a dish. Place in fridge until set.

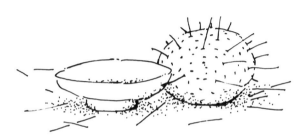

NOTES

Soups

Do not put too much salt in soup before freezing.

To prevent soup boiling away during long cooking, turn lid upside down and fill with water.

When making a milk soup and recipe calls for meat or chicken stock use vegetable cube or marmite.

When a meat soup recipe requires a small quantity of cream add parev whip at last moment.

When an absolutely clear stock is required line the inside of your sieve with a piece of fine material, i.e. a linen handkerchief or old curtain which must overhang the edges. You can also use a coffee filter.

ACCOMPANIMENTS FOR SOUPS

Make thin pancakes then roll them up and cut into slices, unroll them and drop into hot soup.

Sausages can be cut into thin rounds and dropped into vegetable soup.

Puffs. Mix 1 cup matzo meal, 2 tablespoons ground almonds, 1 egg, water to make short paste, salt and pepper. Drop small spoonfuls in hot oil, drain and add to soup.

Croutons. Fry slices of bread cut into small pieces.
Slices of cucumber with cream.
Rice.

ASPARAGUS SOUP
Betty Dill

Serves 6   Preparation 15 mins.   Cook 1 hour   Advance

1 pint of meat or chicken stock (½ litre)
1 pkt. Osem asparagus soup
1 tin of asparagus or asparagus pieces

1-2 tablespoons cornflour
2 tablespoons water
Salt and pepper

Cook packet soup as directed. Make a paste from the cornflour and water. Mix a little of the soup with the cornflour mixture. Add all ingredients to soup and season to taste. Simmer gently for 1 hour. Serve with croutons.

BEAN AND BARLEY SOUP
Susan Stone

Serves 8   Preparation 20 mins.   Cook 1 hour 10 mins.   Advance

2 large tins butter beans
2 sliced large onions
4 cubed large carrots
2 sliced celery sticks
3 pints water (1½ litres)

2 chicken stock cubes
3 tablespoons barley
½ teaspoon soya sauce
1 tablespoon oil
Salt and pepper

Heat oil in large saucepan. Add fresh vegetables and seasonings. Sweat for 5 minutes. Add remaining ingredients. Cook gently for 1 hour.

BORSHT (HOT OR COLD)
Muriel Rosner

Serves 12   Preparation 10 mins.   Cook 15 mins.   Advance

5 bottles clear borsht
4 large eggs

Juice of 2 lemons
Castor sugar to taste
½ teaspoon cornflour

Beat 4 eggs in mixer. Add strained lemon juice. Add castor sugar to taste and the cornflour mixed with a few spoons of the borsht. Add borsht to egg mixture. Heat gently stirring all the time. DO NOT BOIL OR IT WILL CURDLE. Serve hot with a few cubes of boiled new potatoes and beetroot. Serve cold with a few spoons of sour cream in centre.

27

BOUILLABAISE
Claire Jacobs

Serves 6   Preparation 15 mins.   Cook 40 mins.   Freezable   Advance

STOCK

1 lb fish trimmings (450 grms)	1 lb cubed fish fillet (450 grms)
1 pint water (½ litre)	(Haddock, Cod, Whiting)
¼ pint dry white wine (2 dl)	14 oz tin tomatoes (400 grms.)
1 quartered onion	2 medium diced potatoes
2 chopped celery tops	2 tablespoons chopped parsley
A few parsley sprigs	1 crushed clove garlic
1 bayleaf	½ teaspoon basil
¼ teaspoon thyme	Squeeze lemon juice
	Little oil
	Salt and pepper

Put fish trimmings into saucepan with water, wine and other stock ingredients. Add salt and pepper to taste. Simmer for about 20 minutes without lid. Stir and reserve. Heat some oil in a heavy saucepan or casserole. Add potatoes and garlic, cook about 5 minutes before adding tomatoes, fish and stock, lemon juice and some dried basil. Simmer gently for 10 minutes. Stir in parsley just before serving. Taste to check seasoning. Serve very hot with French bread.

RUSSIAN CABBAGE BORSHT
Julia Bennett

Serves 8   Preparation 15 mins.   Cook several hours   Refrigeration 12 hours   Advance

3 pints water (1½ litres)	3 carrots	1 medium red cabbage
Plenty of marrow bones	1 leek	
1½ lb diced soup meat (675 grms)	1 large onion	
1 jar clear borsht	Caraway seeds to taste	
3 lemons	Sultanas (optional)	
Brown sugar	Salt and pepper	

These quantities are approximate and may be altered according to taste.

Cook marrow bones in water with onions, carrots, leek, salt and pepper for 3-4 hours to make basic stock. Strain and refrigerate overnight. Remove any fat and cook diced meat until tender for 1-2 hours. Add shredded cabbage, the jar of borsht, lemon juice and brown sugar to taste. Add a sprinkling of caraway seeds and sultanas. Cook for a further 30 minutes.

CARROT AND ORANGE SOUP
Caroline Posnansky

Serves 6   Preparation 10 mins.   Cook 15 mins.   Advance   Freezable

1 medium chopped onion	6 oz tin frozen orange juice (175 grms)
1 oz butter or margerine (30 grms)	Salt and pepper
1½ pints chicken or vegetable stock (1 litre)	8 fl ozs cream (2¼ dl) if desired
15½ oz tin carrots (430 grms)	Chives

Cook the onion in butter until soft but not coloured. Liquidize drained carrots with onion and a little stock. Put orange juice, the puréed vegetables and remaining stock, seasoning and cream into pan, heat until just below boiling point. Adjust seasoning and decorate with chives. If it is to be served cold use oil instead of butter. If it is to be frozen do not add cream until reheating.

CAULIFLOWER SOUP 1

Carole Chesterman

Serves 6   Preparation 10 mins.   Cook 15 mins.   Advance

1 large cauliflower   3 pints water (1½ litres)
1 chicken stock cube   Salt and pepper

Cut cauliflower into pieces. Add to water with cube and seasoning. Cook for 10 minutes. Liquidize. Excellent for filling up slimmers!

CAULIFLOWER SOUP 2

Evelyn Nymen

Serves 8   Preparation ½ hour   Cook 1 hour   Advance

2 ozs tomor (50 grms)   ½ lb carrots (225 grms)
2 ozs flour (50 grms)   ½ lb cauliflower (225 grms)
2 pints stock (1 litre)   Salt and pepper

Melt tomor and stir in flour, cook for 2-3 minutes stirring all the time. Add hot stock gradually, stirring well. Scrape and slice carrots and add to soup. Simmer for ½ hour. Separate cauliflower into florets and add to soup. Simmer for further ½ hour. Adjust seasoning and serve.

CREAM OF CELERY SOUP

Gillian Fenner

Serves 4   Preparation 10 mins.   Cook 30 mins.   Advance

6 chopped celery stalks   1 or 2 vegetable cubes
1 medium onion   ¼ pint cream (2 dl)
1 pint water (1 litre)   Salt and pepper
                                              Dash of Worcestershire Sauce

Cook celery and onion in cubes and water until tender. Liquidize. Add cream and seasonings. Reheat slowly. Serve with croûtons.

CHICKEN SOUP WITH LEMON

Joyce Keyes

Serves 6   Preparation 15 mins.   Cook 1 hour 15 mins.   Advance   Freezable

Carcass and giblets of 1 chicken   3½ pints water (2 litres)
3-4 sliced celery stalks   Juice of ½ lemon
2 sliced leeks (optional)   2-3 courgettes (optional)
2-3 slivered cloves garlic   4 ozs boiled rice (100 grms)
                                              Salt and black pepper

Put carcass, bones and giblets in large saucepan with celery, leeks and garlic. Cover with water. Bring to boil — skim — add seasonings and lemon juice and simmer for 1 hour. Remove bones etc., trim off pieces of chicken and return. Add courgettes and cook for further 15 minutes. Adjust seasoning adding more lemon juice if necessary. Add rice just before serving. This soup should have a distinctly lemon flavour which with the garlic gives an oriental flavour.

TRADITIONAL CHICKEN SOUP   Rene Massey

Serves 10   Preparation 20 mins.   Cook 4 hours   Advance   Freezable

1 5lb Fowl (2k 250 grms)
Extra giblets and feet
Knuckle of Veal or
2 chicken cubes
1 lump of sugar
Salt and pepper

10 carrots
2 large whole onions
2 leeks
8 sticks of celery
1 root

Using a very large saucepan place fowl and giblets etc. inside and fill saucepan nearly to the top with cold water. Bring slowly to the boil removing scum as it rises to the top. Add vegetables and seasonings and simmer slowly for 3½ hours skimming the fat from the surface at regular intervals. Strain soup and allow to get cold, when it will be easy to remove any remaining fat.

MATZO BALLS   Sally Bloom

Serves 10   Preparation 15 mins.   Refrigeration 2 hours   Cook 15 mins.   Advance   Freezable

4 beaten eggs
3 cups medium matzo meal
2 cups boiling water
Pepper to taste

4 tablespoons chicken fat
2 dessertspoons ground almonds
2 teaspoons salt
1 tablespoon finely chopped parsley
(optional)

Mix eggs with melted fat, add boiling water, matzo meal, ground almonds and seasonings and stir. When cool, refrigerate. With wet hands, roll the mixture into small balls and cook in gently boiling strained chicken soup. For a change you can stuff the balls with a mixture of finely minced cooked meat and fried chopped onion. Cook as before.

COURGETTE AND TOMATO SOUP   Jo Garretto

Serves 4   Preparation 15 mins.   Cook ½ hour   Advance

2 medium courgettes
1 medium tin peeled tomatoes
1 chicken or beef cube

1½ pints boiling water (1 litre)
Salt
Pepper

Add cube to boiling water. Peel and dice courgettes and add to boiling stock with the tomatoes, season to taste. Simmer until cooked then purée or liquidize.

CUCUMBER SOUP

A friendly chef

Serves 6   Preparation 15 mins.   Cook 15 mins.   Refrigeration 2 hours

4 medium sized cucumbers
1 medium sized fennel
4 sprigs dill
4 spring onions
1 tablespoon butter
2 tablespoons flour

½ pint cream (3 dl)
½ pint milk (3 dl)
½ pint water (3 dl)
Carton of yoghurt or sour cream
2-3 crushed black peppercorns
Salt

Slice cucumbers, spring onions, fennel, dill and sauté in butter without colouring. Add cream, milk, water, salt and crushed peppercorns. Cook until cucumbers etc. are tender. Liquidize and reboil. Mix flour with yoghurt or sour cream and stir into soup to thicken. Boil for 4 minutes. Reseason if necessary. Allow to cool, refrigerate. Serve cold garnished with very thin slices of peeled cucumbers, dash of paprika and a helping of chopped chives.

CUCUMBER VICHYSOISSE

Russele Solomons

Serves 4–6   Preparation 10 mins.   Cook ½ hour   Refrigeration 2 hours   Advance

1 peeled and diced large cucumber
½ lb chopped new potatoes (225 grms)
6 chopped spring onions
Chopped chives

1½ ozs butter (45 grms)
1½ pints vegetable stock (1 litre)
4 tablespoons single cream
Salt and pepper

Melt butter in thick saucepan. Add potatoes, cucumber, spring onions and a little salt. Stir. Put on lid and allow to sweat for 10 minutes. Add stock and seasonings. Simmer without lid for 20 minutes. Liquidize. Add cream when cold. Serve cold and garnish with chives and croutons.

FRUIT SOUP

Renata Knobil

Serves 12   Preparation ½ hour   Cook ½ hour   Advance

2 lbs cooking apples (900 grms)
2 lbs rhubarb (900 grms)
2 lbs stewing apricots (900 grms)
2 lbs stewing plums (900 grms)
2 lbs gooseberries (900 grms)

1 Snowcrest raspberry jelly
6 tablespoons Ribena
8 tablespoons sweet red wine
6 tablespoons brown sugar
4 peaches (optional)
5 pints water (3 litres)

Peel and core apples. De-stone apricots and plums. Stew all fruit together with sugar in the water until cooked. The consistency should be fairly thick, if not discard some of the liquid. Liquidize. Add remaining ingredients and cool. Serve cold. Cut up peaches may be added just before serving.

GAZPACHO

Helen Murray

Serves 4–6   Preparation 30 mins.   Refrigeration 1 hour   Advance   Freezable

2 tomatoes
1 green pepper
1 stick celery
1 finely chopped onion
½ cucumber

¼ pint chicken stock (2 dl)
12 fl ozs tomato juice (4½ dl)
1 crushed clove garlic
Salt and freshly ground black pepper

Skin tomatoes, remove seeds from pepper and chop both finely. Chop celery and onion. Peel and chop cucumber. Reserve celery, tomato and a little of the green pepper and onion for garnish. Liquidize rest of ingredients for 2 minutes then chill. Just before serving sprinkle each portion with some of the remaining garnish.

GOLDEN SOUP

Bobby Collins

Serves 4   Preparation 10 mins.   Cook 20 mins.   Advance   Freezable

1 tablespoon Mazola oil
1 chopped onion
6 ozs carrots (175 grms)
1 lb tomatoes (445 grms) or
15 oz tin tomatoes (440 grms)

1 teaspoon sugar
1 teaspoon salt or celery salt
Pepper
1 chicken stock cube
¾ pint water (½ litre)
Chopped parsley or croûtons

Heat oil in saucepan. Sauté onion until golden brown. Add carrots and tomatoes roughly cut into pieces, or strained tinned tomatoes retaining liquid. Stir in sugar and add ½ pint (3 dl) water or liquid from tinned tomatoes. Bring to boil, simmer with lid on for 10-15 minutes. Add remaining ¼ pint (2 dl) water and liquidize for 30 seconds. Strain or mouli if desired. Return to saucepan to reheat, stir continuously. Garnish with chives or croûtons.

LEEK AND TOMATO SOUP

Gillian Fenner

Serves 6   Preparation 15 mins.   Cook 45 mins.   Advance

3 washed and shredded large leeks
1 oz butter or tomor (45 grms)
1 lb halved tomatoes (450 grms)
1 teaspoon castor sugar

½ lb peeled and diced potatoes (225 grms)
1½ pints chicken stock (1 litre)
Salt and pepper

Melt fat in saucepan and sauté leeks with lid on without browning for 5 minutes. Add tomatoes, sugar and seasonings and simmer in covered saucepan for 5 minutes. Add potatoe and stock. Bring to boil and cook gently for 30 minutes. Liquidize. Taste for seasoning. Reheat when required.

M.W.M.H.— C

32

QUICK MINESTRONE

Diane Krais

Serves 6   **Preparation 10 mins.**   **Cook 1 hour**   **Advance**

1½ tubs dried vegetables
1 medium tin tomatoes
1 sliced onion
2-3 carrots
1 small sliced turnip
2 ozs rice (50 grms)

Salt and pepper
Pinch oregano
1 teaspoon dried parsley
1 beef cube (optional)
2 handfuls macaroni
3 pints water (1½ litres)

Add all the ingredients, except macaroni, to boiling water and cook slowly for 40 minutes. Add macaroni and continue simmering for further 20 minutes. Serve with parmesan cheese if beef cube is not used.

QUICK MUSHROOM SOUP

Jackie Garfield

Serves 4–6   **Preparation 10 mins.**   **Cook 25 mins.**   **Advance**   **Freezable**

8 ozs mushrooms (225 grms)
4 small onions
4 small carrots
A dollop of marmite

1 oz margarine (30 grms)
1 stock cube
2 pints water (1 litre)
Salt and pepper

Peel and slice vegetables. Sauté them in the margarine for a few minutes. Add water and cube, seasonings and bring to boiling point, simmer gently for 20 minutes. Liquidize.

ONION SOUP (PRESSURE COOKED)

Valerie Ross

Serves 6   **Preparation 15 mins.**   **Cook 1 min. at 15 lbs or 1 hour ordinarily**   **Advance**

4 Spanish onions
2 ozs margarine (50 grms)
2 beef cubes
3 pints water (1½ litres)

1 tablespoon plain flour
Salt and black pepper
Small rounds of toast to garnish

Peel and slice onions thinly. Melt margarine in pressure cooker and fry onions until golden brown. Keep well stirred so that they brown evenly. Remove from heat and stir in flour smoothly. Gradually add water and beef cubes and seasoning to taste. Put lid on and pressure cook for 1 minute at 15 lbs (6k 75grms) pressure. Serve with toast garnish.

PASTA FAGIOLI

Diana Marks

Serves 8   Preparation 20 mins.   Soak 12 hours   Cook 1 hour   Advance

½ lb dried kidney or haricot beans (225 grms)
or tinned butter beans
4 tablespoons tomato concentrate
4 pints stock or cubes and water (2¼ litres)
1 spanish onion
1 clove garlic
½ lb pasta shells or other pasta (225 grms)

3 tablespoons olive oil
2 tablespoons chopped parsley
1 teaspoon salt
Freshly ground black pepper
Cayenne pepper
1 tablespoon oregano
Grated cheese to garnish

Chop onion and garlic finely and sauté in olive oil until transparent. Add finely chopped parsley, black pepper, salt, cayenne pepper and oregano simmer gently for approximately 10 minutes. Combine beans (soaked overnight) tomatoe paste and stock in large saucepan. Add onion, parsley etc. Simmer for 40 minutes. Add cooked pasta and simmer for further 10 minutes. Serve with grated cheese for garnish.

COLD PEA SOUP

Valerie Selby

Serves 6   Preparation 10 mins.   Advance

2 lbs frozen peas (900 grms)
2 pints vegetable stock or water (1 litre)
½ pint sour cream (¼ litre)

Chopped chives
Croutons to garnish
Salt and pepper

Liquidize peas, mix with liquid. Sprinkle chives on top. Serve with croûtons.

MINT PEA SOUP

Avril Kleeman

Serves 6   Preparation 30 mins.   Advance   Freezable

2 pints white sauce (1 litre)
2 large packets frozen peas
    (mint flavoured)

Fresh mint
½ pint single cream (3 dl)

Cook peas as per packet instructions and liquidize them with the white sauce then heat them together. Add cream. Serve hot or cold and sprinkle with chopped mint at the last moment.

POTAGE CRÈME D'OR

Carolyn Morgan

Serves 4   Preparation 5 mins.   Cook 40 mins.   Advance   Freezable (before adding orange)

1 medium onion
1 lb carrots (450 grms)
1-1½ ozs margarine (30-45 grms)
1 teaspoon arrowroot or cornflour
½ pint fresh orange juice (3 dl)

Nutmeg
Chives or parsley
1 pint chicken stock (½ litre)
Salt and pepper

Peel and thinly slice carrots. Chop onion finely and sauté with carrots in margarine in covered saucepan for 5-7 minutes without browning. Add stock, bring to boil and simmer until tender. Liquidize. Return to saucepan and thicken with cornflour paste. Remove from heat. Add orange juice, seasoning and a little nutmeg. Reheat soup without boiling. Serve with chives or parsley on top.

STRONG MEAT SOUP

Marian Robert

Serves 8   Preparation 15 mins.   Cook 8 hours   Refrigeration 24 hours   Advance

3-4 lbs shin (1 k 350 grms-1 k 800 grms)
1 lb onions (450 grms)
1 lb carrots (450 grms)

Parsnip and turnip (optional)
Salt and black pepper

Cut meat into pieces and put into large saucepan with all other ingredients. Add water to top of saucepan. Bring to boil and skim. Simmer with lid on for 7-8 hours. Strain into large bowl. Allow to cool. Refrigerate for 24 hours. Remove fat before serving. Reheat before serving with vermicelli. A little marmite can be added if necessary.

ST. TROPEZ SOUP

Elaine Greys

Serves 8-10   Preparation 10 mins.   Cook 20 mins.   Advance

Olive oil
1 onion
2 carrots
4 sticks celery
1 green pepper
2-3 courgettes

3 medium potatoes
¼ lb haricot verts (100 grms)
1 clove garlic
Chopped parsley
Salt and pepper

Simmer onions in olive oil. Add finely chopped carrots and celery. Simmer until partly cooked then gradually add the rest of the chopped vegetables and crushed garlic, salt, pepper and parsley. Cover with water and cook until tender.

JOAN'S SUMMER SOUP

Joy Walker

Serves 4   Preparation 10 mins.   Cook 10-15 mins.   Advance   Freezable

1 pint meat stock (½ litre) or
   water and beef cubes
3 chopped sticks celery
1 sliced large onion
1 lb tin tomatoes (450 grms)
2 tablespoons lemon juice

Garlic to taste
Pepper
½ teaspoon sugar
No salt

Add vegetables and seasonings to stock. Simmer for 10-15 minutes.

VEGETABLE SOUP

Tina Greenspan

Serves 6   Preparation 15 mins.   Cook 1½ hours   Advance

1 large onion
1 swede
1 turnip
1 parsnip
1 leek

3 carrots
2-3 sticks celery
5 tomatoes
Marrow bones or chicken giblets
2 chicken cubes
Salt and pepper

Cut all vegetables into pieces except tomatoes. Put giblets or bones into large saucepan of cold water. Bring to boil and skim. Add vegetables and cook until soft. Pour boiling water over tomatoes. Return to saucepan. Add chicken cubes, salt and pepper to taste and cook slowly for a further hour.

CLEAR VEGETABLE SOUP

Jewels Leader-Cramer

Serves 8   Preparation ½ hour   Cook ½ hour   Freezable   Advance

1 leek
6 carrots
2 onions
1 turnip
1 parsnip
4 sticks celery

2 beef cubes
½ pint water (¼ litre)
2 heaped teaspoons mixed herbs
Salt
Pepper

Cut all vegetables into cubes. Extract the juices from vegetables. Double the volume of liquid using the same amount again of water. Dissolve beef cubes in the ½ pint (¼ litre) water. Add to vegetable stock, season to taste. Simmer gently (do not boil as vitamins will be destroyed) for ½ hour. Add herbs 10 minute before end. A chicken cube can be added if desired.

SUMMER VEGETABLE SOUP
Phyllis Kilstock

Serves 6   Preparation 15 mins.   Cook 30 mins.   Advance

1 diced turnip
4 diced carrots
Few lettuce leaves
Some green peas

Few French beans
Few spring onions
Chopped parsley
2 pints water (1 litre)
Salt and pepper

Cut up lettuce, beans and onions. Simmer carrots, beans, peas and other vegetables with seasoning in water until tender. Add chopped parsley before serving. A little cream can be added if necessary.

VEGETABLE AND BARLEY SOUP
Sheila Rosen

Serves 6   Preparation 15 mins.   Cook 1¼ hours   Freezable   Advance

4 potatoes
2 leeks (white part only)
½ head celery
4 carrots

4 onions
Handful washed barley
2 pints (1 litre) stock or cubes and water
Salt and pepper

Clean and cut up all vegetables. Place in saucepan and cover with stock or water and stock cubes, add barley and seasoning. Bring to boil and simmer gently for 1 hour. Blend in liquidizer.

THICK VEGETABLE AND PEA SOUP
Frederica Harris

Serves 8-10   Preparation 20 mins.   Cook 2-3 hours   Advance

½ lb split peas (225 grms)
2 tablespoons barley
½ boiling chicken
1 chicken cube
4 carrots

1 medium parsnip
2 small leeks
1 large onion
1 teaspoon sugar

Place chicken in large saucepan and fill ¾ full with water. Bring to boil and skim. Cut up all vegetables, grate the carrots and add these to saucepan. Bring to boil and simmer gently with rest of ingredients allowing water to bubble slightly. Add more water when necessary and cook until creamy.

VICHYSOISSE

Helen Murray

Serves 6-8   Preparation 20 mins.   Cook 45 mins.   Refrigerate 2 hours.   Freezable   Advance

4 thinly sliced leeks	1 cup milk
(onions can be used as a substitute)	Black pepper
½ cup butter	1 tablespoon chopped chives
2 lbs potatoes (900 grms)	Water
1 cup single cream	Salt

Sauté leeks in butter for 5 min. in a deep saucepan. Add potatoes (thinly sliced) salt and water to barely cover. Simmer for 30 mins. Sieve or liquidize. Chill in refrigerator for at least 2 hours before serving. Stir in chilled cream and milk to desired consistency. Sprinkle with chives and black pepper.

NOTES

Fish

Sprinkle salt on tail of fish to make it easier to grip when removing skin.

To drain fish after frying, place on clean brown paper bags or plain brown paper.

When grilling fish it is much easier to lift for turning if cooked on tinfoil.

An excellent crispy batter for fish (or vegetables). Mix together 5 oz flour (150 grms), salt, pepper, pinch of paprika, pinch bicarbonate of soda and enough water to make a thick batter. Add two whipped egg whites just before using. Frying can be done in advance, then reheat in hot oven Gas No. 6 (400°) for ten minutes.

When grilling fish cutlets, dip both sides in melted butter and season, then only grill one side. This will stop the fish becoming dry.

When serving grilled fish 1) lay 2 or 3 asparagus tips on top and pour some melted butter over. 2) Just before cooking time is up, lay a slice of cheese on fish, return to grill until cheese bubbles.

HEIMISHE STUFFED CARP
Julia Bennett

Serves 6-8   Preparation 40 mins.   Cook 2½ hours   Advance

4 lbs sliced carp (1 k 800 grms)   1 large tablespoon ground almonds
2 lbs chopped haddock (900 grms)   2 eggs
Plenty of fish bones   Salt and pepper
3 large onions   Water for stock
3 large carrots   Medium matzo meal

(Make sure fishmonger knows carp is for stuffing and does not cut belly right through).

Wash carp thoroughly in several waters. Dry with absorbent paper. Place fish bones, carrots and two sliced onions in a fish kettle or shallow pan half full of water and season. Bring to the boil. Skim, simmer for at least 1½ hours. Remove bones. Grate one onion into minced haddock, add beaten eggs, ground almonds and matzo meal to bind. Season, fill each end of carp including head with haddock mixture. Place in fish stock and simmer gently for one hour. Strain liquid off and keep some onions and carrots for garnishing. When cool, place fish in shallow dish, pouring a little sauce over and refrigerate. Place the rest of the sauce in a separate dish and refrigerate. When jelly has set, serve cold with fish.

STUFFED CARP
Bobby Benscher

Serves 4-6   Preparation 40 mins.   Cook 1 hour   Advance

2 lbs carp (900 grms)   Sauce   To decorate
1 large onion   5 cups of water   Hard boiled egg
2 slices soaked white bread   1 large chopped onion   A little parsley
1 teaspoon salt   1 sliced carrot   Olives
1 teaspoon sugar   1 small sliced tomato
½ teaspoon pepper   1 teaspoon salt
Beaten egg to bind   ½ teaspoon pepper
                          1 teaspoon sugar

Soak fish in salt water for 1 hour. Wash thoroughly in vinegar and water. Rinse thoroughly. Cut fish into slices and remove flesh leaving skin intact. Remove bones and keep for sauce. Mince fish and onion finely. Remove excess liquid from bread and add to minced fish with spices and enough beaten egg to bind. Mix well and put back into skins. Put all sauce ingredients into wide shallow pan with fish and cook over very small light for one hour. Test that fish is soft. When cold, lift fish out carefully. Strain liquid and pour on fish. Decorate with wedges of hard boiled egg, parsley and olives.

FISH FILLETS IN CREAM SAUCE WITH MUSHROOMS
Marily Ungar

Serves 4   Preparation 20 mins.   Gas No 6 (400°)   Cook 35-40 mins

12 fillets of plaice or lemon sole   Salt, pepper and nutmeg
12 ozs. sliced and fried mushrooms (350 grms)   Small glass white wine or sherry
Large carton double cream

Wash fillets. Roll and put closely together in oven proof dish. Cook for a few minutes until the fillets are opaque. Sprinkle with the fried mushrooms. Season well with salt, pepper and nutmeg. Stir wine gently into cream. Pour sauce over fish and place in oven.

FISH AND GRAPE CASSEROLE
Rusty Sotnick

Serves 3-4   Preparation 20 mins.   Gas No 6 (400°)   Cook 30 mins.

6 ozs. green grapes (175 grms)
1 lb. cooked and flaked haddock
    or any white fish (450 grms)
¼ pint fresh cream (2 dl.)
Salt and pepper

1 lb. mashed potato (450 grms)
1 beaten egg
2 tablespoons milk
1 oz. butter (30 grms)
4 ozs. grated cheese (100 grms)

Butter casserole. Arrange de-seeded grapes over bottom of dish. Mix fish with cream and seasonings and place over grapes. Mix potatoes with egg and milk - put over fish. Flatten top with fork. Cover with foil and bake for 20 minutes. Remove foil. Sprinkle top with cheese and grill until brown.

FISH PIE
Monica Morris

Serves 6   Preparation 15 mins.   Gas No. 5 (375°)   Cook 45 mins.

2 lbs. fresh haddock (900 grms)
2½ lbs. mashed potato (1125 grms)
Little grated cheese
Butter
Salt and pepper

CHEESE SAUCE
1 oz butter (30 grms)
1 oz plain flour (30 grms)
½ pint milk (3 dl)
3 ozs grated cheese (80 grms)
Salt and pepper

Wash haddock. Cook in covered pan in a little water for 5 mins. Flake fish from skin and remove any bones. Place in a greased casserole dish and season. To make sauce: melt butter. Add flour, milk, salt and pepper and nearly all the cheese (leave remainder of cheese to garnish). Simmer sauce for a few minutes and cover the fish. Top with mashed potatoes, sprinkle with the rest of the grated cheese and a few knobs of butter. Bake in oven.

GEFILTE FISH (1)
Millie Goldston

Serves 8   Preparation 45 mins.   Cook 1½ hours   Freezable   Advance

4 lbs minced fish (1k 800 grms)
3 eggs
2 minced Spanish onion
2 oz ground almonds (50 grms)
Medium matzo meal
¼ cup of oil

Salt, pepper and sugar
A little cold water
Oil to fry
1½ pints of water to boil (1 litre)
2 sliced onions
8 carrots

Mix all ingredients together until the texture is like a hamburger mixture. Take handfuls and shape into balls. If frying dip in matzo meal and fry until brown in oil. To boil - put two sliced onions and carrots with salt, pepper and two tablespoons of sugar in a large saucepan in water. Bring to the boil and put fish balls in. Boil for 1½ hours.

41

GEFILTE FISH (2)

Sally Bloom

Serves 14	Preparation 1 hour	Cook 2 hours	Freezable	Advance

2 lbs small haddock (900 grms)
1 lb tail of carp, lash or pike (450 grms)
1½ lbs bream (700 grms)
1 lb whiting (450 grms)
½ lb halibut flap (225 grms)
1 lb tail of hake (450 grms)
3 medium onions
3 eggs
1 cup of cold water
1 dessertspoon of sugar
Salt and pepper
2 tablespoons medium matzo meal

Fish Stock
1 lb fish bones (450 grms)
2 sliced onions
3 sliced carrots
4 tablespoons of ground almonds
Salt
Pepper
A little sugar
N.B. Ask your fishmonger to skin and
      fillet the fish and reserve the
      bones for the stock.
      All given weights include bones.

Place bones, onions and carrots in fish kettle, cover well with water and bring to boil, skim, add seasoning, cover pan and simmer for 30 mins, strain liquid. Keep carrots. Mince fish and grate onions and add all remaining ingredients. Mix together thoroughly. Form into oval balls with wet hands, make sure that the mixture is of a soft consistency. Cook fish balls in the stock simmering gently in covered pan for 1½ hours. To serve. Allow to cool and place a slice of the cooked carrot on each piece, pour a little of the stock over the fish and serve the remainder separately.

CRISPY BAKED HALIBUT

Jackie Leigh

Serves 2	Preparation 10 mins.	Gas No. 3 (350°)	Cook 20-30 mins.

1 cup crumbled Ritz crackers
1 handful of slivered almonds

Slice of halibut
Butter
Lemon and parsley - to decorate

Dab fish slice with butter and season. Place in buttered ovenware dish and cover with cracker crumbs and almonds. Dot with butter. Bake according to thickness. Decorate with lemon and parsley.

HALIBUT CREOLE

Phyllis Kilstock

Serves 8	Preparation 10 mins.	Gas No. 3 (350°)	Cook 30 mins.

8 good sized steaks of halibut
Cup of white wine
4 tablespoons tomato ketchup
Salt and pepper

2 lemons
Cup of water
Grated cheese
Paprika

Rub the fish on both sides with lemon and place in a greased shallow baking dish. Season with salt, pepper and sprinkle with paprika. Mix ketchup, water and wine together and pour over fish. Cover with greased paper and bake, basting occasionally. Before serving sprinkle with cheese and brown under the grill. This is delicious served with pommes almandine and petits pois.

HALIBUT WITH EGG AND LEMON SAUCE   Ruth Simmons

Serves 4   **Preparation 10 mins.**   **Cook 20 mins.**

4 slices halibut   SAUCE:
2 large sliced carrots   2 lemons
1 large sliced Spanish onion   Castor sugar
Salt   4 beaten eggs
Pepper   1 cup fish liquor

Bring a saucepan of water to the boil together with seasoning, carrots and onion. Wrap each piece of fish individually in greaseproof paper (this keeps each slice of fish intact without flaking) and place gently into saucepan. Return to boil and allow to simmer gently with lid on for twenty minutes. Halfway through cooking time remove one cupful fish liquor. Allow fish to cool slightly in the water before removing from saucepan. Remove greaseproof from fish when cool.
SAUCE: Mix cooled cupful of liquor with eggs slowly. Pour into saucepan and add sugar and lemon to taste. Heat very slowly, stirring continuously until sauce comes to the boil. Continue to simmer, still stirring for one to two minutes until sauce thickens. Serve cold poured over fish. Must be made on day. Sauce cannot be re-heated.

HALIBUT IN GREEN MAYONNAISE   Ann Millett

Serves 4   **Preparation 20 mins.**   **Cook ½ hour Gas No. 4 (350°)**   **Cook 20-30 mins.**

4 halibut or haddock steaks 1" thick   SAUCE:
8 peppercorns   1 ripe avocado
2 blades mace   ¼ pint thick mayonnaise (2 dl)
Salt   4 lettuce leaves
2 tablespoons wine vinegar   1 lemon
2-3 fronds dill   4 feathery fronds of dill
                                        1 level dessertspoon chopped dill

Wipe the fish and arrange in shallow ovenproof dish. Scatter peppercorns and mace over the top and sprinkle with salt. Add enough water just to cover fish, then add vinegar and place dill on top. Cover dish with lid or foil, place in oven until bone will slip out. Leave fish in liquid to cool for at least half an hour. Drain fish on absorbent kitchen paper. Remove skin and small bones. When fish is cold arrange on lettuce leaves. Before serving, peel avocado and remove stone. Cut into quarters and lay on fish. Mix chopped dill into mayonnaise and put a good spoonful on each piece of fish. Decorate with fronds of dill and slices of lemon.

HALIBUT PROVENÇAL   Karol Solomons

Serves 4-6   **Preparation 10 mins.**   **Gas No. 5 (375°)**   **Cook 30 mins.**

2½ lbs halibut (1 k 125 grms)   1 large tin tomatoes
Freshly ground black pepper   3 cloves garlic
Salt   ½ lb stuffed olives (225 grms)
½ lemon   Parsley
2 large onions

Cut halibut into squares. Dry thoroughly then sprinkle with salt, pepper and lemon juice. Fry onion and garlic, add tinned tomatoes and simmer for 15 minutes. Put fish in large dish and pour sauce mixture over fish. Place in oven.

43

BAKED HALIBUT WITH TOMATO AND ONION SAUCE   Ruth Simmons

Serves 4   Preparation 15 mins.   Gas No 4 (350°)   Cook 20 mins.

4 slices halibut
1 large onion
½ lb. tomatoes (225 grms)
4 oz. butter (100 grms)

¾ pint milk (½ litre)
1 level tablespoon plain flour
Parsley
Salt and pepper

Chop onion, fry gently in butter until soft. Butter oven dish and spread half onion and chopped parsley over bottom of dish. Place fish on top, season, add milk (level with fish). Spread other half of onion and parsley on top, dot with butter and bring to the boil. Bake in oven for fifteen minutes. Remove from oven, drain sauce and keep fish warm. Reduce sauce to half pint. Blend one ounce butter and flour to a roux and slowly add sauce until thickened. Meanwhile have tomatoes peeled and chopped, cooked lightly in butter, salt and pepper. Pour sauce over fish and spread tomato mixture on top of sauce. Sprinkle with dots of butter and chopped parsley and place under hot grill until bubbling. Serve with creamed potatoes. Must be made on the day.

SOUSED MACKERELS   Jemma Levine

Serves 4   Preparation 5 mins.   Marinate 4 hours   Cook 10 mins.

4 mackerels
½ pint oil (3 dl)
Mixed herbs

2 bay leaves
1 onion
2 cloves garlic

Soak mackerels in herbs, oil, onion and garlic for 4 hours. Grill on both sides.

MAQUEREAUX À L' HONGROISE   Sheila Shaw

Serves 4   Preparation 15 mins.   Gas No. 7 (425°)   Cook 25 mins.

4 fresh mackerel
1 teaspoonful paprika
2 green peppers
½ lb tomatoes (225 grms)

1 onion
3 large potatoes (optional)
1 cup soured cream or yoghurt
1 oz butter (30 grms)
Salt

Clean fish and remove heads and tails. With sharp knife make incisions on each side at intervals of 1 inch. Rub each fish with a little salt and paprika. Cut peppers, tomatoes and onions into quarter inch slices. Put them alternately into cuts made in fish. Slice potatoes thinly. Grease bottom of shallow fire proof dish with butter. Cover bottom of dish with sliced potatoes and dot with remaining butter. Place fish on potatoes. Pour over a little soured cream or yoghurt. Place dish in hot oven, basting with rest of soured cream or yoghurt occasionally.

MAQUEREAU MARINES   Goldie Allan

Serves 8   Preparation 30 mins.   Gas No. 2 (325⁰) Cook 30 mins.   Advance

8 large fat fillets of mackerel
1 bottle white wine
¾ cup vinegar
2 medium onions
1 large carrot

4-6 shallots
Parsley, thyme, bayleaf
Salt and peppercorns
Small teaspoon oil

Clean and wipe fish dry. Place in earthenware baking dish. Place all ingredients - except oil - in a saucepan and cook for 20 minutes, while still boiling pour over the mackerel. Cover with a piece of oiled or buttered parchment paper and cook in oven. Remove. Pour oil over fish and allow to cool. This should be served cold in the marinade. (DO NOT USE metal baking dish).

MEXICAN FISH   Masha Greenbaum

Serves 10   Preparation 10 mins.   Gas No. 4 (360⁰)   Cook 30 mins.   Freezable   Advance

4 lbs. minced fish (1 k 800grms)
5 beaten egg yolks
5 beaten egg whites
3½ ozs. fine matzo meal (95 grms)
Pepper, salt

Spice or seaweed
2 tablespoons oil
Scant 4 ozs. tomato ketchup (1 dl.)

Reserving a little egg white for topping, mix all ingredients — except oil. Place oil in large pyrex dish. Put mixture in dish and top with beaten egg whites. Place in oven (When freezing do not add topping).

PORTUGESE PLAICE   Jo Garretto

Serves 4   Preparation 10 mins.   Gas No. 4 (360⁰)   Cook 25 mins.   Advance

1 tablespoon chives
3 skinned tomatoes
1 oz. butter (30 grms)

8 fillets plaice
White wine
Salt and pepper

Chop chives and fry in butter with sliced tomatoes for a few minutes. Pour into ovenproof dish. Fold each fillet in three and lay on tomatoes. Cover with wine. Add salt and pepper and bake.

PLAICE AND CHEESE CASSEROLE
Jo Garretto

Serves 4   Preparation 30 mins.   Gas No. 5 (375°)   Cook 20 mins.

8 fillets of plaice
3 ozs. grated cheese (80 grms)
½ lb. skinned tomatoes (225 grms)

Sauce:
1 oz. flour (30 grms)
½ pint milk (3 dl.)
1 oz. butter (30 grms)

Fold plaice in half. Sprinkle with salt and pepper and place in casserole. Cove with half the grated cheese and bake for 10-15 minutes until cooked. To make sauce, melt butter. Add flour then gradually add milk. Bring to the boil stirring constantly. Add almost all cheese. Slice tomatoes and add ½ to sauce. Season well. Allow to cool slowly for 5 minutes, then pour over the fish. Cover with remainder of grated cheese and sliced tomatoes and grill until golden brown.

SCALLOPS OF PLAICE
Carol Hill

Serves 4   Preparation 20 mins.   Gas No. 3 (350°)   Cook 15-20 mins.

4 skinned plaice fillets
¼ lb. mushrooms (100 grms)
1 oz. plain flour (30 grms)
1 oz. margarine (30 grms)
½ pint milk (3 dl.)
1 sliced onion
1 sliced carrot

4 ovenproof scallop shells
¾ pint water (½ litre)
1 plaice bone
Creamed potato for piping
2 peppercorns
GARNISH
Crated cheese and breadcrumbs

Make a fish stock using the bone, onion, carrot and peppercorns and water. Cool and strain. Fold fish into three and place in a casserole. Pour stock over fish and cook until white. Cook mushrooms in milk. Make a sauce with the margarine, flour, milk and mushrooms. Pipe potato border round the shells. Put the fish into shells. Pour sauce over and scatter cheese and crumb mixture on top and grill until golden. Serve with brownbread and butter.

QUENELLES OF FISH
Phyllis Jacobs

Serves 8   Preparation 1 hour   Cook 20 mins.

1 lb. boned halibut or turbot (450 grms) or
1½ lbs. boned whiting (700 grms)
Nutmeg
Salt and pepper

3 eggs
½ pint bechamel sauce (3 dl.)
Accompanying sauce as preferred
To decorate:
1½ lbs. mushrooms (700 grms)

Chop fish and mince twice. When sauce in cold mix with fish, nutmeg, salt, and pepper. Beat 3 eggs into mixture (if too thick add an extra egg white). Put mixture into fridge to chill ½ hour before cooking. Using floured hands roll mixture into small sausage shapes. Drop into boiling water then lower heat so that they do not boil. When cooked they will rise to top of pan (approximately 15-20 minutes). Drain and arrange on platter. Cover with mushrooms, tomato or curry sauce as desired and decorate with fried button mushrooms. Serve hot.

QUENELLES AU FROMAGE

B. Dersch

Serves 8   Preparation ½ hour   Gas No. 4 (360°)   Cook 30 mins.   Freezable   Advance

2 lbs. mixed white fish, haddock,
    hake, etc. (**900 grms**)
3 stale trifle sponges
1 tablespoon ground almonds
2 eggs
2 tablespoons cream or sour cream
1 grated onion
¾ pint water (½ litre)
Salt and pepper
Pinch of saffron (optional)
½ sliced onion
Parmesan cheese

Cheese Sauce:
¼ lb. grated cheddar cheese (**100 grms**)
½ pint milk (3 dl.)
Fish stock:
1 heaped tablespoon flour
½ oz. butter (15 grms)
Eggspoon of mustard
Salt and pepper

Put sponges into mincer followed by skinned and boned fish. Add grated onion, almonds, cream, seasoning and eggs. Mix well (if smoother texture is required put mixture in liquidiser). Put the water into a non stick pan with sliced onion, pepper, salt and saffron. Bring to the boil. Add small oval balls of fish mixture and simmer gently for ¾ hour. Transfer fish to an ovenware casserole. **To make sauce** Strain stock and mix with milk. Make a white sauce using the above ingredients. Fold in the grated cheese. Pour over the fish and shake a little parmesan over the top of the dish. Bake in oven. This dish should be served hot and is suitable for an entree.

LEMON SOLE WITH CHEESE AND ORANGE SAUCE

Ruth Glatman

Serves 4   Preparation 20 mins.   Cook 20 mins.

4 fillets lemon sole or plaice
2 ozs. butter or margarine (50 grms)
1 tablespoon flour
3 ozs. grated cheddar cheese (80 grms)

1 orange
Salt and pepper
Parsley and orange slices to garnish

Grate orange rind. Squeeze and make up to ¼ pint (2 dl.) with water. Melt butter or margarine in frying pan. Add grated orange rind and saute for 1 minute. Add fish and saute gently flesh side down for two minutes then turn and saute for a further 5 minutes. Transfer fish to ovenproof dish and keep warm. Blend flour to remaining fat in pan and slow to cook for one minute. Remove from heat and blend in orange juice. Return to heat and stir until thickened. Add two ounces of grated cheese. Pour sauce over fish. Sprinkle with remaining cheese. Brown under hot grill. Garnish with chopped parsley and twisted orange slices. This dish makes a nice entree. If used for main course serve with creamed potatoes and peas.

SOLE OR PLACE GOUJONS

Benita Silverman

Serves 2   Preparation 15 mins.   Cook 20 mins.

2 medium plaice or
Lemon sole filletted
4 ozs. medium matzo meal (100 grms)

1 beaten egg
Salt and pepper
Oil

TARTARE SAUCE (See Sauce Section)

Cut fish into strips and dip into matzo meal and then into beaten seasoned egg. Dip once more in matzo meal and deep fry in oil until golden brown. Serve with tartare sauce and lemon wedges.

SOLE EN CRÔUTE

Ruth Starr

Serves 4   Preparation 30 mins.   Gas No. 5 (375°)   Cook 45 mins.

8 fillets of sole
1 small finely chopped onion
2 ozs. butter (50 grms)
2 ozs. finely chopped mushrooms (50 grms)
Salt and pepper

A little chopped parsley
A little dried tarragon
A few white breadcrumbs
12 ozs. puff pastry (350 grms)
1 egg

Trim fillets to equal size. Season. Sauté onion until soft. Add mushrooms and cook until tender. Add parsley and tarragon and sufficient breadcrumbs to bind mixture. Leave to cool. Roll pastry into two lengths, one slightly longer and wider than the other. Place fillets on the smallest piece of pastry and spread some filling on each. Moisten pastry between the fillets. Place larger piece of pastry on top and press down between fillets to form eight portions. Cut between each and press gently into shape. Place on slightly damp oven tray and refrigerate for 30 minutes. Glaze with beaten egg and bake until pastry is cooked. Serve with a rich white sauce or cheese and parsley sauce.

SOLE GEORGETTE

Jemma Levene

Serves 4   Preparation 1 hour   Cook 30 mins.

4 baked potatoes
1 cooked sole
½ pint cheese sauce (3 dl.)

4 ozs. cooked mushrooms (100 grms)
1 oz. grated cheese (30 grms)

Scoop out potatoes and fill with flaked fish and mushrooms. Cover with sauce. Pipe remaining potato round edge. Scatter cheese on top and grill.

SOLE A L'INDIENNE

Elaine Machover

Serves 4   Preparation 20 mins.   Cook 20 mins.

2-2½ lbs. skinned & filleted dover sole
    or plaice (900-1k 250 grms)
1 large onion
2 ozs. butter (50 grms)
1 tablespoon curry powder

2 dessert apples (Cox's if possible)
4 medium tomatoes
½ pint single cream (3 dl.)
Salt and pepper
Parsley

Cut each fillet into four strips. Tie each strip into single knot. Chop the onion finely and saute in butter until transparent. Add curry powder and fry together for 1 minute. Add apples and tomatoes which have been peeled, cored and diced. Cook together for 5 minutes. Add fish and cream and cook for further 8 minutes. Serve on dish with freshly chopped parsley.

SOLE WITH ORANGE

Stella Majeran

Serves 4   Preparation 10 mins.   Cook 10 mins.

4 fillets sole
2 ozs. butter (50 grms)
1 large orange

Salt and pepper
Flour

Sprinkle sole with salt and pepper and coat lightly with flour. Heat half the butter in a pan and fry fillets until lightly brown and remove from pan and place on hot dish. Peel orange, remove as much pith as possible and cut into slices. Arranges slices on each fillet. Heat remainder of butter until light brown, pour over fish and serve at once.

FILLETS OF SOLE À LA PORTUGAISE

Mrs. S. Solk

Serves 4   Preparation 35 mins.   Gas No. 3 (350⁰)   Cook 20 mins.   Advance

2 lbs. lemon or dover sole (900 grms)
4 teaspoons grated cheese
2 small grated onions
Tomato sauce (see Sauce Section)

4 ozs. breadcrumbs (100 grms)
2 large tomatoes
Egg or milk
Margarine

Skin fish. Peel tomatoes and mash to pulp and mix with crumbs, cheese and grated onion. Season and add sufficient beaten egg or milk to bind. Spread fish with some mixture and roll tightly commencing at the wide end of the fillet. Stand fillets in well greased oven dish and if there is any stuffing left over roll it into small balls and place around fish. Place small pieces of margarine in dish and cover with greaseproof paper and bake. When ready pour tomato sauce over and serve.

TRUITES FARÇIES

Carolynn Morgan

Serves 4   Preparation 1 hour   Gas No. 3 (350⁰)   Cook 30 mins.

4 trout
1 lb. whiting or fresh haddock (450 grms)
3 small lightly beaten egg whites
1½ gills double cream (2 dl.)
Salt and pepper

1½ ozs. butter (45 grms)
1-2 finely chopped shallots
1 glass white wine
1 dessertspoon chopped parsley
Brandy

Split trout down back and carefully remove backbone and head. To prepare stuffing remove skin from whiting or haddock before passing fish through mincer or blender. Gradually mix egg whites into fish. Place mixture into a bowl and beat in cream by degrees. Season. Fill the trout with stuffing and reshape. Lift into buttered oven-proof dish. Pour over a little melted butter and cook in oven for 15-20 minutes. Place under hot grill to crispen the skin. To make sauce, soften shallots in butter and cook till pale golden. Add wine and seasoning and cook rapidly for 1 minute. Add a dash of brandy and parsley to the pan and pour over fish — serve immediately. It is advisable to cook the trout in the dish from which they will be served since they are delicate to move once cooked.

TUNA CASSEROLE

Estelle R. O. Lewis

Serves 4   Preparation 30 mins.   Gas No. 6 (400⁰)   Cook 20 mins.

1 x 7 ozs. tin tuna fish (200 grms)
1 x 8 ozs. box egg noodles (225 grms)
1 onion

1 tin condensed mushroom soup
4-5 ozs. grated cheddar cheese (100-150grms)
Milk

Boil noodles in salted water with lid off for 10 minutes (do not overcook). Strain oil from tuna and break up into large bowl. Chop onion and add to tuna. Mix tin of soup with ⅓ tin of milk over low heat. Stir soup into tuna and onion. Strain noodles and add to tuna mixture. Stir mixture very gently try not to break noodles. Pour into buttered casserole and cover with grated cheese. Cook in hot oven.

50

Meat

When a recipe needs a strong wine taste but only a very little liquid, reduce wine by fast boiling to concentrate the flavour. It's a good way of using up remains, and a wonderfully effective tenderizer for the less tender cuts of meat.

Keep salt and pepper and plain flour ready mixed in plastic container for Schnitzels etc.

To coat cut-up meat in seasoned flour speedily and evenly, place both in a plastic bag, hold it firmly closed and toss the meat up and down.

If recipe for meat meal requires SMALL quantity of cream use parev whip instead.

Meat balls are nicer if minced veal is used with minced beef in equal quantities.

Mix sausage meat with egg and matzo meal and grated onion and make into a fat roll. Cover with puff pastry, brush with egg and prick with fork. Cook in hot oven for fifty five minutes. Serve with sweet and sour sauce or tomato sauce.

Mince any left-over cold meat, add seasonings, Worcester sauce, grated onion and moisten with gravy or stock and (A) stuff green peppers or scooped out tomatoes and bake in moderate oven for ¾ hr. or (B) stuff pancakes, cover with tomato sauce and heat through in the oven. Sprinkle with parsley.

Lamb or veal chops are delicious when fried having been dipped in egg and breadcrumbs first.

A nice change for coating meat is to use equal quantities of matzo meal, breadcrumbs and crushed cornflakes.

Quick way to thicken a soup or casserole is to add a little instant potato mix.

Quick way to slice liver really thinly: pour a cup of boiling water over it, leave for 1 minute, then drain and slice with a sharp knife.

Beef

CHOLENT
A Slow Cooker

Serves 6   Preparation 20 mins   Gas No 5 (375°)   Cook 18 hours approx.   Advance

2 lbs. brisket of beef (900 grms)
8 ozs. haricot or butter beans (225 grms)
(Beans must have been soaked in
    water for 5 hours)
4 tablespoons oil
1 chopped onion
6 ozs. rice (175 grms)
6 tomatoes
6 peeled potatoes
Pinch of cinnamon
Salt and black pepper
1 tablespoon of sugar

DUMPLINGS
3 tablespoons chicken fat
4 ozs. Self Raising flour (100 grms)
1 oz. semolina (30 grms)
1 egg
¼ teaspoon nutmeg
1 small grated onion
2 teaspoons chopped parsley
Salt
Pepper

Drain the beans and reserve. Fry the onion until soft in the oil, add the rice and fry gently until it is slightly golden not brown. Add peeled and sliced tomatoes and cook stirring for 5 minutes. Put half the beans, the tomato mixture and the potatoes in the bottom of a large casserole dish, sprinkle with half the seasonings. Place the meat on top. To make the dumplings:– Combine all ingredients until well mixed and divide into the required amount of dumplings. Roll into balls with wet hands. Place them round the meat. Add rest of ingredients and pour over enough boiling water to cover, sprinkle top with sugar. Cover with greasproof paper and casserole lid and cover whole with tinfoil. Place in the middle of the oven for 30 minutes then reduce heat to Gas No ½ (275°) and leave until required.

BEEF CHOW MEIN
Valerie Green

Serves 4-6   Preparation 40 mins.   Cook 30 mins.   Freezable   Advance

¾ lb. bola (325 grms)
1 teaspoon salt
2 teaspoons sugar
1 tablespoon soy sauce
Pinch accent
4 Chinese dried mushrooms
16 oz. can bean sprouts (450 grms)
5 oz. can bamboo shoots (150 grms)

2 tablespoons cornflour
¾ pint beef stock (½ litre)
3 tablespoons nut oil
4 oz. Chinese dried egg noodles (100 grms)
Oil for deep frying
1 beaten egg
4 spring onions

Cut beef into long strips approx. 2″ x ¼″ x ¾″ (5cms x ¾cm x ¾cm). Mix together in a bowl the salt, sugar, accent and soy sauce. Marinate the beef in this for 30 minutes. Soak mushrooms in warm water for 20 minutes. Rinse and squeeze dry and slice – discarding stalks. Drain bean sprouts, rinse in cold water and drain again. Slice bamboo shoots into thin strips. Cut spring onions into 1″ lengths. Mix cornflour and stock together. Drain beef and reserve any remaining marinade. Heat oil in pan and fry beef, stirring constantly. Cover for 10-15 minutes and simmer gently until beef is soft. Add prepared vegetables and simmer another 5 minutes. Cook noodles in boiling water for 5 minutes, drain thoroughly. Deep fry just before needed in hot oil. Drain well on absorbent paper. Beat egg with 1 tablespoon water and pour into heated highly oiled omelette pan. Make small omelette and cut into strips. To serve – place noodles on heated serving dish, top with beef mixture and garnish with strips of omelette. – Delicious!!
Omit noodles if freezing.

BEEF FONDUE

Faith Duke

Serves 6   **Preparation ½ hour.**

3 lbs. Ball of the Rib (1 kilo 350 grms)   **1 pint corn oil (½ litre)**
Salt and Pepper

Trim all fat off the meat and cut in 1" cubes. Season with salt and pepper. Divide into six portions. Heat oil in Fondue Pan in centre of table. Each guest then cooks their own meat according to their own taste in the oil. Serve with a variety of sauces from the sauce section, accompanied by banana pieces, onions, olives, gherkins etc. and a mixed salad.
A variety of ready made sauces are available in the shops.

BEEF STEW

Val Ross

Serves 4-6   **Preparation 20 mins.**   **Pressure Cook 25 mins.**   **Freezable**   **Advance**

2 lbs. cubed chuck steak (900 grms)   **6 quartered potatoes**
1 Spanish onion   **2 tablespoons Worcester sauce**
1 x 1 lb. 3 oz. tin carrots (530 grms)   **Salt and pepper**
1 x 1 lb. 3 oz. tin tomatoes, larger if liked   **A little fat**
Any left over peas or other vegetables

Peel and slice onions. Fry onions and meat in a little fat until brown all over. Add tin of carrots and tomatoes, strained, keeping juices. Add ¼ pint (2 dl.) juices, Worcester sauce and seasonings. Cook at 15 lb. pressure for 15 minutes. Allow cooker to cool slowly. Add quartered potatoes stir in well. Close cooker and cook for further 10 minutes at 15 lb. (6 k 750 grms).

BOEUF À LA MODE DE LA BARONESE DE ALMEIRIM Ilda Dentith

Serves 10   **Preparation ½ hour.**   **Gas No 5 (370⁰)**   **Cook 2 hours**

6 lbs. best steak – cubed (2 kilos 700 grms)   **1 tablespoon cornflour**
3 chopped very fine large onions   **¼ cup very fine chopped parsley**
2 grated large carrots   **4 tablespoons olive oil**
¼ pt. Madeira wine (2 dl.)   **Pinch of nutmeg**
¼ pt. brandy (2 dl.)   **Flour & water paste for sealing**
¼ pt. port wine (2 dl.)   **Salt and pepper**
2 cups stock

This dish must be made in a large oven to table casserole dish. Sprinkle meat with salt and pepper and nutmeg, fry it in the oil, in a very large pan all at once, until golden brown. Take the meat from the fat and place in the casserole. Fry the onions in the same fat for a few minutes until golden brown. Add to the steak and the grated carrots. Flambé the beef with the brandy add the port, the Madeira, cornflour and stock, season to taste, and cover with lid. Make a flour and water paste dough to seal rim, roll out and cover lid of the casserole (this is for the steam to stay in the meat instead of getting out while the meat is cooking). Put the casserole in a medium hot oven and cook for two hours, just before serving take off the pastry, it is not good to eat. Leave the lid on until you serve the dish. It should be served very hot with chopped parsley.

BOEUF BOURGIGNON

Wendy Max

Serves 8	Preparation 20 mins.	Cook 2½ hrs.	Freezable

3 lbs. stewing steak (1k 350 grms)
1 large onion
½ lb. button mushrooms (225 grms)
3 tablespoons oil
3 tablespoons plain flour

½ bottle red wine
1 pint stock (½ litre)
1 tablespoon tomato purée
Salt, pepper, bay leaf
Garlic (optional)

Cube the steak. Slice the onion. Trim the stalks of the mushrooms and chop trimmings, wipe the whole mushrooms with a damp cloth. Fry the steak with the sliced onion and the chopped mushroom trimmings in the oil until the meat is brown and the onions soft. Add the flour, stir and cook for a minute. Heat the wine and add gradually to the mixture, blending well. Add enough stock to cover the meat. Add tomato purée, salt, pepper, bayleaf and garlic (crushed with salt with the tip of a round knife) and lastly the whole mushrooms. Simmer gently for 2 hours. Serve with plain boiled rice.

BOEUF EN CROÛTE

Martin Spears

Serves 4-6	Preparation 1 hour 40 mins.	Gas No 6 (400°)	Cook 1 hr.

2 lbs. beef (900 grms)
Salt and pepper
Other seasonings
2 oz. fat (50 grms)
String to tie

1 tablespoon oil
½ lb. liver paté (225 grms)
¾ lb. puff pastry (350 grms)
1 beaten egg

Trim meat, make sure there is no fat, season and tie in a roll very firmly, mix the oil with 1 oz. (30 grms) of fat. Fry the beef, to seal, until brown all over and then pop in oven in the remaining fat for 15 minutes. Remove from oven and leave till cold then take off binding string. Spread paté over joint, roll out pastry place meat on pastry, paté side down, cover the top with the rest of paté, fold pastry round meat, seal edge of pastry with beaten egg, place meat in cooking tin with the join underneath, brush with the rest of the beaten egg, decorate the top with pieces of cut out pastry. Bake for 40 minutes.

BRISKET OF BEEF SAUERKRAUT

Mrs. L. Ableson

Serves 6	Preparation ½ hour	Cook 3 hours	Advance

3 lbs. boneless brisket (1k 350 grms)
1 large potato
1 teaspoon caraway seeds

2 pints sauerkraut (1 litre)
2 tablespoons flour
1 teaspoon brown sugar

Peel and grate potato. Put half the sauerkraut in a saucepan and sprinkle with flour. Lay the meat on top and cover with the rest of sauerkraut and grated potato. Sprinkle over sugar and caraway seeds and pour over sufficient boiling water to cover. Put on lid and simmer gently for 3 hours.

CHINESE PEPPER STEAK

Debbie Smith

Serves 4   Preparation 20 mins.   Cook 20 mins.

4 round thinly cut steaks
¼ cup melted margarine
1 crushed garlic clove
¼ teaspoon salt
¼ teaspoon pepper
4 tablespoons soy sauce
Pea pods or mushrooms optional

1 cup bean sprouts (fresh or canned)
2 large tomatoes (quartered)
2 finely sliced peppers
½ tablespoon cornflour
2 tablespoons cold water
4 spring onions, shallots or chives

Tenderise meat. Heat margarine and add garlic, salt and pepper. Add beef and lightly brown. Add soy sauce. Cover and cook over high heat for 5 minutes. Add bean sprouts, tomatoes and peppers. Cover and cook for further 5 minutes. Stir cornflour in little cold water and add, stirring to thicken. Sprinkle with onions. Serve with rice.

DANISH GOULASH

Mrs. V. Knobil

Serves 5-6   Preparation 20 mins.   Cook 2½ hours   Advance   Freezable

2 lbs. chuck steak – cubed (900 grms)
2 tablespoons oil
2 large onions peeled & chopped
1 clove garlic crushed
1 oz. flour (30 grms)

1 bayleaf
Pinch of thyme (if liked)
Seasoning
½ pint stock, or water (3 dl.)
Parsley for decoration

Fry meat in hot oil to seal, set aside. Lightly brown the chopped onions and crushed garlic, then stir in the flour and cook for 2-3 minutes. Add the liquid, return the meat to the pan and stir in seasoning and bayleaf. Bring to the boil, cover and simmer for about 2 hours, stirring occasionally and adding more water when necessary. Garnish with finely chopped parsley before serving.

TURKISH MEAT BALLS WITH AUBERGINE PURÉE

Marion Cohen

Serves 4-5   Preparation 15 mins.   Cook 30 mins.   Freezable   Advance

4-6 Aubergines
2 lb. finely minced beef (900 grms)
2 eggs
3 tablespoons breadcrumbs
1 teaspoon ground cumin
1 teaspoon ground allspice

Salt and black pepper
Flour
3 tablespoons oil
1 large sliced onion
2 tablespoons tomato purée

Wash aubergines. Grill aubergines until skin is charred all over. Cool and rub skins off under cold water. Drain off as much bitter juices as possible and mash flesh with fork. Combine mince, eggs, seasoning, breadcrumbs and shape into small balls. Roll in flour and fry in oil until cooked through. Remove and drain. In same oil fry the sliced onion until soft and golden. Add aubergine purée and tomato purée. Season to taste and cook gently for 10 minutes. Drop in meat balls and simmer for final 10 minutes. Serve with plain rice of bread and salads.

MEAT BALLS AND PICKLED WALNUT STEW
Carole Jay

Serves 5-6   Preparation 30 mins.   Gas No 4 (350°)   Cook 3 hours   Freezable   Advance

1½ lb. lean chuck steak (500 grms)
6 large carrots
4 sliced large onions
Salt and pepper
4 tablespoons oil or margarine
Flour
1 jar pickled walnuts

MEAT BALLS
1 large chopped onion
Small bunch chopped parsley
½ squeezed lemon
1 lb. minced meat (450 grms)
Salt and Pepper
Fine matzo meal
1 egg

Cut meat into 2″ (5cms) cubes and roll in flour. Heat oil or margarine in pan. Gently sweat sliced onions and carrots for 15 minutes. Add floured meat and stir occasionally — about 10 minutes. Flavour — add cold water to cover. Put on lid and simmer until nearly cooked (or in oven for 2 hours). Add the small meat balls and cook for another 30 minutes. Crush 8 pickled walnuts in the juice. Stir in gently and let simmer.

STEAK FLAMBÉ WITH MADAGASGAR GREEN PEPPERS
Fernand Burn

Serves 4   Preparation 10 mins.   Cook 10 mins

4 thick steaks
Brandy
Salt
2 soup spoons Madagascar Green Pepper (in juice)

Beef stock cube
Parsley Margarine
(Mix finely chopped parsley into tomor and
    make into small pats)

Fry steaks in hot fat to seal. Pour over brandy and flame. When flame is dead, season. Remove steaks to hot service plate. Take one spoonful of peppers and mash with a fork. Add to sauce and replace steaks. Place remaining pepper on top of each steak. Place a pat of parsley margarine on top of each steak and serve immediately. If there is not sufficient gravy add a stock cube and a little extra water after removing the steaks.

STUFFED MARROW
Muriel Rossner

Serves 4   Preparation 15 mins   Gas No 3-4 (300°-350°)   Cook 2 hrs.

2 lb. minced beef (900 grms)
2 large onions (minced)
2 slices wet bread (crustless & minced)
Salt and pepper
1 nicely shaped marrow
1 tablespoon tomato purée

½ pint stock or water (3 dl.)
2 beef cubes
1 medium tin tomatoes
¼ lb. mushrooms (100 grms)
1 green pepper

Peel marrow and slice lengthways through middle. Remove pips. Mix all the other ingredients and fill both halves of the marrow as full as possible. Put halves together and put into baking dish. Crumble two beef cubes into dish with diced green pepper, peeled tomatoes, sliced mushrooms and a spoonful of tomato purée and stock or water. Put all together and pour over marrow. Cover with foil and cook in oven for about 2 hours. Baste two or three times. Check gravy to see if seasoning needs adjusting or more stock added.

SWEET MINCED MEAT
Renata Knobil

Serves 4　　　　Preparation 15 mins.　　　　Cook 25 mins.　　　　Freezable　　　　Advance

2 lb. best minced meat (900 grms)
1 large chopped onion
2 tablespoons ketchup
2 eggs

Salt and pepper
Matzo meal
Dutch honey cake
Little oil

Mix minced meat with onions, ketchup, eggs, salt and pepper. Add enough matzo meal to be able to roll mixture into balls. Fry the minced balls in shallow oil. Remove balls and crumble honey cake into remaining oil. Add water to make a smooth fairly thick sauce. Put meat balls in sauce and cook watching and turning continually. If necessary add more water during cooking time.

SWEET AND SOUR POT ROAST
Vivienne Seymour

Serves 6-8　　　　Preparation 30 mins　　　　Cook 2½ hours　　　　Advance

4 lbs. cubed beef (1k 800 grms)
2 large sliced onions
1 crushed clove garlic
½ cup stock or water
2 bay leaves
6 quartered potatoes

2 tablespoons vinegar OR
Lemon juice
1 tablesppon brown sugar
3 tablespoons ketchup
½ cup raisins

Brown meat on all sides in hot fat in large pan. Brown onions and add the garlic, vegetable stock or water and bay leaves, cover and simmer for 1 hour. Add more stock if necessary to prevent burning. Add potatoes, vinegar and brown sugar, cover and simmer another hour. Add salt, ketchup and raisins. Cover and cook ½ hour longer. Serve hot.

Lamb

LAMB CURRY
Vivienne Seymour

Serves 8　　　　Preparation 10 mins　　　　Cook 1 hour 45 mins.　　　　Freezable　　　　Advance

4½-5 lb. shoulder of lamb (2 kilos 250 grams)
2 tablespoons cooking fat
3 teaspoons curry powder
¼ teaspoon dry mustard
2½ teaspoons salt

2 chopped medium sized onions
½ cup chopped parsley
1 small chopped garlic clove
1 medium sized tin tomatoes
½ teaspoon sugar

Cut lamb into 1″ (2½cms) cubes. Heat fat. Add all ingredients except meat and tomatoes. Fry gently until onions are soft. Add meat. Fry vigorously for 20 minutes stirring well. Add solid part of tinned tomatoes. Cover and cook on low flame for 1 hour stirring occasionally. Add liquid from tomatoes. If necessary, skim excess fat. Thicken to desired consistency with a little flour and water. Gently cook for 25 minutes, Serve with boiled rice.

BARBECUED KEBABS

Hatty Kleeman

Serves 8-10   **Preparation 30 mins.**   **Marinate 24 hours**   **Cook 30 mins.**   **Advance**

4 lbs. cubed lamb or beef (1 k 800 grms)
3 green peppers
10 small tomatoes
1 lb. mushrooms (450 grms)
Skewers

SAUCE
6 tablespoons olive oil
4 tablespoons sherry
1 chopped onion
2 tablespoons chopped parsley
1 level teaspoon oregano
Salt and pepper

Mix sauce ingredients together and marinate meat in it for 24 hours. Thread meat and vegetables alternately onto the skewers and barbeque over hot charcoal basting with the sauce during cooking.

MORROCAN COUSCOUS

Joyce Keyes

Serves 6   **Preparation 30 mins**   **Cook 2½ hours**   **Advance**

2 lb. stewing lamb (900 grms) or
1 lb. stewing lamb and 1 lb. beef (900 grms)
1 lb. couscous (450 grms)
(obtainable Atheniian Grocery,
   Moscow Road, W2
½ chicken
2 chopped onions
2 oz. chick peas (soaked overnight) (50 grms)
2 turnips (quartered)
2 sliced large carrots
2 tablespoons olive oil
1 teaspoon paprika

Salt and black pepper
¼ teaspoon ground ginger
¼ teaspoon saffron (optional)
3 sliced courgettes or
1 marrow cut into chunks
¼ lb. fresh or frozen broad beans (100 grms)
2 tomatoes
4 tablespoons finely chopped parsley
Cayenne or chilli pepper
2 tablespoons tomor

This is a genuine Morrocan dish and is definately worth the effort involved. The basic process for the preparation of couscous is the steaming of the grain over a stew or broth of chicken or beef and a variety of vegetables. To improvise a couscousere use a double steamer or a colander or sieve fitting exactly over a saucepan.

Place in bottom of the pan the cubed meat, chicken, onions, chick peas, turnips and carrots. Cover with water. Add oil, salt, pepper, ginger and saffron. Bring to the boil skim and simmer for about 1 hour. Moisten the couscous with a little cold water working it in with the fingers to prevent lumps. Turn into the top of the steamer. Place steamer over pan but do not cover. Rake the grains occasionally to air them. Steam for ½ hour. Add raisins, courgettes, broad beans, tomatoes and parsley to stew in pan and cook for a further ½ hour. Moisten again to prevent lumps by removing steamer. Replace and steam for a further ½ hour.

To serve: Pile the couscous on a large wooden or earthenware dish. Add tomor and work it in until it melts. Arrange the meat and vegetables on top and pour the broth over reserving 1 cupful. Serve this separately mixed with cayenne and chilli pepper to make it strong and fierce.

REGENTS PARK HOT POT
Anita Elman

Serves 4   Preparation 20 mins.   Gas No 5 (350°)   Cook 2 hours

4 lb. lean neck of lamb cut
   into chops (1 kilo 800 grms)
Seasoned flour
1 large onion
Margarine or oil
1 beef cube

½ pint boiling water (3 dl.)
1 carrot
2 sticks celery
Salt and pepper
2 lb. peeled and sliced potatoes (900 grms)

Put flour in plastic bag and shake chops in it to coat well. Fry chops on both sides to seal. Drain on absorbent paper. Lay in ovenproof dish approx. 14″ x 12″ (35½cms x 30½cms) and sauté sliced onion, celery and carrots. Arrange over meat. Make stock with cube and water and pour over. Season well. Cover with sliced potatoes in overlapping layers. Season. Brush with melted margarine. Cover with lid or foil and cook in oven for 1½ hours. Remove lid and cook for further ½ hour to brown top.

GLAZED LAMB RIBS
Sandra Connelley

Serves 4   Preparation 10 mins.   Gas No 7 (425°)   Cook 1 hour 15 mins.

2 racks of lamb
2 tablespoons lime marmalade
2 tablespoons vinegar

2 tablespoons brown sugar
Salt and pepper
Dash of Worcestershire Sauce

Cut ribs downwards with sharp knife to separate. Put into moderately high oven uncovered for 1 hour turning occasionally. Put all other ingredients into saucepan over small light add half cup of gravy from lamb and stir. Pour mixture over ribs and continue to cook basting frequently until crisp.

ROAST CROWN OF LAMB
Phylis Kilstock

Serves 6   Preparation 20 mins.   Gas No 5 (375°)   Cook 1½ hours

1 Crown of Lamb (16 cutlets)
Salt and pepper
Rosemary
Tin-foil

1 onion
10 small carrots
10 small potatoes
Paper frills

Ask your butcher to arrange chops into the shape of a crown. Place meat in an oven-proof dish that you can take to the table. Cover each bone end with tin-foil. Lay a little lamb fat in centre of crown then fill centre with sliced onions and carrots. Arrange potatoes over them and season well to taste. Cover vegetables with foil and roast. Remove centre foil for the last 15 minutes of cooking to brown potatoes. Slip a paper fril on each cutlet end and serve.

ROAST SHOULDER OF LAMB
Phyllis Kilstock

Serves 6   Preparation 15 mins   Gas No 6 (400°)   Cook 1 hour 15 mins.

3 lb. shoulder of lamb (350 grms)
1 crushed clove garlic
½ teaspoon salt
¼ teaspoon cayenne pepper
¼ teaspoon mustard
½ teaspoon thyme

4 oz. margarine (100 grms)
5 peeled and sliced apples
1 onion sliced into rings
3 sliced tomatoes

Combine the garlic, salt, cayenne pepper, mustard and thyme. Rub into lamb. Coat the seasoned lamb with 2 oz. margarine (50 grms). Grease baking tin with the remaining margarine and add lamb. Cover with slices of apple, onion and tomato. Roast in hot oven for 20 minutes then lower temperature to No 5 (350°) and roast for 50 minutes. Serve with rice or creamed potatoes.

SPICED LAMB
Janet Cohen

Serves 6   Preparation 30 mins.   Gas No 1-2 (250°)   Cook 3-4 hours   Freezable   Advance

2 finely cut double fillets of lamb
2 large onions
1 small tin tomatoes
2 peeled aubergines
1 medium leek
Salt and pepper

1 large cinnamon stick
Pinch ground coriander
Pinch cumin seed
Water
¼ pint white or red wine (2 dl.)
Flour
Oil or fat

Slice onions and sauté in oil until tender. Cut up leek and add to onions. Leave pan on low light. Dredge meat in flour and add salt and pepper and tomatoes. Peel and dice aubergines and add to pan. Add cinnamon stick, cumin seed, ground coriander and wine. Bring to boil then leave to simmer for 10 minutes. If too dry add water. Place in oven and cook until tender.

Veal

VEAL BIRDS
Mrs. Nettie Smith

Serves 4   Preparation 15-30 mins.   Gas No 3-4 (350°)   Cook 1½ hours   Advance

4 escalopes veal
2 ozs. margarine (50 grms)
Salt and pepper
1 oz. flour (30 grms)

1 can tomato soup
1 pkt. Rakusan's apple and celery stuffing
Cocktail sticks to secure

Flatten slices of veal until very thin. Make stuffing according to directions on packet. Place a portion of stuffing on each slice of veal. Roll up and secure with 2 cocktail sticks. Coat each roll in seasoned flour. Fry in hot fat until browned all round. Dilute can of soup if necessary put veal rolls in casserole. Cover with tomato liquid, cover casserole and cook in centre of oven.

STUFFED BREAST OF VEAL

Anita Elman

Serves 4   Preparation 20 mins.   Gas No 4 (350⁰)   Cook 2 hours

1 baby breast of veal
1 lb. minced veal (450 grms)
1 large onion (½ grated, ½ sliced)

1 egg
Salt and pepper
½ cup water or stock

Mix minced veal with grated onion, egg salt and pepper. Open pocket on side of breast and fill with mince meat mixture close securely — sew up with thread if possible. Place meat in roasting tin. Cover with sliced onion. Season and pour in liquid, cover with foil and cook in oven for 1½ hours. Remove foil and cook a further ½ hr. to make crisp. You can stuff the breast with a breadcrumb and herb stuffing for a change. Remove thread before serving.

VEAL CHOPS EN PAPILLOTE

Anne Moss

Serves 4   Preparation 10 mins.   Gas No 6 (400⁰)   Cook 25 mins.   Freezable   Advance

4 large veal chops (lean)
4 tablespoons oil
2 teaspoons chopped parsley
2 teaspoons chopped onion
2 tablespoons chopped chives

4 ozs. mushrooms (100 grms)
Salt
Pepper
Margarine
Greaseproof paper or tin foil

Leave chops to marinate overnight in oil. Mix parsley, onion, chives and mushroom and leave to blend for 1 hour. Cut 4 pieces of greasproof paper or foil large enough to take chops. Spread foil with margarine and herbs and mushroom mixture. Place chop on each and cover with more mixture. Season and wrap up. Bake No 6 (400⁰) for 25 mins. Serve chops in paper.

VEAL FRICASSÉE

Goldie Allan

Serves 4   Preparation 30 mins.   Cook 2¼ hours

1 lb. stewing veal (450 grms)
1 pint well-flavoured chicken stock (½ litre)
1 oz. cornflour (30 grms)
2 medium carrots
2 sticks celery

Mixed herbs
A few sliced mushrooms
Sherry to taste
2 tablespoons artificial cream or 2 egg yolks

Cut veal into cubes and place in saucepan with flour, salt and pepper, chicken stock, sliced carrots, celery and mixed herbs. Bring to boil slowly and simmer until meat is cooked (approx. 2 hrs.) Add sherry and mushrooms and cook a further 10 minutes. Lastly add cream and serve with rice.

VEAL GOULASH (OR BEEF)
Linda J. Sharpe

Serves 8   Preparation 30 mins.   Cook 3½ hours   Freezable

3 tablespoons oil
2 Spanish onions
5 lbs. veal or chuck steak (2k 250 grms)
1 heaped teaspoon paprika — more if desired
1 tablespoon vinegar

Marjoram
Dash of salt
3 cups water & beef cube
1 flat tablespoon flour
1 teaspoon tomato purée

Heat oil. Fry sliced onion rings until golden. Cut meat into 2″ (5cms) cubes. Add to oil, add paprika, vinegar, marjoram and salt. Add water, and beef stock cube gradually as needed. Simmer until meat is tender, about 2½-3 hours, (or cook in moderate oven.) Add flour, blend well. Boil for few minutes.

SAUTÉ DE VEAU MARENGO
Lesley Bennett

Serves 4-6   Preparation ½ hour   Cook 1½-2 hours   Freezable

3 lbs. stewing veal (1kilo 350 grms)
3 tablespoons flour
Salt, black pepper
2 finely chopped onions
½ pt. veal stock (3 dl.)
1 strip orange peel

Bouquet garni
Small tin tomato purée
¼ pint white wine (2 dl.)
1 tablespoon margarine
2 tablespoons finely chopped parsley
Oil

Dice veal. Dredge with flour seasoned with salt and pepper. Sauté in hot oil, until brown on all sides. Add finely chopped onions and garlic. Simmer for a few minutes. Bring veal stock to boil. Add orange peel, bouquet garni, tomato purée and dry white wine. Pour over meat. Cover pan and simmer till meat is tender. Remove herbs. Knead tablespoons of flour and tablespoon of margarine together and drop bits into sauce to thicken — if necessary. Sprinkle with finely chopped parsley.

OSSOBUCO
Hazel Kaye

Serves 4   Preparation ¼ hour   Gas No 2-3 (300⁰)   Cook 2 hours   Advance

½ cup corn oil
4 veal shin bones with meat,
    4″ long (10cms)
½ teaspoon salt
Fresh ground black pepper
½ cup dry white wine

1 cup stock
½ clove garlic
4 strips lemon peel
1 anchovy fillet
1 teaspoon chopped parsley
2 tablespoons flour

Heat oil in frying pan. Season bones and roll in flour, fry until meat is golden brown. Place in casserole and add wine. Cook until wine evaporates on high light. Add stock and cover casserole. Cook until meat leaves bone easily, adding more stock if necessary. Five minutes before serving add garlic, lemon peel, chopped anchovy fillet and parsley, add more salt and pepper if necessary.

HAWAIIN RICE

Mavis Goldberg

Serves 4   Preparation 15 mins.   Cook 15 mins.

1 lb. thin veal steak (cut into strips) (450 grms)
1 teaspoon salt
¼ teaspoon pepper
½ cup margarine
½ pint hot curry sauce (3 dl.)
20 drained pineapple chunks or 4 rings

½ cup diced pimento
2 bags boil in the bag rice
Banana
Small tin sliced peaches
Parsley

Season veal strips with salt and pepper. Sauté in margarine until tender and lightly brown. Stir in curry sauce, pineapple and pimento. Simmer 3 to 4 minutes. Meanwhile cook the rice. Drain. Place in a hot dish with the meat on top. Garnish with parsley, banana sliced lengthwise and peach slices.

VASIKAN PYYT   STUFFED VEAL

V. Interesting

Serves 10   Preparation 15 mins.   Cook 1½ hours

15 very thinly sliced and beaten
    escalopes of veal
1 large tin stoneless prunes
Juice of 1½ lemons
Parsley
Oil

5-6 gherkins
2-3 cloves of garlic
Flour
Salt and black pepper
A little mustard

Cut escalopes in half. Squeeze the lemons. Chop parsley finely. Chop gherkins and press garlic. On each escalope squeeze some lemon juice, season and put on one prune, a little garlic and few pieces of gherkin and parsley. Roll and tie with cotton. Roll the veal in flour. Fry in oil until golden brown. Place in thick based saucepan and add juices from pan. Pour over some prune juice and add left over ingredients if any. Simmer gently until tender, approx. ¾ hour. Take out the rolled veal and remove cotton. Strain liquid in saucepan and thicken with flour, add mustard and season to taste. Put the veal back in the same saucepan and heat thoroughly and serve.

VITELLO TONNATO

Barbara Green

Serves 4   Preparation 30 mins.   Advance

2 lbs. cooked veal-chicken-turkey (900 grms)
1 large egg yolk
Juice of 1 lemon
1 tin of tuna fish in oil
1 breakfast cup of olive oil

Little salt & pepper
Gherkin, capers
Lemon whirls to decorate

Sauce — Put tuna fish, lemon juice, egg yolk and salt & pepper into liquidizer — beat well. Add oil gradually (as if making mayonnaise) — when thick and creamy, about 2-3 minutes, pour over meat or poultry which has been skinned and boned and laid on serving dish. Make sure meat is completely covered. Flavour is improved if dish is prepared the day before using, decorate with lemon whirls and capers.

WIENER SCHNITZEL

Mrs. V. Knobil

Serves 4   **Preparation 10 mins.**   **Cook 10 mins.**

4 escalopes of veal
Fresh breadcrumbs
A little beaten egg

2 ozs. margarine (50 grms)
1 sliced lemon
Salt & pepper

Ask the butcher to beat the escalopes until really thin. Season and coat each with beaten egg and fresh breadcrumbs, patting the crumbs into the meat. Melt the margarine in a clean frying pan, and gently fry the veal for about 5 minutes on each side. Garnish with a slice of lemon and serve with salad.

FEGATO ALLA VENIZIANA

Mrs. L. Jacobson

Serves 4   **Preparation ½ hour**   **Cook 15 mins.**   **Freezable**   **Advance**

2 lbs. calves liver (900 grms) (in one piece)
2 sliced onions (large)
½ cup Marsala wine

½ cup flour
Oil
Salt and pepper

Slice liver ¾" (2cms) thick. Cut each slice in strips ¾" (2cms) thick. Sprinkle liver with salt and pepper and roll in flour. Pour oil into frying pan and fry onions until soft — remove onions from pan and in the same oil fry liver for about 3 minutes over a high flame, stirring all the time. Put onions back in pan add Marsala wine and cook on a very high flame for one minute, lower heat and simmer for about 5 minutes. This dish can be placed in oven for reheating directly from freezer. Add one hour to reheating process if food is frozen.
If no Marsala available a very good substitute is sweet Kiddush wine.

APRICOT TONGUE

Frances Welt

Serves 8   **Preparation 30 mins.**   **Cook 3 hours**   **Advance**

1 tongue
Small teacup brown sugar
Heaped teaspoon dry mustard
Large tin apricot halves
$\frac{1}{3}$ cup sultanas

½ cup white vinegar
½ teaspoon salt
1 tablespoon flour
Enough water to make paste

Boil tongue until tender. Slice thinly and set aside. Sieve apricots and juice into saucepan. Add all other ingredients, except flour. Bring to boil. Add paste made of flour and water and stir until thickened. Place alternative layers of tongue and sauce in oven dish. Heat well before serving.

Poultry

Mince, left over boiled or roast chicken, add beaten egg, matzo meal, tomato sauce and soup or stock to bind, shape into balls, dip in batter and fry in oil.

To roast a chicken that has been cleaned and deep frozen, place unthawed in roasting tin put in oven No 6 (400°) for ½ hour. Then take out, rinse tin and roast chicken in normal way.

To make light work of lifting a heavy turkey from the roasting tin, first lay two long strips of folded foil into the tin under the bird crossways. (To make strips, tear two lengths of wide foil approx. 48″ (122cms) long, fold in half lengthways again and again until approx 4″ (10¼cms) (wide). Before cooking in normal way, place strips under the bird 3″ (7½cms) apart and roll long ends towards tin so that they rest on edge. After cooking unroll strips and hold the two ends on one strip in one hand and the other two ends in the other hand. Hold tightly and lift easily.

To oven-fry chicken dip portions in seasoned flour, then egg, lastly breadcrumbs and put into ½″ (1½cms) of hot oil in a roasting tin. Allow 40 minutes each side. Remove from oil and drain well. No 5 (375°).

Turkey Schnitzels bought from the butcher taste delicious. They are cheaper than meat.

Cube left oven chicken or turkey, mix with equal quantities of cubed cucumber, green pepper and a few chopped spring onions. Mix well with mayonnaise and serve on lettuce leaves.

A good way to use left over boiled chicken is to lay the boned pieces on a layer of fried onions and add 2 teaspoons Worcester Sauce. Pour over 2 cups of chicken soup, cover with foil and cook in Gas No 4 (360°) for 45 mins.

Alternatively, cover the left over chicken pieces with a mixture of fried onions, a tin of tomatoes, some of your favourite herbs and a little chicken soup. Cover and cook as before until liquid is well reduced.

Chicken

CHICKEN ADOBÉ
Lina Jacobson

Serves 6   Preparation 30 mins.   Gas No 3 (350°)   Cook 1½ hrs.   Freezable   Advance

3 poussins (3 x 450 grms)
2 large onions
1 lb. carrots (450 grms)
1 teaspoon ground ginger
Soya sauce

½ teaspoon ground allspice
Salt and pepper to taste
½ cup chicken stock
1 tablespoon oil

Peel onions and cut into 6 or 8 quarters. Put onions and chickens into pan of boiling water and par boil. Remove onions and chickens from water and divide each chicken in half. Peel and slice carrots. Place onions and carrots in roasting dish or big pyrex dish. Place chickens skin side up on top of vegetables. Mix chicken stock (or liquid from par boiled chickens) with ginger, soya sauce, allspice, salt, pepper and oil. Pour over chickens. Cover dish with tin foil and cook in the oven. Method for reheating. Place in oven on lowest heat one hour before serving. Chicken must be thoroughly thawed before reheating. This recipe is very nice served with rice — preferably pilaf rice.

ASPARAGUS CHICKEN
Mrs. J. Shapiro

Serves 4   Preparation 30 mins.   Gas No 3-5 (350°–375°)   Cook 1-1½ hrs.   Freezable   Advance

1 3½ lb. chicken (1k 575 grms)
½ cup chopped onions
½ cup wine (white)
1 crushed clove of garlic

1 tin asparagus soup
Salt and pepper
1 tin asparagus

Cut chicken up into serving portions. Season. Brown in casserole in hot oil. Take chicken out. Add ½ cup chopped onions and soften in same oil. Place chicken in casserole again with the onions. Pour ½ cup wine and tin of asparagus soup over the chicken. Add salt and pepper and crushed clove of garlic. Put into medium oven for 1 hour. Before serving add tin of asparagus to the casserole.

CHICKEN CACCIATORIA
Karol Solomons

Serves 6   Preparation 30 mins.   Cook 1-1½ hrs.   Freezable   Advance

1 5 lb. roasting chicken (2k 250 grms)
2 chopped onions
4 diced carrots
4 diced sticks of celery
Seasoned flour

Paprika
1 large tin tomatoes
1 tablespoon olive oil
¼ lb. chopped mushrooms (100 grms)

Cut chicken into six pieces and dredge with seasoned flour. Cover with paprika. Fry in oil until brown both sides. Place in large casserole. Sauté onions, add mushrooms, carrots and celery. Cook together about ¼ hour. Add tomatoes, then pour over chicken. Cook slowly on top of cooker. Serve with rice.

AUNT HARRIET'S CHINESE CHICKEN
Lillian Ressler

Serves 8   Preparation 30 mins.   Gas No 3 (350°)   Cook 1 hour   Advance

Chicken pieces
8 oz. cup vinegar (2½ dl.)
8 oz. cup pineapple juice (2½ dl.)
2 (sliced) green peppers
8 oz. cup sugar (225 grms)
1 tablespoon soya sauce

2 tablespoons tomato ketchup
¾ teaspoon salt
1½ teaspoons accent
3 tablespoons cornflour
6 large tomatoes
1 large tin pineapple cubes

Dip chicken pieces in seasoned flour and fry till golden brown in oil. Make sauce with all ingredients (except tomatoes) and cook ¾ hour in oven. Add tomatoes cut into wedges for last 15 minutes. Serve with chinese fried rice.

FRIED CHICKEN CHINESE STYLE
Susan Stone

Serves 6   Preparation 30 mins.   Cook 15 mins

1 5 lb. roasting chicken (2k 250 grms)
Deep oil to fry
BATTER
4 oz. plain flour (100 grms)
Pinch salt
1 egg yolk
1 tablespoon oil
¼ pint water or chicken stock (2 dl.)

1 whisked egg white
SAUCE
¼ pint water or stock (2 dl.)
1 level teaspoon cornflour
2 level tablespoons brown sugar
1 tablespoon cranberry sauce
1 tablespoon soy sauce
2 tablespoons vinegar

Remove flesh from chicken bones in large pieces. Cut in cubes. Season well. To make batter — put water, salt, egg yolk and oil into bowl, beat well. Add flour, one spoon at a time. Beat in each addition. When smooth leave to stand in fridge 30 minutes. Before using fold in beaten egg white. Dip pieces of chicken in batter. Deep fry until golden. To make sauce — Blend cornflour with water in saucepan and rest of ingredients. Bring slowly to the boil stirring constantly. Simmer for 5 - 10 minutes. Serve with plain boiled rice. Do not brown chicken cubes too fast or the flesh might not be cooked through.

CHICKEN CHOW MEIN
Claire Jacobs

Serves 4   Preparation 20 mins.   Cook 20 mins.   Freezable   Advance

½ cup oil
4 ozs. mushrooms (100 grms)
Small green pepper
1 onion
1½ cups cooked chicken pieces
Tin bean sprouts

3 tablespoons soy sauce
1 tablespoon cornflour
1 pkt. crispy fried noodles
   or 1 pkt. noodles
½ pint chicken stock (3 dl.)
   or ½ pint water (3 dl.) & 1 cube

Sauté onions till soft. Do not brown. Add mushrooms, sliced green pepper. Fry gently for 5 minutes. Add chicken, sprouts, stock and sugar to taste (this is the chow mein). Mix soy sauce and cornflour to a thin paste. Stir into chow mein and cook for 3 mins. Serve immediately with crispy fried noodles or soft noodles. Fry crispy fried noodles in oil or boil noodles in usual way. Any cooked meat can be used.

CICASSIAN CHICKEN

Renee Elkabir

Serves 6   **Preparation 20 mins.**   **Cook 2-3 hours**   **Freezable**   **Advance**

1 6 lb. boiling chicken (2k 700 grms)
8 oz. soft breadcrumbs (225 grms)
4 oz. ground walnuts (100 grms)
Peas

1 dessertspoon sweet paprika
3 large cups of water
Salt and pepper
Cooked beetroot

Boil seasoned chicken in covered pan for about 2 hours until cooked. Reduce stock from chicken to ½ pint (¼ litre). Taste and re-season. Soak the crumbs in stock while hot. Leave for about half an hour, drain and keep remaining stock. Add walnuts to crumbs and mix well. Gradually add the stock to make a thick sauce. Add paprika. Cut chicken into small pieces removing bones. Arrange on a dish and pour over sauce to cover. Decorate with boiled green peas and boiled beetroot which you cut in the form of petals to make flowers. Complete design by making the peas as stems.

CHICKEN OR MEAT CURRY

V. Musty

Serves 6-8   **Preparation 30 mins.**   **Gas No 2 (300°)**   **Cook 1½-2 hours**

2 large sliced onions
4-6 cloves crushed garlic
1-2 tablespoons madras curry powder
1-2 teaspoons garam masala (indian spice)
1-2 teaspoons chilli powder (optional)
2 oz. tin tomato purée (50 grms)
¼ cup water if needed
1 5½ lb. roasting chicken cut into
   eight pieces (2k 275 grms)

or 2 lbs. braising veal beef or lamb (900 grms)
Salt
1 tablespoon vinegar
Large green or red pepper
or ½ lb. frozen peas (205 grms)
or 1 tin bamboo shoots cut into thin pieces
Oil

Sauté onions in oil until lightly browned. Add garlic. Add meat or chicken, curry powder, garam masala and chilli powder. Stir on low flame until meat is browned. Add tomato purée and water if needed. Cover and cook. Add salt and vinegar and continue cooking until meat is tender. Just before serving add slivered pepper or peas or bamboo shoots.

SUMMER CHICKEN CURRY

Helene Littlestone

Serves 4   **Preparation 30 mins.**   **Advance**

2 lb. cooked boiled chicken (1 k 125 grms)
1 large onion
Oil for frying
1 large cooking apple
1 dessertspoon curry powder

Miracle whip or
Hellman mayonnaise
2 ozs. long grain rice (50 grms)
Juice of ½ lemon

Cook rice in salted water for 12 mins. and strain under cold water. Heat oil in pan — chop onion and fry until golden. Chop apple and add to pan for five minutes. Add curry powder and lemon juice and mix gently but thoroughly for 5 minutes. Remove from heat and allow to cool. Put mixture in bowls add 2 dessertspoons of mayonnaise and mix, then add rice and chicken which has been cut into bite sized pieces. Pile on a dish lined with lettuce and serve cold.

DEVILLED CHICKEN
Susan Stone

Serves 6   Preparation 30 mins.   Gas No 3-4 (350°)   Cook 1 hour

4 tablespoons French mustard
1 tablespoon tomato sauce
1 tablespoon Worcestershire sauce

5 lb. jointed chicken (2k 250 grms)
Salt and pepper
1 cup chicken stock or water

Lay chicken pieces in oven proof dish. Mix all other ingredients together in a bowl and spread over chicken. Put in oven, turning after ½ hour. Remove from oven turn over. Place under hot grill till brown on top. This can be done with boiled chicken in which case leave in oven for only ½ hour, turning after ¼ hour.

FRIED CHICKEN WITH RICE
Phyllis Kilstock

Serves 6   Preparation 30 mins.   Gas No 3 (350°)   Cook 30 mins

5 lb. large chicken (2k 250 grms)
4 breakfast cups rice
8 cups water
6 tinned tomatoes
2 teaspoons sweet paprika

1 chicken cube
1 green pepper
2 tomatoes
Salt and pepper
Flour

Cut chicken into pieces, dip in seasoned flour and fry. Cook tinned tomatoes with sweet paprika slowly for 5 minutes. Put rice in an ovenproof dish with boiling water and salt. Put chicken on top and cover with cooked tomatoes and paprika. (Take one chicken cube put in boiling water with peas and cook for 5 minutes). Pour over chicken and cook in oven. Decorate with slices of tomato and paprika.

HAWAIIAN CHICKEN
Hilary Brass

Serves 4   Preparation 15 mins.   Gas No 3 (350°)   Cook 1½-2 hours   Freezable   Advance

1 4½ lb. boiler (2 kilo)
1 tin pineapple chunks
1 tin Chinese bean shoots
1 green pepper
1 tin Chinese Water Chestnuts

Bay leaves
1 tin peeled tomatoes
Salt and black pepper
1 pint water

Put chicken either whole or jointed in casserole. Cover with water. Add bean shoots, water chestnuts, tomatoes, pepper, bayleaves and salt and pepper. Cook until tender. Add pineapple chunks ¼ hour before serving. Remove bay leaves before serving.

JAFFA CHICKEN

Estelle Gaunt

Serves 4   Preparation 30 mins.   Gas No 4 (360°) Cook 1½-2 hours   Freezable   Advance

½ teaspoon salt
3 ozs. margarine (80 grms)
1 oz. flour (30 grms)
$\frac{1}{8}$ teaspoon cinnamon
Dash of ginger

¾ pint fresh orange juice (½ litre)
2 ozs. blanched almonds (50 grms)
2 oz. seedless raisins (50 grms)
2 Jaffa oranges
4 ozs. hot cooked rice

Wash chicken well in cold water pat dry. Sprinkle with salt. Melt margarine in saucepan, brown chicken lightly and remove. Mix flour, remaining salt, cinnamon and ginger. Blend with margarine in pan to make a smooth paste. Add orange juice, cook stirring constantly until sauce bubbles and begins to thicken. Return chicken to pan with almonds and raisins cover and cook in oven until chicken is tender. Add orange sections, heat through. Serve chicken and sauce on bed of rice.

CHICKEN A LA KING

Esther Taub

Serves 6   Preparation 20 mins.

4 tablespoons schmaltz or margarine
4 tablespoons flour
2 cups well seasoned chicken stock
1½ cups diced cooked chicken

6 ozs. sautéed mushrooms (175 grms)
$\frac{1}{3}$ cup canned diced pimento
1 egg yolk
Salt and pepper

Melt fat. Blend in flour and slowly add stock. When sauce is smooth and boiling add chicken, mushrooms and pimento. Reduce heat. Add egg yolk and cook stirring carefully until slightly thickened. Season to taste. Can be served with rice or used to fill vol au vents.

CHICKEN MARENGO

Gillian Fenner

Serves 4   Preparation 30 mins.   Gas No 3 (350°)   Cook 1¼ hours   Freezable

4 lb.roasting chicken (1k 800 grms)
½ bottle dry white wine
Chicken stock cube
Salt and pepper
Pinch mixed herbs

2 sliced medium onions
2 sliced medium green peppers
1 15 oz. tin tomatoes (425 grms)
Small jar black olives

Cut chicken in quarters. Roll in seasoned flour and fry until slightly firm. Drain. Place in deep casserole. Add all other ingredients. Cover and cook in oven, adjusting seasoning as necessary. Draw off any fat that comes to the surface. ¼ hour before serving add drained olives. Can be kept hot until ready to serve. Serve with rice.

CHICKEN A L'ORANGE
Mrs. West

Serves 6   Preparation 30 mins.   Gas No 7 (425°)   Cook 50 mins

¾ pint orange juice (½ litre)
Grand Marnier to taste
2 tablespoons grated orange rind
4 ozs. brown sugar (100 grms)
1½ ozs. melted margarine (45 grms)

1 tablespoon prepared mustard
4 lb. young chicken split down back (2 kilos)
1½ tablespoons cornflour
Orange slices to garnish
2 tablespoons cold water

Mix orange juice, rind and brown sugar. Mix melted margarine and mustard and rub over the chicken. Open up the chicken and put it skin side down in a greased baking pan and pour over the orange juice mixture. Bake in a hot oven until chicken is tender. Baste frequently. For the last 15 minutes of baking have the skin side up to brown and glaze. Remove chicken and place on warmed serving dish. Dissolve cornflour in cold water. Add to gravy and cook until thick. Add Grand Marnier if desired.

ORANGE GLAZED CHICKEN   Madeleine Cope Thompson

Serves 4   Preparation 30 mins.   Gas No 5 (375°)   Cook 1½ hours

4 chicken joints
¾ cup orange juice
2 oranges
½ cup lemon juice
1 tablespoon grated orange rind

½ cup brown sugar
2 tablespoons corn oil
1½ teaspoons dry mustard
1 teaspoon mixed spices
1 teaspoon salt

Combine warm orange juice with the lemon juice, orange rind, sugar, oil, mustard and mixed spices (this makes the glaze). Place seasoned chicken joints in a casserole. Pour the glaze over the chicken; top with thick orange slices and bake until well glazed, brown and tender. Baste frequently.

CHICKEN WITH MUSHROOM SAUCE   Patricia Miller

Serves 6-8   Preparation 20 mins.   Gas No 6 (400°)   Cook 40 mins.   Freezable   Advance

6 lb. cooked boiled chicken (2k 700 grms)
6 ozs. mushrooms (175 grms)
¾ pint chicken stock (½ litre)

2 oz. flour
Salt, pepper, bayleaf
2½ tablespoons oil

Cut chicken into small pieces. Place in casserole dish. Melt oil in saucepan, add flour and stock to form thick sauce. Add coarsley chopped and washed mushrooms to sauce and seasonings. Pour sauce over chicken in casserole. Put in oven for ten minutes. Reduce heat to No 2 (325°) when boiling. Cook for further 30 minutes. Serve with boiled rice.

CHICKEN PIE

E. Nyman

Serves 4   **Preparation 30 mins.**   **Gas No 7 (425°)**   **Cook 20 mins.**

Left over chicken
¼ lb. mushrooms (100 grms)
2 teaspoons potato flour
¼ pint stock (2 dl.)

½ oz. tomor margarine (15 grms)
Small onion
1 packet vegetarian puff pastry
Beaten egg

Dice and soften the onion in margarine. Add potato flour, stock and stir. Add sliced mushrooms. Dice chicken and place in oven proof dish. Pour sauce over. Roll out pastry to fit dish and place on top. Brush with egg and bake near top of oven until brown. Can use mashed potato instead of puff pastry if desired.

CHICKEN IN PORT AND BRANDY

Nettie Smith

Serves 6   **Preparation 5 mins.**   **Gas No 6-7 (400°–425°)**   **Cook 1-1½ hours**

5 lb. roaster (2k 250 grms)
½ wine glass brandy
1 wine glass port

Salt and pepper
1 oz. margarine (30 grms)

Season chicken. Heat margarine in oven. Roast chicken for 30 minutes breast down. Turn chicken and pour over brandy. Set alight and then douse with port. Continue roasting for a further 30-45 minutes, basting often until cooked. Dubonnet can be used instead of port. This recipe is very easy and always popular.

BABY POUSSIN WITH SHALLOTS

Susan Mandell

Serves 6   **Preparation 30 mins.**   **Gas No 6 (400°)**   **Cook 1-1½ hours**

3 baby chickens
1½ lbs. baby shallots (675 grms)
½ pint water (¼ litre)
Watercress

Salt and black pepper
Paprika, garlic, rosemary
Honey, orange juice (optional)

Cut chickens into halves and place in large baking dish with shallots and water. Season chicken well and place knob of margarine or chicken fat on top of each portion. Roast in oven basting frequently. A little honey and orange juice gives added flavour. Add a little extra water if necessary. Serve garnished with watercress.

ROAST CHICKEN AMERICAN STYLE Rosalind Gilbert U.S.A.

| Serves 6 | Preparation 10 mins. | Gas No 3 (350°) | Cook 2 hours |

5 lb. roast chicken (2k 250 grms)
Garlic or garlic powder
Pepper
Ground ginger
Seasoned salt
Chicken fat and tomor mixed

Ground oregano
Thyme
Sweet basil
2 bay leaves
Spanish onion

Rub chicken with garlic and ground ginger. Season with salt and pepper. Sprinkle with oregano, thyme and sweet basil. Place in roasting dish together with bay leaves and onion. Pour over a little melted chicken fat and tomor. Cook in preheated oven, basting frequently. Last half hour turn chicken breast down to make it all crispy.

SWEET AND SOUR CHICKEN Valerie Green

| Serves 6 | Preparation 15 mins. | Cook 15 mins. | Freezable |

5 lb. boned chicken (2k 250 grms)
Flour for cooking
2 egg whites

2 bottles sweet and sour sauce
Salt and pepper
Nut oil

Cut chicken flesh into squares. Dust chicken with seasoned flour. Drop floured chicken pieces into beaten egg whites. Heat oil and fry chicken until golden. Dry on absorbent paper. Heat sweet and sour sauce in separate pan. Put chicken into heated serving dish and pour over sauce. Can be prepared in advance and re-heated for 10-15 minutes, in oven Gas No ¼ (250°).

CHICKEN TETRAZZINI Marilyn Unger

| Serves 8-10 | Preparation 20 mins. | Gas No 6 (400°) | Cook 45-60 mins |

1 large roasted chicken
2½ pints chicken stock (1¼ litre)
Salt and pepper
Pinch of paprika and curry powder

2 glasses sherry
2 packets of ribbon noodles
12 ozs. unpeeled and sliced mushrooms
   (350 grms)
Little flour to thicken

Cut chicken into small pieces. Keep juices from roasting tin, having removed any fat. Add chicken stock. Thicken and season, cook for a few minutes. Add sherry. Cook noodles and drain well. Place noodles, chicken and mushrooms in a greased oven proof dish, finishing with a layer of noodles. Pour over sauce. Cook in moderate oven.

CHICKEN VERONIQUE

Letitia Leigh

Serves 4   Preparation 40 mins.   Gas No 6 (400°)   Cook 1 hour

3 lb. roasting chicken (1k 250 grms)
3 ozs. margarine (90 grms)
2-3 sprigs tarragon
½ pint giblet stock (3 dl.)
1 lb. potatoes (450 grms)
¼ lb. muscat grapes (100 grms)

1 glass of white wine (optional)
1 teaspoon arrowroot
2 tablespoons lightly whipped imitation
     cream
Salt and pepper
Lemon juice

Rub chicken well with 2 ozs. (30 grms) of the margarine. Put salt, pepper and tarragon inside the bird and cover with greased paper. Pour half stock into tin. Roast for 1 hour, basting from time to time. Meanwhile peel potatoes and cut into julienne strips. Dry well. Rub remaining margarine round a small thick frying pan. Press in potatoes, seasoning well. Cover with greased paper and a lid and cook slowly on top of cooker, or in oven for about 40 mins. Peel and de-pip grapes. Squeeze over a few drops of lemon juice and keep covered. Cut chicken into portions and keep hot. Strain juices into small saucepan. Deglaze roasting tin with wine and allow to reduce by half. Add to pan with remaining stock. Bring to boil and adjust seasoning. Thicken with arrowroot (mixed with little water). Turn out "Paillasson" of potatoes and arrange chicken on it. Add cream to gravy and grapes at last minute and serve over chicken. (This recipe can also be made with individual poussins or a large roaster, altering other ingredients proportionately per 1 lb. (450 grms weight of chicken).

COQ AU VIN

Jackie Segall

Serves 4-6   Preparation ½ hour   Cook 3¼ hours

5 lb. roasting chicken (2k 250 grms)
4 ozs. tomor (100 grms)
SAUCE
1 large tin tomatoes
¼ bottle red wine
2 bay leaves
2 onions
Salt and pepper

2 carrots
1½ pints chicken stock (1 litre)
or 2 cubes and water
½ lb. button mushrooms (225 grms)

Simmer sauce ingredients — except mushrooms — for 1½ hours then add mushrooms and simmer for further ½ hour. Liquidize in blender and season with salt and pepper. Whilst sauce is cooking; Fry skinned portions of chicken in margarine until brown on both sides. Add chicken to prepared sauce and simmer for about ¾ hour or until tender.

Duck

DUCK WITH APRICOTS
Caroline Posnansky

Serves 6   Preparation 1 hour   Gas No 7 (425⁰)   Cook 1½ hours   Freezable   Advance

5 lbs. large Duck (2k 250 grms)
4 ozs. dried apricots (100 grms)
¼ pint water (2½ dl.)
Grated rind & juice of 1 orange
1 finely chopped onion
1½ oz. flour (45 grms)

¾ pint stock (½ litre)
2 level tablespoons Demerara sugar
Salt and pepper
To finish
4 tablespoons brandy
15 ozs. can apricot halves (425 grms)
1 oz. chopped walnuts (30 grms)

Roast duck in centre of oven basting occasionally. Gently stew dried apricots in orange juice with rind and water for 20 minutes until soft, purée in blender. Remove cooked duck, joint it and place in casserole, keeping it warm. Drain excess fat from roasting tin and fry onions until coloured. Add flour and continue cooking for 3 minutes, stirring all the time. Gradually add stock, apricot purée and sugar, boil for 2-3 minutes, still stirring. Season to taste, add brandy and pour over duck. To serve. Heat apricot halves with juice in saucepan, drain and sprinkle top of duck with chopped walnuts. To freeze Store in ovenproof casserole, before using, heat in oven – Gas No 7 (425⁰) for 1¼ hours.

DUCK WITH APRICOTS & GINGER
Faith Duke

Serves 6   Preparation 15 mins   Gas No 8 (450⁰)   Cook 1½ hours

2 x 4 lb. ducks (1k 800 grms each)
½ level teaspoon salt
½ level teaspoon ground ginger
8 tablespoons clear honey
1 lb. 12 oz. can apricot halves (800 grms)

4 tablespoons apricot juice
3-4 pieces sliced stem ginger
2 tablespoons redcurrant jelly
Watercress to garnish

Prick ducks all over and then rub the skin with salt and ground ginger. Put the ducks on a rack in a roasting tin and cook for 15 minutes. Pour off fat. Heat together honey and apricot juice and pour over the ducks. Reduce heat to Gas No 4 (350⁰) and cook ducks allowing approx 20 minutes per pound, basting frequently. 15 minutes before the end of cooking time, place apricots under ducks. Serve ducks on a platter, pour over glaze and surround with apricot halves which have been filled with redcurrant jelly. Garnish with watercress and place slices of ginger on the breasts.

GALANTINE OF DUCK
Terry Segal

Serves 4   Preparation 20 mins.   Gas No 6 (400⁰)   Cook 1½ hours

1 boned 3-4 lb duck (1k 800 grms)
1 oz. margarine (30 grms)
1 finely chopped onion
12 ozs. minced veal (350 grms)
Salt and pepper

1 teacup fresh breadcrumbs
1 dessertspoon chopped parsley
1 teaspoon dried sage
1 small glass dry sherry
1 beaten egg

Stuffing Melt margarine, add onion and cook until soft, but not coloured. Add to minced veal and breadcrumbs. Mix well with herbs and sherry and bind with egg. Put stuffing into duck and sew with strong thread. Place in roasting tin with fat and cook for 1½ hours basting frequently. Can be sliced hot or cold.

CANETON du PYRENEES (DUCK IN ORANGE)   Carole Chinn

Serves 12   Preparation 20 mins.   Gas No 3 (350°)   Cook 2 hours   Freezable   Advance

3 ducks
5 oranges (Bitter Seville are best)
10 tablespoons wine vinegar
2 lemons

6 lumps sugar
Brandy or Cointreau
1 extra orange for decoration

Roast duck in usual way, draining fat frequently. Whilst this is cooking peel skin from oranges and lemons and cut into julienne strips and squeeze fruit for juice. Drop strips into a saucepan of boiling water for 1 minute and drain with care. In another saucepan reduce vinegar and lump sugar till it begins to caremelise. Add fruit juice and reduce a little. Add peel. Carve duck as required and place on serving dish. Remove fat from baking tin and dissolve brown juices with a little Brandy or orange flavoured liqueur. Add this to sauce and simmer together for a few minutes. Pour sauce over duck and garnish with decoratively cut orange slices. Alternatively garnish duck and serve sauce separately. If freezing, sauce can be kept in separate container to keep in flavour of liqueur.

PEKING DUCK WITH PANCAKES   Jane Manuel

Serves 8   Preparation 45 mins.   Cook 15 mins.

2 cooked ducks
Spring onions to garnish
Pancakes
1 lb. plain flour (450 grms)
2 tablespoons sesame seed oil
1 pint boiling water (8 dl.)

Sauce
4 rounded tablespoons plum jam
1 level dessertspoon sugar
1 dessertspoon sesame oil
1 tablespoon water

Roast ducks in usual way making sure that as much fat as possible is poured off during cooking and that the skin is very crisp.
Pancakes. Sift flour into a bowl and mixing all the time add boiling water to make a soft dough that leaves the sides of the bowl clean. Knead the dough for 10 minutes on a lightly floured board, adding more flour to the dough if necessary, until it becomes rubbery. Cover with cloth and leave for 20 minutes. Roll out dough ¼" thick and cut into 2" rounds. Brush half the rounds with oil and place an unbrushed round on top. Roll out each pair of pancakes (about 14) into as thin a round as possible. Heat an ungreased frying pan for 30 seconds, then lower heat and put in the first pancake, turning it when bubbles appear and underside is flecked brown and looks floury. Cook all pancakes in this way (they may puff up). Allow to cool. Wrap the cooked pancakes in foil parcels and store them in fridge until needed. Reheat pancakes over saucepan of hot water. Keep warm on hot plate covered with napkin. Serve ducks on a platter and cut into small pieces at the table. Place pieces of duck, spring onions and sweet and sour sauce on each pancake and roll up.
Sauce Mix the ingredients in a small pan (except water). Add 1 tablespoon of cold water and bring to boil. Stir over low heat for 2-3 minutes. If desired use a sweet and sour sauce instead. (see sauce section)

PINEAPPLE DUCK

Gillian Fenner

Serves 3-4   Preparation 1 hour   Gas No 5-6 (375°-400°)   Cook 2 hours

1 large roasting Duck
15 ozs. tin pineapple slices (425 grms)
1 glass red wine
1 clove garlic
Salt and pepper
1 medium onion
½ orange

Sauce
1 tablespoon cornflour or flour
Juice and rind of 1 orange
Gravy from duck
2 oz. raisins (50 grms)
Lemon juice
Juice from pineapple tin
Garnish
Cooked rice and a few cashew nuts
Light fried onions

Place duck in roasting tin, together with onion and with half an orange inside. Season with salt and pepper. Rub garlic over breast and roast in oven for 1½ hours. Pour away excess fat. Remove from oven, cut into portions. Reserve juices from pan, straining off fat. Keep warm until ready to serve. **Sauce.** Mix cornflour to smooth paste with orange juice, duck juices, pineapple syrup and red wine to make ¾ pint (½ litre). If necessary to increase sauce to this amount use a chicken cube mixed with water. Return to pan and thicken. Season, adding squeeze of lemon if necessary. Add chopped pineapple pieces, raisins and orange rind. Pour sauce over duck and serve with cooked rice to which a few cashew nuts and fried onions have been added.

Miscellaneous

ROAST GOOSE

Faith Duke

Serves 8   Preparation 15 mins.   Gas No 4 (360°)   Cook 20-25 mins per lb.

1 Goose
¼ teaspoon sage
¼ teaspoon thyme
Salt and pepper

To make stock
All giblets (except liver)
1 onion
Salt and pepper
Bayleaf
Water

Rub inside of the goose with salt, thyme and sage. Pricking all over to allow fat to escape. When cooked place on a hot platter. Meanwhile cook giblets, onion, bay leaf in water till tender. Remove fat from pan juices and stir in the strained stock. Reduce sauce and serve separately.

LEFTOVER TURKEY WITH CHERRY SAUCE   A Russian Exile

Serves 4   **Preparation 10 mins.**   **Cook 30 mins.**   **Freezable**   **Advance**

Sliced breast of turkey
8 oz. cherry jam
Cinnamon/ginger

Cloves
2 oz. margarine
1 glass Madeira wine or Sherry

Heat the jam slowly with a little water, a pinch of cinnamon and ginger and 2 cloves. Rub through a sieve. Melt the margarine, heat the turkey slices in it, add the wine or sherry and cook again for 1 minute. Pour the sauce into the middle of a dish and arrange the turkey round it.

Vegetables

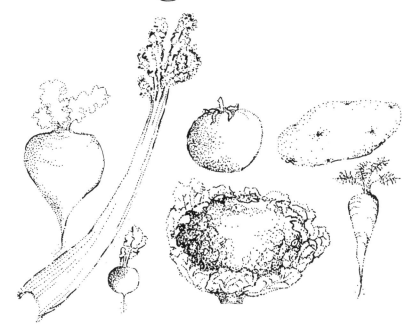

When cooking cauliflower, put a piece of bread in saucepan to prevent smell.

Vegetable bread baskets — Butter or Marge both sides of sliced bread. Cut into rounds and put into muffin tins and bake in moderate oven for 10-15 minutes. Fill with cooked peas or corn (cooked in usual way) and serve.

When roasting potatoes, peel, dry and scrape with fork before seasoning and putting in hot fat.

Put a pinch of Bicarbonate of Soda in water when cooking greens to keep colour bright.

When chopping onion, grip a spoon in your mouth and run cold water to prevent watering eyes.

To store parsley well, wash it, shake most of moisture off and keep in covered plastic container.

An easy way of chopping parsley is to put the required amount in a narrow glass or jar and then hold scissors with the blades inside jar.

To skin button onions easily, plunge in boiling water for 2 minutes and then into cold.

Parsley can be frozen then crumbled between thumb and fingers to obtain instant chopped fresh parsley.

To make jacket potatoes look pretty. Cut a visible cross about ¼" deep into skin. Bake in usual way. After removing from oven squeeze sides of potato together and the centre will come into a flower. Decorate with knob of butter and sprig of parsley.

For faster boiling, halve potatoes lengthwise instead of across; for faster frying slice and dredge them with flour.

To quick-fry onions and keep them juicy, place chopped onion in a pan with a little butter, just cover with water and boil briskly until water evaporates. Reduce heat and the onions will soon be an even golden brown.

For speedy chopped onion without tears, skin and coarsely out the onion, place in a blender goblet with just enough cold water to cover. Switch on and, when chopped, drain off liquid.

ALMOND VEGETABLES MANDARIN
Lesley Bennett

Serves 6   Preparation 15 mins.   Cook 5 mins.

1 cup thinly sliced carrots
2 tablespoons salad oil
1 cup water
Garlic to taste
1 vegetable or stock cube

1 cup green beans cut into 1" pieces
1 cup thinly sliced cauliflower
½ cup sliced spring onions
2 teaspoons cornflour
½ cup unbalanced whole almonds

Cook and stir carrots and beans in oil over medium heat for about two minutes. Add cauliflower and onion and toss for a further minute or two. Add water to cube and cornflour, cook and stir until thickened. If further cooking is necessary, reduce heat, cover and steam for a minute or two. Vegetables should be crisp. Add almonds just before serving.

AUBERGINES À LA PROVENCAL
Delia Kramer

Serves 4   Preparation 15 mins.   Gas No. 5 (375°)   Cook 30 mins.   Freezable   Advance

1½lbs. aubergines (575 grms)
Vegetable oil
1 peeled onion
1 crushed clove garlic
1 dessertspoon flour

Salt and pepper
Sugar to taste
Few stoned olives
4-6 ozs. grated cheese (100-175 grms)
15 ozs. tin tomatoes (425 grms)

Wipe, slice and sauté aubergines in oil on both sides until tender. Remove from pan and arrange in large flat dish, seasoning well. Fry onion and garlic until soft, add flour and cook for two minutes. Mash tomatoes and add to flour mixture. Return to heat and stir until thickened, season and pour sauce over aubergines. Sprinkle with olives and scatter with cheese. Serve with soufflé potatoes and spinach.

GREEK BEANS AND SPINACH
Joy Walker

Serves 4   Preparation 30 mins.   Cook 10 mins.

4 ozs. black-eyed beans (100 grms)
1 tablespoon lemon juice
Salt

Pepper
½ lb. fresh spinach (225 grms)
2 tablespoons olive oil

Boil beans until tender, add spinach and cook five to ten minutes covered. Add salt, pepper, oil and lemon juice, mix well. This can be served as a vegetable, or cold as a starter or salad.

BROCCOLI AND MUSHROOM SURPRISE Jill Gluckstein, U.S.A.

| Serves 4 | Preparation 15 mins. | Gas No. 4 (350°) | Cook 45 mins. |

1 broccoli head
1 tin condensed mushroom soup
Butter

Breadcrumbs
½ lb. muchrooms (225 grms)
Grated parmesan cheese

Boil broccoli for about seven minutes until just cooked. Drain and arrange in round casserole dish. Slice mushrooms and fry in a little butter, when sufficiently cooked, place over broccoli. Spread tinned soup over and sprinkle with breadcrumbs and parmesan cheese. Bake until heated right through. This can also be served as a supper dish.

CABBAGE AND NOODLE CASSEROLE Beryl Kramer

| Serves 4-6 | Preparation 30 mins. | Gas No. 4 (350°) | Cook 45 mins. |

1 small head cabbage
4 ozs. butter or margarine (100 grms)
Salt

Pepper
2 onions
8 ozs. noodles (225 grms)
Oil

Shred cabbage finely and wash in salted water. Put in bowl, pour boiling water over, and set aside. Slice and fry onions gently in oil until soft. Strain water from cabbage and fry together with onions until translucent. (about ten minutes). Cook noodles as directed on packet. Mix together, season to taste, put in greased casserole and bake.

CABBAGE AND NUTS Carole Ross

| Serves 4 | Preparation time 15 mins. | Cook 20 mins. |

1 whole cabbage
Butter or margarine

2 ozs. plain cashew nuts (50 grms)

Cook cabbage in usual manner. Fry nuts in butter or margarine until brown, add to cabbage before serving.

WHITE CABBAGE Renata Knobil

| Serves 8 | Preparation 10 mins. | Cook 20 mins. |

1 white cabbage (Dutch or Savoy)
2 medium onions
2 sliced and peeled cooking apples
4 tablespoons corn oil

3 tablespoons white vinegar
3 tablespoons sugar
Salt
Pepper

Slightly boil whole cabbage leaves, then cut cooked cabbage into shreds. Sauté sliced onions in oil. Add apples to shredded cabbage and mix, then add remaining ingredients and a little water, cook with lid on until ready.

CHINESE CABBAGE WITH MUSHROOMS
Valerie Green

| Serves 4-6 | Preparation 10 mins. | Cook 10 mins. | Advance |

1 lb. cabbage (450 grms)
2 tablespoons nut oil
1 green pepper
1 teaspoon sugar
4 tablespoons water

4 ozs. button mushrooms (100 grms)
1 tablespoon soy sauce
Salt
Pepper
Pinch Accent

Wash cabbage and chop roughly. Heat oil in saucepan, add cabbage and sauté two-three minutes stirring constantly. Cut pepper into strips, add to pan. Add mushrooms, soy sauce, sugar, accent and water. Cover pan and cook five-seven minutes, shaking pan occasionally. Place in hot serving dish and serve immediately.
To prepare in advance — do everything EXCEPT add water. Just before serving add boiling water and cook five minutes only.

RED CABBAGE
Carol Stone

| Serves 8 | Preparation 20 mins. | Cook 1 hour | Freezable | Advance |

1 medium sized red cabbage
1 tablespoon corn oil
1 large onion
2 sliced apples
1 tablespoon sultanas

1 teaspoon caraway seeds
1 tablespoon vinegar
½ teaspoon salt
Black pepper
1 tablespoon brown sugar

Using an ovenproof casserole or a large saucepan, fry sliced onions in oil, add salt and pepper and cook until soft. Slice cabbage (discarding the thickest white stalks) then add it to the onions, with all the remaining ingredients. Simmer gently, with the lid on stirring occasionally.
Alternatively the casserole can be transferred to a medium oven Gas No. 3 (350°) instead of simmering on top of oven.

RED CABBAGE WITH APPLE
Valerie Ross

| Serves 6 | Preparation 10 mins. | Cook 25 mins. |

1 small red cabbage
1 large cooking apple
1 small onion

1 level teaspoon sugar
Salt and pepper
Pinch of ground nutmeg

Cut the cabbage into shreds, discarding the thick white stalk. Rinse and put into a large saucepan. Cover with cold water. Bring to the boil. Skin and slice the onion, into rings and add to the cabbage. Season with salt and pepper and cook for 15 minutes. Peel, core and roughly chop the apple. Add to the cabbage with the sugar and nutmeg, and continue to cook until the cabbage is tender — 10 to 15 minutes more. Drain well and serve at once.

SPEEDY RED CABBAGE

Bobby Bensher

Serves 6   Preparation 10 mins.   Gas No. 3 (300°)   Cook 20 mins.

1 tin Felix red cabbage
Juice ½ lemon
Salt and pepper

1 cup slightly sweetened stewed apple
Pinch garlic powder
½ oz. margarine (15 grms)

Mix all ingredients, place in greased casserole and cover. Bake until warmed through. Delicious served with duck.

CARROTS

Norma Cutner

Serves 6   Preparation 10 mins.   Cook 25 mins.

3 lbs. carrots (1 kilo)
½ or 1 small onion (optional)
1 clove garlic (optional)
1 oz. margarine (30 grms)
2 dessertspoons sugar

1 chicken or vegetable cube.
Salt
Pepper
1 dessertspoon cornflour
1 pint water (½ litre)

Crush garlic. Dice carrots and onions very small. Melt margarine in heavy saucepan and add garlic, onions and carrots. Fry on low light covered for a few minutes. Dissolve sugar in cold water, add to saucepan. Drop in chicken or vegetable cube, stir and add salt and pepper to taste. Replace lid and simmer slowly for fifteen minutes. Dissolve cornflour in a little cold water, add to saucepan and stir until thickened. This can be reheated.

SWEET SOUR CELERIAC

Susan Stone

Serves 4   Preparation 5 mins.   Cook 5-7 mins.

1 celeriac
1 teaspoon salt
Juice ½ lemon

1 tablespoon sugar
Water

Peel and cube celeriac, cover with water in saucepan with rest of ingredients and boil until tender.

CELERY WITH ALMONDS

Audrey Stone

Serves 6   Preparation 10 mins.   Cook 10 mins.

1 dessertspoon olive oil
2 ozs. skinned almonds (50 grms)
1 lb. celery (450 grms) chopped into
1″ lengths
1 chopped clove garlic

2 dessertspoons soy sauce
Good sprinkle tabasco
Small glass dry sherry (optional)

Fry almonds and put aside. Saute celery in hot oil, add all other ingredients. Stir, cover and cook five-seven minutes. Serve with almonds sprinkled over.

CHESTNUT VEGETABLE

Renata Knobil

Serves 4.   Preparation 5 mins.

15½ ozs. tin chestnut puree (440 grms) or
Fresh chestnuts, shelled boiled and mashed.

Sugar
1 tin prunes.

Mix everything together with some prune juice. (Must not be too liquid) Heat and serve.

STUFFED COURGETTES

Faith Duke

Serves 4   Preparation 30 mins,   Gas No 5 (375°)   Cook 30 mins

1 lb. thick courgettes (450 grms)
Salt and pepper

½ lb. grated carrot (225 grms)
Little margarine
Little corn oil

Peel courgettes and core with apple corer. Mix grated carrot with the oil, salt and pepper. Stuff courgettes with carrot mixture and place in shallow casserole. Dot with margarine, cover with foil and bake.

CREAMED CORN PUDDING

Pauline Israel

Serves 8   Preparation 15 mins.   Gas No 4 (350°)   Cook 45 mins

2 tins creamed corn
2 tablespoons plain flour
6 tablespoons milk or water

2 eggs
2 ozs. butter or margarine (50 grms)
Salt and pepper

Melt butter or margarine gently in saucepan, remove from heat. Stir in flour, gradually add milk or water to make roux. Add eggs to creamed corn and mix together with roux. Put into greased tin and bake until golden.

SWEETCORN FRITTERS

Faith Duke

Serves 8   Preparation 15 mins.   Cook 15 mins.

10-11 oz. tin of sweetcorn (257-300 grms)
2 oz. plain flour (50 grms)
Cooking oil

1 large egg
Salt
Pepper

Drain corn well, lightly beat egg into flour, season and mix in corn. Heat a little oil in thick frying pan and drop spoonfuls of the mixture into frying pan cooking until golden brown on both sides.

LEEKS IN WHITE SAUCE
Elissa Bennett

Serves 4   Preparation 15 mins.   Cook 1¼ hours approx.

2½ lbs. fresh leeks (1 kilo)   2 ozs. salted butter (50 grms)
6 ozs. milk   Heaped teaspoon cornflour
Salt and pepper

Slice leaks crosswise, discarding only the toughest outer leaves. Wash very thoroughly and
drain well. Melt butter in heavy saucepan and put in leeks. Cover, sweat until tender on very
low heat (about one hour). Shake and stir occasionally. Mix cornflour with plenty of salt and
pepper and blend with milk. Add to leeks and bring to boil. Gently cook a further five minutes.
Serve with fish meal.

LEEK AND POTATO BAKE
Susan Stone

Serves 8   Preparation 15 mins.   Gas No 6 (400°)   Cook 45 mins

2 large potatoes   Oil
5 large leeks   8 ozs. grated cheddar cheese (225 grms)
2 eggs   Salt, fresh ground pepper, celery salt

Cut prepared vegetables into large chunks. Boil in well salted water fifteen minutes, strain.
(reserve water for vegetable soup). Return vegetables to empty saucepan. Add beaten eggs and
mix with wooden spoon. Add cheese (reserving some to sprinkle on top) add seasonings. Oil a
roast tin or gratin dish (12" x 14"). Heat in oven. When sizzling press vegetable mixture in, and
sprinkle with remaining cheese. Bake until crispy brown (approx. thirty minutes). Cut in
squares and serve hot or cold. Can be made with spinach also.

BRAISED LEEKS WITH RICE
Jewels Leader-Kramer

Serves 4-6   Preparation 30 mins.   Cook 40 mins.

2 lbs. firm fresh leeks (900 grms)   ½ teaspoon sugar
3 tablespoons olive oil   7 ozs. water (3 dls.)
4 ozs. finely chopped onions (100 grms)   2½ tablespoons uncooked rice
1 scant teaspoon flour   2 lemons cut lengthwise in
1 teaspoon salt   6 or 8 wedges

Wash and prepare leeks, discarding all but about 2" of green tops. Slice crosswise into 1"
lengths. Heat oil in large heavy casserole over moderate heat. Sauté onions until transparent.
Add flour and water and raise heat. Cook briskly stirring constantly until the mixture comes to
the boil and thickens lightly. Add the rice and leeks, turning with a spoon to coat them evenly
with sauce. Reduce heat to low, cover tightly and simmer for about thirty minutes until rice
and leeks are tender but intact. Season and serve from casserole accompanied by lemon wedges.

BAKED PEA SAVOURY
Sandra Blackman

Serves 6   Preparation 15 mins.   Gas No 4 (350°)   Cook 30-40 mins   Freezable   Advance

1 lb. shelled and cooked peas (450 grms)
or 1 lb. frozen peas
3 ozs. ground hazelnuts (80 grms)
1 teaspoon marmite
1 large onion

1 oz. dried breadcrumbs (30 grms)
2 eggs
Salt
Pepper
1 oz. margarine (30 grms)

Peel and grate onion. Fry in margarine until just brown. Mash peas, add hazelnuts and breadcrumbs, marmite, seasoning and eggs. Mix together and put in greased baking dish. Bake. Serve as main course with potatoes, marrow, carrots and brown gravy.

BAKED POTATO AMANDINE
Phyllis Kilstock

Serves 4   Preparation 30 mins.   Gas No 4 (350°)   Cook 15 mins.

1½ lbs. boiled potatoes (700 grms)
1 egg
1 oz. flaked almonds (30 grms)
Salt

Pepper
2 ozs. margarine (50 grms)
3 ozs. ground almonds (80 grms)
Little fine matzo meal

Cool potatoes. Mix ingredients together except flaked almonds. Put into icing bag with large nozzle. Pipe into pyramids and sprinkle with flaked almonds. Bake.

BAKED POTATOES WITH CHEESE
Mrs. Boston

Serves 6   Preparation 30 mins.   Gas No 2 (325°)   Cook 1 hour

2 lbs. new potatoes (900 grms)
12 tablespoons freshly grated gruyère
Salt and freshly ground black pepper

½ pint well flavoured stock (¼ litre)
4 tablespoons freshly grated parmesan
Butter

Butter a heat-proof shallow oven dish. Peel and slice potatoes thinly and soak in cold water for a few minutes. Drain and dry. Place layer of sliced potatoes in bottom of dish in overlapping rows. Pour over stock. Sprinkle potatoes with four tablespoons of the mixed cheeses, dot with butter, season. Continue this process until the dish is full, finishing with a layer of cheese. Dot with butter and bake.

DEEP FRIED POTATO BALLS
Faith Duke

Serves 4   Preparation 10 mins.   Cook 10 mins.

6 large peeled potatoes
Corn oil

Salt
Pepper

Make as many potato balls as possible with a melon ball cutter. Keep in cold water until required. Heat oil, drain potatoes and season well. Deep fry the potatoes until golden brown.

BOULANGERIE POTATOES
Wendy Max

Serves 10   Preparation 20 mins.   Gas No 4 (360°)   Cook 40-50 mins.

8 lbs. potatoes (3k 600grms)   Salt
6 medium onions   Pepper
Bayleaf   Stock

Slice onions, bring to the boil in unsalted water and drain well. Grease two fire-proof dishes and arrange potatoes in layers, seasoning each layer of onion and potato, ending with a layer of potatoes neatly arranged. Fill dish two thirds full with stock, add bayleaf and bake until potatoes are well browned.

POTATOES WITH MUSHROOMS
Valerie Selby

Serves 6   Preparation 30 mins.   Gas No 3 (350°)   Cook 1½ hours approx

2 lbs. potatoes (peeled and sliced) (900 grms)   1½ lbs. Mushrooms (700 grms)
½ pint cream (3 dl)   Salt
Chopped parsley   Pepper

Butter a 2 pint soufflé dish or gratin dish. Fill dish with alternate layers of mushrooms and potatoes, beginning and ending with mushrooms, and well seasoning each layer. Pour cream over and bake. Sprinkle with parsley before serving.

BAKED POTATOES AND RICE
Frieda Stewart

Serves 4-6   Preparation 15 mins.   Gas No 5 (375°)   Cook 1 hour

2 cups rice   1 onion
3 medium potatoes   Salt
1 oz. chicken or beef fat (30 grms)

Wash rice and place in glass oven dish. Cover with water, salt and sliced onion. Peel potatoes and slice crosswise. Place on top of rice mixture, dot potatoes with fat and bake.

ROSTI POTATOES
Devorah Freeman

Serves 4   Preparation 5 mins.   Cook 30 mins (approx).

1¾ lbs. potatoes (825 grms)   4 ozs. butter or margarine (100 grms)
1½ tablespoons water or milk   Salt and pepper

Boil the potatoes in their skins the previous day and leave overnight in refrigerator. Peel potatoes and shred with coarse grater. Heat large frying pan, let fat get hot, put in potatoes, sprinkle with salt and pepper and fry turning them constantly. When potatoes have soaked up the fat add a little more. Form a kind of cake by pushing the potatoes from the edge of the pan towards the middle and flattening the top. Sprinkle with a little milk or water reduce heat and cover tightly. Shake covered pan occasionaly to prevent the potatoes from burning and leave on a low heat for at least fifteen minutes. The potatoes must stick together, but not to the bottom of the pan. When cooked, turn over carefully and slightly brown the other side.
Variations. Sauté approximately 2 tablespoons chopped onions in fat before placing potatoes in pan. Onions should not be allowed to brown.
Or, before potatoes are done, sprinkle with 3 dessertspoons of grated Gruyère cheese and continue frying for a few more minutes.

RATATOUILLE
Gloria Brown

Serves 4   Preparation 10 mins.   Cook 1¾ hours.   Advance

1 tablespoon oil   1 lb. sliced courgettes (450 grms)
1 sliced Spanish onion   1 lb. tomatoes or large tin strained (450 grms)
2 green peppers   1-2 crushed cloves garlic

Heat oil in ovenproof casserole, add onion and garlic. Season with salt and pepper. Cook gently until soft and golden, add tomatoes, courgettes and de-seeded and sliced peppers. Stir well and place in moderate oven for 1½ hours. Flavour improves if kept until the following day.

FRIED RICE — Chinese Style
Valerie Green

Serves 4   Preparation 20 mins.   Cook 10 mins.

6 ozs. boiled rice (175 grms)   2 tablespoons nut oil
1 oz. blanched almonds (30 grms)   1 tablespoon soy sauce
1 oz. smoked beef (30 grms) optional   3 spring onions
2 eggs   ½ teaspoon salt

Allow rice to cool. Split almonds in half and toast by placing them under very hot grill until golden. Shake occasionally making sure they do not burn, or toast them by placing in medium oven for fifteen minutes. Cut beef into strips and chop spring onions in ¼" lengths. Beat eggs and add salt. Heat oil in large frying pan. Half cook eggs, add rice and coat the grains in egg stirring briskly. Keep stirring and turning rice over and over. Add beef and onions and sprinkle with soy sauce. Fry three to four minutes stirring continuously, serve in heated platter and sprinkle with almonds.

HAWAAIN RICE
Faith Duke

Serves 6   Preparation 5 mins.   Cook 25 mins.

¾ lb. rice (350 grms)   1 onion
2 cloves garlic   ½ pint chicken stock (3 dl.)
Salt and black pepper   Juice of 1 orange
6 tablespoons margarine   2 teaspoons grated orange rind
2 sliced bananas   2 teaspoons finely chopped parsley

Melt four tablespoons margarine and sauté finely chopped onion and garlic until soft but not brown. Add rice and fry, stirring constantly until golden. Add parsley, orange juice, chicken stock and season to taste. Cover and simmer for twelve to fifteen minutes until rice is cooked but still firm. Melt remaining margarine in separate pan and sauté bananas until golden, add these gently into rice mixture.

RICE WITH ALMONDS

Bernice Burr

Serves 8   Preparation 30 mins.   Cook 2½ hours.

8 ozs. long grain rice (225 grms)
1 finely sliced large onion
1 chopped celery stalk
Stock or water
4 ozs. finely sliced mushrooms (100 grms)
Salt and pepper

Herbs or saffron (optional)
2 ozs. chopped toasted almonds (50 grms)
Oil
Lemon juice
Tin foil

Fry onion and celery slowly in oil. When soft, add rice and fry until lightly golden. Using twice the volume of water or stock as rice, pour on half to begin with, add remainder as required. (When liquid is absorbed). Add seasoning and herbs. Using a small pan, put a tablespoon of oil and two tablespoons of lemon juice to heat gently, add mushrooms without stalks. Toss carefully so that they are coated but do NOT boil. Add to rice mixture and mix through with a fork. Decorate with nuts and parsley and keep warm in low oven. If this dish is made the day before required, slightly undercook rice, add mushrooms and allow to cool, then turn onto foil and fold loosely. The foil parcel can be placed in a steamer for about two hours. Nuts and parsley can be added when rice is in the dish.

SPRING ROLLS

Jane Manuel

Serves 6   Preparation 35 mins.   Cook 30 mins.   Advance

BATTER
3 tablespoons flour
7½ fl. oz. water (¼ litre)
FILLING
1 medium onion
2 ozs. cooked shredded chicken
    (50 grms) (optional)

1½ tablespoons cornflour
1½ tablespoons oil
4-6 ozs. bean sprouts (100-125 grms)
Salt and pepper

Batter. Make, and allow to stand thirty minutes before using. Heat a small frying pan and brush with oil. Turn off heat and pour one tablespoon of batter into pan until dry and uncoloured. Peel it off and put on plate. These can be frozen in foil with small piece of greaseproof separating pancakes.
Filling
Fry chopped onion in oil until transparent. Add shredded chicken and cook for one minute. Add drained bean sprouts, salt and pepper. Cook for a further one or two minutes and drain off excess liquid. Spread two tablespoons of filling on uncooked side of each pancake, then fold pancake over, tucking in it's ends to form a neat parcel. Press edges together and seal with uncooked batter. Leave for fifteen minutes then fry in deep oil until golden. If made in advance just re-heat before using.

SWEDES BAKED IN OVEN
Marian Boston

Serves 4   Preparation 30 mins.   Gas No ¼ (200°)   Cook 6-7 hours   Freezable   Advance

8 medium swedes	2 eggs
Butter	½ pint milk (2½ dl.)
Salt	2 tablespoons breadcrumbs (topping)
Pepper	5 tablespoons black treacle
8 tablespoons breadcrumbs	

Peel, and cook swedes until tender. Liquidise. Whilst still warm add milk, breadcrumbs, beaten eggs, treacle and seasoning and mix well. Put mixture into greased baking tin and sprinkle with breadcrumbs. Turn up heat to brown at end of cooking time.

STUFFED VINE LEAVES
Anastasia Ninnis

Serves 4-6   Preparation 1 hour   Cook 30 mins.   Advance

1 lb. vine leaves (450 grms)	2 cups water
1 lb. chopped onions (450 grms)	Juice of 1½ lemons
Olive oil	1 heaped cup long grain rice
Parsley	Dill

Vine leaves may be bought from any Greek or Cypriot store. It is not necessary to cook these. If fresh leaves are used then:—
Boil in water for thirty minutes to soften. Fry onions in oil to soften. Add rice and fry for a few minutes. Remove from heat and add water, salt, pepper, parsley, dill and lemon juice. Do not use all the water at once as the rice will absorb water as you are stuffing the leaves and it may be necessary to add more liquid. It must not be stiff or watery, but moist enough for rice to cook. Spread the vine leaves on the table separately. Place on each leaf a small amount of mixture. Roll into a small loose parcel. Arrange in rows in saucepan, add enough water to cover — cover with a plate, bring to the boil and simmer long enough for rice to cook but remain firm.

TSIMMUS
Mrs. S. Solk

Serves 6   Preparation 30 mins.   Gas No 6 (400°)   Cook 5 hours   Freezable   Advance

6 lbs. thinly sliced carrots (2½ kilos)	Dumplings
1 lb. sliced potatoes (450 grms)	4 ozs. margarine (50 grms)
1½ lbs. beef for stewing (700 grms)	8 ozs. self raising flour (100 grms)
Marrow bone	Cinnamon
Stuffed neck	Sugar
3 tablespoons golden syrup	Water
4 teaspoons sugar	

Put half of the carrots into a very large pan, add meat, salt, bone, stuffed neck, syrup and dumplings, then add remainder of the carrots. Cover with boiling water. Cover with lid and place in oven for two hours, then lower the heat to Gas No 2 (325°) for three hours. Keep topping up with boiling water and do not allow to become dry. Sprinkle top with sugar and place potatoes over, leave in the oven one hour longer. Before serving remove lid to allow potatoes to brown in oven.

Salads

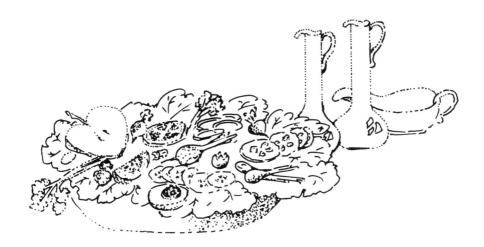

Wash and score sides of cucumber with fork before slicing, looks most attractive.

To refresh lettuce that has gone limp, place in fridge with a few ice cubes on top.

Cover peeled and sliced tomatoes with a good vinaigrette sauce and sprinkle with oregano and chopped chives.

Sour cream and cherries poured over a salad is delicious.

Plain yoghurt and chopped nuts make a useful original dressing.

Green salad decorated with slices of peach or pineapple, prunes, apricots, pears and sliced apples or a mixture of these tastes delicious.

Rub salad bowl with cut clove of garlic before filling with salad.

Use small star cutter on slices of cucumber or unpeeled slices of cucumber for decorations.

Cut small carrots through from tip to within ½ inch of base at three angles, stand in bowl of iced water and flower will open. The same treatment can be given to radishes.

AVOCADO MELON AND TOMATO SALAD   Valerie Selby

Serves 8   Preparation 20 mins.   Advance

1 green melon
3 avocados
1 lb. tomatoes skinned and sliced (450 grms)

12 small spring onions
½ pt. vinaigrette (3 dl.)
Salt and pepper

With a ball scoop make balls of melon and avocado, add sliced tomatoes. Mix well with vinaigrette. Season to taste, arrange in dishes and sprinkle with scissored onions. Note. Can all be prepared in advance omitting avocado.

BEAN SALAD   Simone Prendergast

Serves 4   Preparation 5 mins.   Advance

1 lb. haricots verts (tinned or cooked)
                              (450 grms)
2 oz. blanched almonds (50 grms)
McCormick salad supreme seasoning

Thousand Island dressing
Mazola Oil

Mix beans, almonds and seasoning together, add thousand island dressing and thin down with extra oil. Should be made the day before.

BEETROOT AND ONION SALAD   Sally Bloom

Serves 4   Preparation 10 mins.   Advance

¼ pt. malt vinegar (2 dl.)
1 dessertspoon sugar
½ teaspoon salt

1 large spanish onion
1 large cooked beetroot
¼ pint water (2 dl.)

Mix vinegar and water together. Add sugar and salt and stir in sliced rings of onion then sliced beetroot and spoon over liquid. Leave for 2 days.

RED CABBAGE SALAD   Faith Duke

Serves 10   Preparation 1 hr. 10 mins.

2 lb. red cabbage (900 grms)
Tarragon or wine vinegar
Salt and pepper
4 hardboiled egg yolks

½ pt. single cream (3 dl.)
Juice of large lemon
Handful of raisins
½ cucumber thinly sliced

Shred cabbage, wash and drain, then marinate in vinegar with salt and pepper for 1 hour approx. Drain well, combine cream with finely chopped egg yolks, lemon juice, raisins and more seasoning. Pour dressing over salad and decorate with cucumber slices.

CARROT AND POTATO MOULD
Ann Millett

Serves 10   Preparation 45 mins.   Advance

2 lbs. new potatoes (900 grms)
1 lb. carrots peeled (450 grms)
6 tablespoons French dressing
2 oz. spring onions (50 grms)

¼ pint Mayonnaise (2 dl.)
Watercress or parsley to garnish
1 hard boiled egg to garnish

Rinse potatoes then boil in skins, when cool, peel. Grate carrots into bowl and marinate for ½ hour in French dressing. Dice potatoes into ½" squares, chop spring onions finely. Drain excess dressing from carrots. Mix gently potatoes, carrots, onions and mayonnaise. Scoop into a 3 pint (1½ litres) ring mould. Leave in cool place until required. Turn out and garnish with watercress or parsley and egg.

CELARIAC SALAD
Susan Stone

Serves 4   Preparation 10 mins.

1 celariac
½ cup mayonnaise
½ cup French dressing
Salt

Fresh milled black pepper
Celery salt
½ cup sultanas
½ cup peanuts

Wash and peel celariac and grate coarsely. Mix mayonnaise, French dressing and seasonings, stir into celariac with peanuts and sultanas and mix well. Chill.

GEFLUGELSALAT – CHICKEN SALAD
Sigrid Harris

Serves 4   Preparation 15 mins.   Advance

12 oz. chicken meat (500 grms)
2 gherkins
1 small tin asparagus
1 large tin of mixed fruit

MAYONNAISE
1 egg
Juice of 1 lemon
Salt, pepper sugar to taste
1 teaspoon redcurrant jelly
1 teaspoon mustard
Oil

Mix all the mayonnaise ingredients together to form a mayonnaise and add it to the diced fruit and meat making sure it is well mixed.

CHICKEN AND APPLE SALAD
Katie Adler

Serves 3-4   Preparation 10 mins.

Left over chicken
2 apples

Lemon juice
1 cup mayonnaise

Cut up left over chicken. Cut and peel apples, mix mayonnaise, add little lemon juice and black pepper.

COLE SLAW

Gillian Burr

Serves 8   Preparation 20 mins.   Advance

1 small white cabbage
2 coarsely grated carrots
Salt and black pepper

½ cup French dressing
¾ cup mayonnaise
Dessertspoon of finely grated onion

Shred cabbage, mix dressing ingredients and pour over cabbage. Stir well. Decorate top with grated carrot just before serving.

CUCUMBERS PICKLED

Mrs. J. Sokel

Serves 8   Preparation 10 mins.

1½ large cucumbers
2 oz. acetic acid (50 grams)
1 tablespoon salt

2 bay leaves
1 clove garlic
1 teaspoon mixed pickling spice

Wash and cut cucumber into 2″ pieces and wedge into an 8 oz. (225 grms) size jar. Mix salt and acid. Add water to ¾ pint (½ litre) total. Put pickling spice, bay leaves and garlic in the jar. Pour liquid over. Screw top on jar hard. Leave for 48 hours.
Adjust liquid according to taste.

CUCUMBER SALAD

Karen Segall

Serves 8   Preparation 1 hour 15 mins.

2 cucumbers
¾ carton sour cream
Salt

4 tablespoons salad oil
2 tablespoons wine vinegar
1 teaspoon Dijon mustard

Slice cucumber thinly, put in salted water for 1 hour then strain. Mix other ingredients together and pour over the cucumber. Keep in fridge until required.

CUCUMBER AND YOGHURT SALAD

Sonia Ingram

Serves 4   Preparation 15 mins.

1 cucumber
1 carton plain unsweetened yoghurt
Salt and black pepper

Clove of crushed garlic
2 teaspoons chopped fresh mint

Peel cucumber and dice or slice very thinly using a mandolin or very sharp knife. Combine all ingredients and refrigerate until desired.

EGG, TOMATO AND ANCHOVY SALAD

A. Slimmer

Serves 6-8   Preparation 15-20 mins.   Refrigeration 1 hour.

6 large tomatoes
6 hard boiled eggs
1 tablespoon capers
1 tablespoon sliced gherkins
2 small tins anchovy fillets
1 small cup mixed herbs (chives,
mint, parsley etc.)

6 tablespoons oil
2 tablespoons vinegar
3 desertspoons tomato ketchup
Mustard
Salt and pepper

Skin, halve and seed tomatoes and fry quickly (so as not to lose their shape) in oil with salt and pepper. Leave till cold. Slice hard boiled eggs and put on bottom of dish sprinkle with mixed capers and gherkins. Put the tomatoes cut side down on top. Arrange the drained anchovy fillets in criss-cross pattern on top of tomatoes. Add the two tablespoons of vinegar to the salt, pepper, mustard and tomato ketchup add the 6 tablespoons of oil and lastly the chopped herbs. Spoon over the salad and chill for 1 hour before serving.

FISH SALAD

Bernice Burr

Serves 6   Preparation 30 mins.   Cook 30 mins.   Advance

2 lbs. white fish (900 grms)
Oil
Lemon
1 teaspoon sugar
Salt & pepper
Tomato ketchup

1 teaspoon grated onion
1 green pepper
1 gherkin
Mayonnaise
1 cup finely sliced celery
1 crisp lettuce
A few radishes to garnish

Poach fish (turbot, haddock or hake) — drain — flake when still warm. Make sauce to taste using mayonnaise, oil, lemon, sugar, tomato ketchup, 1 teaspoon each of chopped green pepper, sweet gherkin and grated onion. Mix in celery and mix altogether. (Fish should not be mashed.) Serve on shredded crisp lettuce and garnish.

ISRAELI MIXED SALAD

Joyce Keyes

Serves 8   Preparation 15 mins.

2 tomatoes
2 small cucumbers
6 olives pitted
1 large carrot
1 raw peeled beetroot
1-2 avocados peeled and stoned

2 firm boiled potatoes
1 large mild onion
1 sweet pepper
2 hard boiled eggs
Sour cream or vinaigrette sauce

Peel all the ingredients and cut them into very small cubes. Mix them together in a bowl and dress with sour cream or vinaigrette sauce.

WEBB LETTUCE AND AVOCADO SALAD   Charlotte Davis

Serves 4-6   Preparation 5 mins.

2 hearts of Webb lettuce	French dressing
2 avocados	Salad Herbs

Shred the lettuce hearts. Peel the avocados and dice. Combine with lettuce. Toss with French dressing immediately. Sprinkle with black pepper and herbs.

FRESH MUSHROOM SALAD   Monica Winner

Serves 8   Preparation 10 mins.   Advance

1 lb. mushrooms (450 grms)	2 ozs. almond niblets (50 grms)
¼ cup corn oil	1 tablespoon butter
¼ cup lemon juice	1 tablespoon oil
Salt and pepper	

Wash, peel and slice mushrooms. Mix oil and lemon juice and pour over mushrooms, season to taste. Fry almond niblets in oil and butter till crisp and sprinkle over before serving. Salad can be prepared in quantity beforehand and stored in airtight container.

MUSHROOM À LA GREQUE   Bernice Sion

Serves 8   Preparation 15 mins.   Cook 20 mins   Refrigeration 1 hour   Freezable   Advance

1 lb. button mushrooms (450 grms)	2 tablespoons finely chopped parsely
½ lb. peeled and seeded tomatoes (225 grms)	4 tablespoons olive oil
1 coarsely chopped onion	2 tablespoons corn oil
1 clove coarsely chopped garlic	Salt and black pepper
½ pint dry white wine (2 dl)	

Heat the corn oil and 2 tablespoon of olive oil. Fry onions and garlic until soft and golden. Add white wine and coarsely chopped tomatoes, salt and pepper. Add trimmed mushrooms and cook for 10-15 mins. When cool add additional olive oil and parsely. Serve cold.

96

MUSHROOM AND OLIVE SALAD

Helen Klyne

Serves 6-8   **Preparation 45 mins.**

1 teaspoon salt
1 tablespoon water
1 clove crushed garlic
8 tablespoons oil
3 tablespoons vinegar
2 teaspoon lemon juice
1 tablespoon parsley
2 ozs. stuffed olives (50 grms)

1 teaspoon castor sugar
½ teaspoon dry mustard
½ teaspoon rosemary
½ teaspoon Worcester sauce
4 ozs. tin button mushroom (100 grms)
1 medium lettuce
½ cup celery
3 spring onions

Dissolve salt in water, add garlic and leave for ½ hour. Mix oil, vinegar, lemon juice, sugar, mustard, Worcester sauce, rosemary and mushrooms. Strain garlic water into dressing. Shred lettuce finely. Chop spring onions, parsley and celery. Slice olives. Arrange vegetables in bowl add dressing and mushrooms and toss.

SALADE NIÇOISE

Cynthia Clore

Serves 4   **Preparation 30 mins.**

7 ozs. tuna fish or tinned salmon (200 grms)
1 cucumber
1 lb. tomatoes (450 grms)
½ lb. French beans (225 grms)

Black olives
2 tins of anchovy fillets
French dressing
Chopped herbs or mixed herbs
2 hard boiled eggs (optional)

Cook the French beans and drain and refresh in cold water. Cut the cucumber in chunks and sprinkle with salt. Skin the tomatoes, cut half in thick slices, quarter the remainder and squeeze away the pips. Arrange the beans, sliced tomatoes, cucumber chunks and fish in layers in a serving dish and moisten with the French dressing. Slice most of cucumber over the top, cover with a lattice of anchovy fillets and decorate with stoned black olives and tomato chunks. Hard boiled eggs can be added if desired.

ORANGE AND BRAZIL NUT SALAD

Wendy Max

Serves 6   **Preparation 15 mins.**

1 lettuce (round)
5 good oranges
¼ lb. brazil nuts (shelled) (100 grms)
3 tablespoons oil

1 tablespoon lemon juice
1 tablespoon double cream
Salt and pepper
Sugar

Wash and dry lettuce put in serving dish. Peel oranges and remove pith, cut into segments or slice. Arrange on lettuce. Cut nuts into 3 or 4 pieces sprinkle over oranges. Combine lemon juice, salt, pepper and sugar (to taste) add the oil and then the cream and spoon over salad.

PALM HEARTS WITH THOUSAND ISLAND DRESSING   Faith Duke

Serves 4   **Preparation 5 mins.**

1 large tin Palm Hearts   Chopped parsley
Thousand island dressing

Halve palm hearts and arrange on hore d' oeuvres plates. Pour dressing across centre of hearts and garnish with chopped parsley.

PASTA BOWL SALAD   Phylis Owen

Serves 8-10   **Preparation 30 mins.**   **Refrigeration 1 hour.**

8 ozs. macaroni bows (225 grms)   **DRESSINGS**
1 tablespoon oil   1 clove crushed garlic
¼ lb. frozen peas (100 grms)   Salt
4 slices white bread   6 tablespoons oil
Oil for frying   2 tablespoons vinegar
1 red pepper   Paprika and pepper to taste
1 green pepper
7 ozs. can sweet corn kernels (200 grms)
6 ozs. piece worst (175 grms) (optional)
8 stuffed olives

Cook macaroni bows in plenty of boiling salted water until just tender about 8 minutes. Drain and toss in oil. Leave to cool. Cook peas and drain. Dice bread discarding crusts. Heat oil in pan and fry until crisp and golden, drain. Discard stalks and seeds from peppers and chop coarsely. Drain sweetcorn. Discard skin from worst and dice. Slice stuffed olives. Mix all ingredients together. Toss salad in the prepared dressing and served chilled.

RICE SALAD   Renata Knobil

Serves 6-8   **Preparation 30 mins.**

1½ cup rice   15 ozs. can cut pineapple (425 grms)
2 red apples   4 tablespoons mayonnaise
4 sticks celery   2 tablespoons pineapple juice
¼ lb. walnuts (100 grms)

Boil rice and cool. Cut other ingredients into small pieces (do not peel apples); add mayonnaise and juice and mix together.

SIX DAY SALAD

Shirley Byre

Serves 10   Preparation 20 mins.   Advance

1 green cabbage
½ red cabbage
½ onion
1 green pepper
3 cups olive oil

½ cup wine vinegar
Sugar to taste
Pepper salt
Mustard seed

Shred cabbage, onion and pepper together in large bowl. Put olive oil and vinegar in saucepan and bring to boil. Add handful mustard seed, sugar, salt and pepper. Toss liquid over shredded cabbage etc. and leave to marinate. This lasts in fridge for 6 days.

SKEWER SALAD

Judith Baron-Cohen

Serves 8   Preparation 25 mins.

½ a large white cabbage
8 small tomatoes
8 pitted green olives
8 chunks of Swiss cheese or Edam
8 radishes
8 pitted black olives   8 long skewers

1½ lbs. Sauerkraut (700 grms)
8 large button mushrooms
Lemon juice
8 chunks of green peppers
8 chunks unskinned cucumber
Emerald avocado dressing (page 101)

Brush the mushrooms with lemon juice. Place cabbage (domed side up) in large deep salad bowl, cover with sauerkraut. Thread each skewer with one of each of the remaining ingredients. Stick skewers into the cabbage base forming a circle. Each person should help themselves to a skewer and some sauerkraut. Serve dressing separately.

SALAD WITH SPINACH AND DILL

Phyllis Rubin U.S.A.

Serves 6   Preparation 10 mins.

Raw spinach
Endive
Lettuce - any sort
Battavia
Any other green salad

DRESSING
1½ teaspoons coarse salt
1 teaspoon sugar
½ teaspoon ground black pepper
2 cloves garlic
¼ small onion
1 tablespoon dried dill seed
9 tablespoons salad oil
3 tablespoons lemon juice
1 teaspoon dry mustard

Wash and dry salad. Liquidize dressing ingredients and toss with salad.

TABOULÉ

Helen Klyne

Serves 4   Preparation 30 mins.   Refrigeration 2 hours   Advance

7 ozs. couscous (200 grms)
17½ ozs. tomato juice (500 grms)
6 small tomatoes
12 spring onions
Salt and pepper

2 lemons
2 soupspoons chopped parsley
1 soupspoon chopped mint
6 tablespoons olive oil
Garnish with tomatoes and mint

Put couscous into bowl with 8 chopped onions. Skin tomatoes and cut (with their juice) add to couscous. Add parsley, mint, lemon juice, oil, salt and pepper. Mix well. Chill about 2 hours. Mix occasionally. Serve cold. Decorate with quarters of tomatoe 4-6 spring onions and sprigs of mint.

TOMATO SALAD

Carol Stone

Serves 6-8   Preparation 10 mins.

2 lb. tomatoes (900 grms)
½ cup French dressing (page102)
Salt and pepper

Pinch of oregano
Chopped chives or
Spring onions

Skin tomatoes and slice them thinly. Add remaining ingredients and chill.

DIETERS LUNCH
or TUNA SALAD

Stephen Krygier

Serves 4   Preparation 15 mins.

1 large tin of tuna
2 chopped hard boiled eggs
Salad cream to bind
1 large tablespoon Branston Pickle

Salt & pepper
Mustard & cress
Lettuce leaves
Sliced cucumber

Mix tuna, eggs, pickle, salt & pepper to taste. Add salad cream to bind. Serve on a bed of lettuce and surround with cucumber slices.

SILLISALATTI-
VEGETABLE SALAD

Karina Boston

Serves 10   **Preparation 30 mins**   **Refrigeration 1 hour**   **Advance**

1 large fillet of herring
5-6 potatoes
5-6 carrots
2 large apples (preferably sour)
¼ finely chopped onion
3 hard boiled eggs
5-6 gherkins
2 cooked beetroots

Little parsley
White pepper & salt
SAUCE
1 pint single cream (½ litre)
3 tablespoons sugar
3 tablespoons white vinegar

Cut fillet of herring into small pieces. Cook carrots and potatoes and let them cool. When cool cut into cubes. Cut gherkin also into cubes. Boil eggs, peel and separate whites from yolks. Chop very finely. Put all the vegetables in a large bowl with the exception of the beetroots. Stir gently, season and chill. Just before serving decorate with parsley, egg yolks and whites. **Sauce** -- Whip the cream, sugar and vinegar until of a thick consistency. Serve together with salad.

VIENNA SALAD

Wendy Max

Serves 8   **Preparation 15 mins.**

½ lb. viennas (225 grms)
8 tomatoes
2 green peppers
Lettuce

4 ozs. liver sausage (100 grms)
4 ozs. wurst (100 grms)
French dressing
Paprika
Chutney
French Mustard

Cook the viennas, cool and slice. Dice the liver sausage and wurst. Skin the tomatoes, remove seeds and cut into eight. Slice pepper, remove core and seeds, plunge into boiling water for a few moments and then into cold water. Season a French dressing with paprika, chutney (tomato if possible) and French mustard to taste. Mix all ingredients and moisten with dressing. Serve on a bed of lettuce.

Salad Dressings

EMERALD AVOCADO DRESSING

Judith Baron Cohen

Serves 8   **Preparation 15 mins.**

1 peeled avocado
½ cup natural yoghurt
½ cup buttermilk
¼ cup chopped watercress
¼ cup chopped fresh parsley

2 diced spring onions
½ teaspoon garlic powder
¼ teaspoon sea-salt
¼ teaspoon dill
Soft cheese to thicken if desired

Mix all ingredients in blender at high speed for 1 minute. Refrigerate until needed.

FRENCH DRESSING OR VINAIGRETTE

Susan Stone

Serves 8   Preparation 10 mins.   Advance

1 tablespoon dry mustard
1 teaspoon French mustard
1 teaspoon salt
1 teaspoon fresh milled black pepper

½ pint corn oil (3 dl)
½ pint vinegar (3 dl)
2 tablespoons sugar
1 scored glove of garlic

Combine all ingredients and shake well. Place in a container and store in the fridge.

LIMEY GINGER DRESSING

Judith Baron-Cohen

Serves 8   Preparation 15 mins.   Advance

½ cup sunflower oil
3 tablespoons fresh lime juice
Grated rind of 1 lime
1 tablespoon crystallized honey
¼ teaspoon powdered ginger

¼ teaspoon sea-salt
$\frac{1}{8}$ teaspoon garlic powder
1 tablespoon beetroot juice
1 tablespoon minced ginger

Combine all but last ingredient in blender for 30 seconds at medium speed, add ginger and pour into storage container. Refrigerate until needed and shake well before using.

MAYONNAISE 1

Anne Aubrey

Serves 8   Preparation 10 mins.   Advance

2 egg yolks
¼ teaspoon salt
1 tablespoon wine or garlic vinegar
1 tablespoon lemon juice

½ teaspoon mustard powder
1 teaspoon sugar
Pepper
½ pint oil (3 dls.)

Put egg yolks and salt in liquidizer and beat at high speed for 30 seconds. Reduce speed and add everything else except oil. Pour oil very slowly into mixture, beating all the time, until mixture thickens. Will keep for up to one week in refrigerator. N.B. If mayonnaise curdles — wash liquidizer retaining curdled mixture. Put one whole egg into liquidizer and beat at medium speed, slowly adding curdled mixture. Raise speed and beat until mayonnaise is formed.
Variations:—
Garlic Mayonnaise — Add 6 smoothly crushed cloves of garlic.
Curry Mayonnaise — Add sufficient curry powder to taste.

MAYONNAISE 2

Pamela Kaye

Serves 8   Preparation 10 mins.   Advance.

2 egg yolks
2 tablespoons vinegar

Salt and black pepper
½ pint oil (3 dl.)

In a blender or with a hand mixer beat the egg yolks, vinegar and seasoning until well mixed. Gradually add the oil until it thickens.

MUSTARD MAYONNAISE   Faith Duke

Serves 6   Preparation 10 mins.   Advance.

1 cup home made mayonnaise
1 teaspoon finely chopped spring onion
A few drops of lemon juice

1 teaspoon French mustard
2 teaspoons finely chopped parsley

Mix all ingredients thoroughly together.

PINK AND PRETTY DRESSING   Judith Baron-Cohen

Serves 12   Preparation 15 mins.   Advance.

1 cup sour cream
¼ cup skimmed milk
⅔ of a cup sliced cooked beetroot
2 chopped spring onions

¼ cup diced cucumber
¼ teaspoon sea-salt
½ teaspoon allspice
¼ teaspoon garlic powder

Combine all ingredients in blender at medium speed for 30 seconds. Refrigerate until needed.

NOTES

Sauces & Stuffings

To thicken sauces easily, mix 2 teaspoons of arrowroot with a little water, add to ½ pint of sauce. Bring to boil stirring constantly until thickened.

To use surplus mint from garden, wash and dry thoroughly chop well and put in glass jar. Cover with golden syrup and mix well. To make mint sauce, dilute required amount of mint mixture with vinegar.

To make a quick mousseline sauce, fold 1 stiffly beaten egg white into 1 cup of mayonnaise flavoured with lemon juice to taste. Add chopped parsley if required.

Use up ends of chollas to make breadcrumbs for stuffings.

Any mixture of the following makes a nice stuffing: Rice or breadcrumbs with chopped onion, pineapple pieces and celery. Rice or breadcrumbs with chopped onion, prunes and chestnut puree. Rice or breadcrumbs with chopped onion, mushrooms, celery and parsley. Rice or breadcrumbs with chopped onion, part cooked chicken livers, mushrooms and raisins.

Chinese Sweet and Sour Sauce

This is very good with roast chicken or can also be poured over raw chicken joints, lamb cutlets or breast of lamb, and put in a medium oven until cooked through.

SAVOURY SAUCES

BARBEQUE SAUCE
Valerie Green

Preparation 10 mins.   **Cook 30 mins.**   **Freezable**   **Advance**

4 tablespoons oil
4 ozs. grated onion (100 grms)
1 tablespoon flour
2 tablespoons tomato purée

2 teaspoons dried tarragon
1 teaspoon salt
½ teaspoon tabasco sauce
3 tablespoons lemon juice

Fry onions in oil, until mixture starts to bloom, turn down heat. Add flour and allow to cook, add tomato puree, tarragon, salt, tabasco and lemon juice. Simmer and serve hot.

HOLLANDAISE SAUCE
A. Clog

Serves 4   Preparation 30 mins.

2 tablespoons wine vinegar
2 egg yolks
Salt

1 tablespoon water
3-4 ozs. butter (100 grms)
Pepper

Put the vinegar and water in a pan and boil until reduced to approx. one tablespoon, cool slightly. Put the egg yolks in a basin and stir in the vinegar. Put over a pan of hot water and beat gently stirring all the time, until the egg mixture thickens. (Never let the water go above simmering point) Cut the butter into small pieces and gradually whisk into the sauce, add seasoning to taste. Serve warm, not hot.

SPICY MANDARIN SAUCE FOR DUCK
Nicole Davoud

Serves 6   Preparation 10 mins.   Cook 20 mins.   Advance

2 11 oz. cans mandarin oranges (300 grms each)
½ cup white wine
2 tablespoons soya sauce
1 can tomato sauce or
1 bottle tomato juice

½ teaspoon ginger
½ cup melted margarine
1 clove crushed garlic

Drain the orange segments reserving the juice. Combine the wine, margarine and soya sauce, add juice. Add tomato sauce, garlic and ginger, thicken slightly if desired. Ten minutes before serving add oranges, place in a bowl and spoon generously on each helping of duck.

MARINADE FOR CHICKEN
Sandra Gold

Serves 6   Preparation 5 mins.   Freezable

½ pint soya sauce (¼ litre)
1 tablespoon mustard
5 crushed cloves of garlic

½ pint maple syrup (¼ litre)
1 tablespoon honey
¼ pint brandy (1½ dl.)

Mix honey and mustard together thoroughly then add other ingredients, stirring all the time. Marinate chicken over night. Also useful for meat.

REMOULADE SAUCE
Pauline Israel

Serves 8   Preparation 10 mins.   Advance

1 pint mayonnaise (½ litre)
1 small onion
1 tablespoon basil
2 pickled cucumbers
2 tablespoons chopped capers
2 tablespoons chopped parsley
Salt and pepper

1 tablespoon tarragon
2 tablespoons horseradish
1 tablespoon hot mustard powder
1 tablespoon paprika
2 cloves minced garlic
½ cup tomato ketchup

Mix all ingredients together, put in fridge for at least 12 hours before using. (Very good served over cooked fish).

SWEET AND PUNGENT SAUCE
Claire Jacobs

Serves 6   Preparation 10 mins.   Cook 10 mins.   Freezable   Advance

1 small tin of pineapple
1 small green pepper
2 teaspoons sugar
1 tablespoon cornflour

1 cup of chopped pickled cucumber
(optional)
3 tablespoons soya sauce
2 tablespoons vinegar

Drain the juice from the pineapple into a small pan. Simmer sliced pepper in the juice for 5 minutes, add sugar, mix soya sauce with the cornflour until a smooth paste then gradually stir into the saucepan. Simmer for 5 minutes then add pineapple and chopped pickled cucumber. (Can be served with rice).

SWEET-SOUR SAUCE (CHINESE STYLE)
Susan Stone

Preparation 15 mins.   Gas No 6 (400°)   Cook 15 mins.   Freezable   Advance

½ pint water or stock (3 dl.)
3 tablespoons vinegar
1 teaspoon soya sauce
1 tablespoon tomato ketchup

3 tablespoons sugar
3 teaspoons arrowroot mixed with
a little water
Strips of raw onion, spring onion and
green pepper (optional)

Mix all the ingredients together in a saucepan stirring with a wooden spoon all the time until thick and clear then simmer for ten minutes. (Very good with roast chicken.)

TARTARE SAUCE
Ann Aubrey

Preparation 10 mins.   Advance

1 teaspoon lemon juice
3 small gherkins
1 sprig parsley

4 oz. capers (100 grms)
½ pint mayonnaise (3 dls.)
1 tablespoon chopped chives

Chop all ingredients finely and blend well with mayonnaise.

TOMATO COCKTAIL SAUCE
Gillian Burr

Preparation 5 mins.   Advance

¼ pint mayonnaise (2 dl.)   Few drops of tabasco sauce
Tomato ketchup   Good squeeze lemon juice
Salt and pepper

Blend mayonnaise with sufficient tomato ketchup to give a good colour. Season to taste.

TOMATO RELISH
Rose West

Preparation 10 mins.   Cook 35-45 mins.   Freezable   Advance

3 large chopped onions   A small amount of oil
2 medium cans of Italian tomatoes   Salt
Sugar   Black pepper

Fry the onions in oil in a large pan until golden. Cut the tomatoes into small pieces and add with salt, pepper and sugar to taste. Simmer uncovered until the liquid is well reduced. Adjust seasoning and stir often. (This is delicious served with any grilled meat and can also be put on top of fish when being cooked in the oven.)

TOMATO SAUCE
Ann Aubrey

Preparation 5 mins.   Cook 1-2 hours.   Freezable   Advance

1 finely chopped Spanish onion   2 cloves finely chopped garlic
2 tablespoons butter or margarine   4 tablespoons olive oil
6 tablespoons tomato purée   1 large tin peeled tomatoes
¼ teaspoon oregano   2 tablespoons finely chopped parsley
Salt and freshly ground black pepper   6 tablespoons water
6 tablespoons chicken stock   1 tablespoon Worcestershire sauce
                                           ½ chopped green pepper
                                           2 sticks of grated celery

Sauté the onion in butter or margarine and olive oil in a large pan until transparent and soft but not coloured. Stir in tomato concentrate and cook for 1-2 minutes stirring constantly. Pour in tomatoes, celery, green pepper, parsley and oregano. Add stock and water, salt and pepper to taste, and simmer gently stirring occasionally for 1-2 hours. Just before serving add the Worcestershire sauce.

SWEET SAUCES

APRICOT LEMON SAUCE
Carol Stone

Preparation 5 mins.   Cook 5-10 mins.   Freezable   Advance

6 tablespoons apricot jam
6 tablespoons water

Grated rind and juice of 2 lemons
1 oz. sugar (30 grms)

Simmer jam and lemon rind in the water for five minutes. Add sugar and lemon juice then reheat.

BRANDY SAUCE
Charlotte Davis

Preparation 5 mins.   Cook 10 mins.

5 tablespoons brandy
5 tablespoons water
1 tablespoon sugar

5 tablespoons double cream
2 egg yolks

Put all the ingredients into the top of a double boiler or bowl over a saucepan of hot but NOT boiling water. Beat with a small whisk for 8 minutes until thick and frothy. DO NOT BOIL or this sauce will curdle.

BUTTERSCOTCH SAUCE
Gillian Burr

Preparation 5 mins.   Cook 15 mins.

1 cup soft brown sugar
2 tablespoons butter

2 tablespoons golden syrup
¼ cup of milk or cream

Boil all ingredients together stirring constantly, until it forms a soft ball when a little is dropped into a glass of cold water. Pour over ice cream or sponge pudding.

CARAMEL RAISIN SAUCE
Susan Stone

Preparation 10 mins.   Cook 10 mins.

¼ pint water (2 dl.)
1 oz. margarine (30 grms)
½ oz. cornflour (15 grms) blended with
2 tablespoons water in cup

1 teaspoon lemon juice
6 ozs. soft brown sugar (175 grms)
½ teaspoon vanilla essence
1½ ozs. raisins (40 grms)

Put sugar and water in saucepan and heat carefully till sugar is dissolved. Add margarine and boil rapidly for 3 minutes. Mix a little of the hot liquid to the cornflour mixture then pour back into the saucepan, stirring all the time, bring back to the boil and simmer for 2 minutes. Add vanilla, raisins and lemon juice. Serve hot or cold with ice cream or sponge pudding.

HOT CHERRY SAUCE

Carol Stone

Preparation 5 mins.   **Cook 10 mins.**

1 tin black cherries	1 teaspoon arrowroot
1 tablespoon brandy or sherry	3 tablespoons water

Strain cherries, putting juice in a saucepan. Dissolve arrowroot in water and add to juice. Bring slowly to boil stirring with wooden spoon. When thick and clear add cherries and liqueur. Re-heat when needed. If too thick add a little more water. Serve with ice cream, sponge puddings or soufflés.

COFFEE SAUCE

Lesley Bennett

Preparation 5 minutes   **Cook 5 mins.**

½ lb. soft brown sugar (225 grms)	5 tablespoons strong black coffee
4 tablespoons water	2 tablespoons Tia Maria

Place sugar and water in thick based saucepan and bring slowly to boil, stirring all the time, make sure sugar has melted before you allow to boil — boil for 2 minutes. It should be dark and syrupy — DO NOT OVERBOIL -- Stir in coffee and liquer. Keep warm.

FRUIT SALAD DRESSING
(see Fresh Fig Salad, Meat Dessert Section)

FUDGE SAUCE

Linda Stone

Preparation 2 mins.   **Cook 5 mins.**

4 ozs. fudge (100 grms)	2 tablespoons milk or cream

Put ingredients into a basin and stand over a saucepan of hot water. Heat well, stir, serve hot or cold.

MARSHMALLOW SAUCE

Charlotte Davis

Preparation 15 mins.   **Cook 5 mins.**

12 cut white marshmallows	¼ cup water
½ cup sugar	1 stiffly beaten egg white

Boil sugar and water together until syrupy — about 5 minutes. Press in marshmallows. Remove from heat and leave to stand without stirring. Pour gradually onto egg white and beat until smooth.

MELBA SAUCE

Charlotte Davis

Preparation 10 mins.   **Cook 10 mins.**

1 cup Raspberries
2 level tablespoons Redcurrant or Apply jelly

2 tablespoons water
2 teaspoons sugar

Put jelly and water into saucepan and heat for a few minutes. Put into liquidiser with raspberries and sugar. Beat at high speed for 1 or 2 minutes. Cool and serve with fruit and/or ice cream. Strain to remove pips if preferred.

MOCK CREAM

Rusty Sotnick

Preparation 5 mins.

½ lb. Golden Syrup (225 grms)

2 egg whites

Beat egg whites until frothy then fold in warmed golden syrup and pour as cream. Use at once.

ORANGE SAUCE

Valerie Ross

Preparation 5 mins.   **Cook 10 mins.**

Grated rind of 1 orange
Juice of 2 oranges
Juice of ½ lemon
1 tablespoon arrowroot
½ pint of cold water (¼ litre)

1½ tablespoons castor sugar
1 tablespoons butter
1 egg yolk
1 dessertspoon Grand Marnier

Put rind, orange and lemon juice in a measuring jug, make up to ½ pint (¼ litre) with cold water. Mix arrowroot with some of this liquid. Put all together in saucepan and bring to simmering point, simmer for 3 minutes. Turn heat down, add butter and sugar, keep stirring until sugar dissolves. Beat egg yolks in bowl, add a little of hot liquid, beating all the time, then add rest slowly, still beating. Rinse saucepan, return sauce to pan and stiry away over very low heat for 1-2 minutes to thicken. DO NOT BOIL. Strain, add Grand Marnier. Serve hot or cold.

STRAWBERRY SAUCE

Ann Dietz U.S.A.

Preparation 5 mins.   **Cook 5 mins.**   Advance

1 cup sugar
½ cup water

1½ cups sliced strawberries
½ teaspoon vanilla essence

Boil sugar and water for 5 minutes. Add vanilla essence. Pour over strawberries. Cool. Sauce can be kept for a few days. Any sliced or crushed berries can be used. Similarly sliced apricots, peaches etc can be used for this delicious sauce.

WEINSCHAUMTUNKE (SWEET WINE SAUCE)

Sigrid Harris
W. Germany

Preparation 5 mins.   **Cook 10 mins approx.**

½ pint white wine (¼ litre)
1 tablespoon lemon juice
2½ ozs. sugar (65 grms)

2 eggs
1 teaspoon cornflour
Grated lemon peel

Beat up all the ingredients with a whisk. Heat, while beating steadily, in a basin over a pan of boiling water. When the liquid begins to stiffen, remove from heat. DO NOT BOIL or it will become too runny. As the volume of this sauce almost doubles in the beating make sure the bowl is plenty big enough for this expansion. Serve hot with puddings, custard, ice cream etc. Extra sugar may be added for a sweet tooth.

STUFFINGS

BREAD STUFFING

Karol Solomons

Serves 6-8   **Preparation 15 mins.**

1 small loaf white bread
2 ozs. fresh or dried parsley, (50 grms)
4 large onions

Salt and pepper
Chicken fat

Cut crusts off bread, liquidise into crumbs. Cut onions into small pieces. Mix all ingredients together to form a ball. Use for stuffing poultry.

CHESTNUT STUFFING

Phyllis Millet

Serves 14   **Preparation 30 mins.**   **Gas No 6 (400°)**   **Cook 45 mins**

3 lbs. Chestnuts (1 kilo, 350 grms)
1 pint water (½ litre)
1 chicken cube

2 lbs. Spanish onions (900 grms)
Black pepper
1 tablespoon sugar

Bake chestnuts in oven for 20 minutes. Shell them and put in a saucepan with remaining ingredients. Simmer until all liquid has been absorbed. Liquidise or mince.

EASY CHESTNUT STUFFING

Angela Howard

Serves 16   **Preparation 10 mins.**   **Advance**

2 x 1 lb. tins natural chesnut purée
    (450 grms each)
4 ozs. fresh breadcrumbs (100 grms)
4 ozs. melted margarine (100 grms)

3 lightly beaten eggs
Salt
Pepper

Combine all ingredients and stuff body cavity of turkey, leaving a little space for stuffing to expand during cooking.

111

FRUIT STUFFING FOR GOOSE

Faith Duke

Serves 16   **Preparation 30 mins.**

2 chopped onions
3 tablespoons margarine
Salt and pepper
2 tablespoons sugar
1 tablespoon brandy
1 tablespoon Madeira
1 peeled coarsely chopped orange
3 coarsely chopped apples

1 chopped goose liver
½ teaspoon thyme
½ teaspoon marjoram
¼ teaspoon cinnamon
¼ teaspoon nutmeg
2 cups coarse dry breadcrumbs
14 pitted chopped prunes
¼ cup water

Sauté the onions in the margarine until soft, season and add chopped orange. Simmer for 3 minutes, then add apples and prunes with sugar, spices, brandy and Madeira. Soak the breadcrumbs in water and add to the mixture with chopped liver, a little more salt and pepper and mix thoroughly. Suitable for any poultry.

STUFFED NECK (HELZEL)

Jewels Leader-Cramer

Serves 3-4   **Preparation 10 mins.**   **Cook 30 mins.**   **Advance**

1 neck skin of chicken
3 tablespoons plain flour
3 tablespoons tomor
1 onion

Seasoned pepper
Salt
A little chicken soup

Sew up one end of neck after cleaning. Mix flour with chopped onion and tomor and seasoning. Fill neck and sew other end. Boil in a little of the chicken soup for half an hour or roast with chicken for 1 hour.

NOTES

Meat Desserts

Tip-Top Tips:—

Meringue case filled with raspberry sorbet, and pureed raspberries with Kirsch.

Orange and lemon sorbet with orange sauce and Cointreau.

Add 2 tablespoons of Grenadine to liquid when packing pears or peaches, gives lovely flavour and colour.

To halve a peach easily — hold fruit with stalk scar uppermost. Cut all round horizontally. Hold one half in each hand and screw apart as though undoing a jar.

When making a chestnut dessert for meat meal top with a layer of morello cherries to counteract the excessive sweetness.

Pineapple is delicious cut in slices and sprinkled with Kirsch for 1 hour before needed.

When making pancakes for meat meals, in place of milk, substitute ½ water and ½ parev whip.

When making pies brush pastry with egg white or sprinkle with semolina before putting in filling to prevent pastry from going soggy.

Sainsburys make a good kosher cream substitute.

A little crème de menthe added to chocolate mousse is excellent.

To melt chocolate without overheating, place in pan with a little water in the warming drawer on a low setting.

To make fruit slices — roll out a packet of vegetarian puff pastry into a strip approximately 5″ wide and 11″ long. Bake on Gas No 7 (425°) until golden. Remove from oven and cut in half horizontally, replace in oven to brown cut sides. When cool decorate with fruit and cover with fruit glaze. Serve hot or cold.

Heat lemons a little before squeezing and you'll get a lot more juice.

Don't bother to put apple sauce through a sieve: use your potato masher to purée the apple in the saucepan.

When glazing pastry, a shake of salt added to beaten egg speeds the browning.

When making a jelly use a little hot water to dissolve the jelly and then make up to required quantity with ice cubes.

Light Desserts

AUSTRIAN FRUIT SALAD
Terry Segal

Preparation 10 mins.   **Refrigeration 1 hour.**

Various tinned fruits. ie.   Raspberries
Plums, morello cherries,   Little arrowroot to thicken
Red and Blackcurrants   Lichees

Mix arrowroot with some of the juice. Add remainder of juice and bring to boil stirring all the time until slightly thickened. Put fruit into serving bowl, pour juice over drained fruit. Stir gently and serve cold.

CHOCOLATE AND BRANDY SWEET
Kathy Jennings

Serves 4-5   Preparation 20 mins.   Advance

8 oz. plain chocolate (225 grms)   2 oz. grated chocolate to decorate (50 grms).
5 large eggs, separated   ¼ pint double cream, whipped (optional) (2 dl.)
1 tablespoon brandy

Melt the chocolate in a bowl over hot water. Add beaten egg yolks and brandy to melted chocolate. Beat mixture until smooth. Whisk whites of eggs until stiff. Fold into chocolate mixture. Put into individual dishes and chill. Decorate with grated chocolate and/or cream.

CHOCOLATE RUM MOUSSE
Ruth Perl

Serves 4-6   Preparation 30 mins.   Refrigeration 2 hours   Freezable   Advance

6 oz. plain chocolate (175 grms)   1 tablespoon hot water
5 eggs separated   10 oz. Snowcrest parev whip (275 grms)
1½ teaspoons vanilla essence   4 tablespoons rum
1 teaspoon instant coffee

Melt chocolate in the top of double saucepan over hot water. Beat egg yolks lightly and add to slightly cooled chocolate, beating well. Add vanilla essence and coffee diluted with water. Whip cream until thick, add rum and fold into chocolate. Beat egg whites until stiff and fold into mixture a little at a time, pour into individual soufflé dishes or a larger serving bowl. Chill for 2 hours or longer. Decorate with grated chocolate.

CITRUS SORBET

Mrs Brian Levy

Serves 10   Preparation 25 mins.   Freezable   Advance

10 oranges
2 tablespoons rum
1 tablespoon demerra sugar

Boiling water
1 large block lemon sorbet

Lightly score each orange and place in bowl. Cover with boiling water and leave for 5 minutes. Remove all pith and skin from each orange and allow to cool a little. Slice oranges into serving bowl. Measure the rum and demerra sugar into heatproof bowl. Dissolve the sugar with some of the hot water. Pour mixture onto oranges and leave to cool. Just before serving cover the oranges with the lemon sorbet, roughing up the surface with a fork. The sorbet must be left out at room temperature for a few minutes before using otherwise it is impossible to serve.

FRESH FIG SALAD

Faith Duke

Serves 6-8   Preparation 10 mins.   Refrigeration 2 hours.

18 fresh purple figs
Juice of 1 orange

5 lemons
½ lb. castor sugar (225 grms)

Melt sugar in orange and lemon juices, bring to boil and simmer until it becomes a syrup, cool. Quarter figs and add to syrup. Refrigerate. This syrup is also very good with fruit salad.

FRUIT SALAD

Wendy Max

Serves 8   Preparation 30 mins.

2 apples
¼ lb. grapes (100 grms)
½ pineapple
2 oranges
½ melon

2 pears
2 bananas
¼ lb. strawberries (100 grms)
½ pint water (3 dl.)
6 ozs. granulated sugar (175 grms)

Boil the sugar and water together until syrupy, cool. Prepare the fruit, i.e. cut fruit into similar small pieces, bananas and applies should be cut last as they brown, and quickly moistened with juice of other fruit. Put into large bowl and pour over cold syrup to moisten well. Cover with two layers of silver foil. Before serving remove foil and transfer sald to serving bowl. Avoid fruits with a red juice that will stain the rest of the salad.

GRAND MARNIER SOUFFLÉ

A Soufflé Lover

Serves 8	Preparation 20 mins.	Gas No 8 (450°)	Cook 15 mins.

8 egg yolks	Small pinch of cream of tartar
10 egg whites	$\frac{2}{3}$ cup granulated sugar
½ cup Grand Marnier	

Beat yolks of eggs in the top of a double boiler until they are lemon coloured, then gradually beat in the sugar. Cook the mixture over barely simmering water whisking constantly. When the yolks have thickened place the top of the double boiler in a bowl of cracked ice and stir in the Grand Marnier. Beat the egg whites with cream of tartar until they stand in peaks but are not dry. Transfer the yolk mixture to a bowl and with a rubber spatula fold in 1/3 of the whites thoroughly — fold in the rest very lightly. Pour batter into a greased and light sugared 4 pint (3 litres) souffle mould. Tie a strip of waxed, greased paper around the top of the mould like a collar. Bake in a preheated oven. Sprinkle top lightly with sugar, remove collar and serve immediately.

GRAPEFRUIT SORBET

Jacqueline Leigh

Serves 6	Preparation 10 mins.	Freezing time 4 hours

3 grapefruits or	8 ozs. castor sugar (200 grms)	
14 oz. tin grapefruit (400 grms)	¼ pint dry gin (2 dls.)	¾ pint water

Liquidise the peeled segments of grapefruit after removing the pith. Bring the water and castor sugar to boil for 5 minutes. Combine the syrup and liquidised grapefruit and gin. Freeze for 1 hour or so until the sides are frozen up to ½" thick. Whip very well and return to freezer. Serve piled high in a crystal bowl on a tray garnished with mint and some green glace cherries.

HONEYED FRUIT

Elaine Hallgarten

Serves 8	Preparation 20 mins	Cook 5 mins	Advance

8 oranges or peaches	Rind of 1 orange or 1 lemon
5 oz. clear honey (130 grms)	Juice of 1 lemon
6 oz. water (2 dl.)	

Slice fruit and sprinkle with lemon juice. Mix together the honey, water and fruit rind and heat slowly until the honey melts then boil for 5 minutes. Strain juices over fruit, chill and serve.

JELLY FRUIT WONDER

Cinnie Winton

Serves 8	Preparation 10 mins.	Setting time 2 hours.	Advance

1 medium tin pitted cherries	2 raspberry jellies
1 medium tin loganberries	1 pot parev whipped cream (optional)
1 medium tin raspberries	

Drain all fruit well, place in a large glass bowl. Make 1½ pints (1 litre) of jelly using the 2 jellies and the liquid from the tinned fruit. When cool pour over the fruit and refrigerate. To serve decorate with piped cream rosettes if desired.

116

LEMON MOUSSE

Wendy Max

Serves 5   Preparation 30 mins.   Setting time 2 hours.   Freezable   Advance

3 eggs
6 ozs. castor sugar (175 grms)
Rind and juice of 1 large lemon

½ oz. gelatine (15 grms)
2 ozs. chopped walnuts (50 grms)

Separate eggs. Beat egg yolks, lemon rind, sugar and half of lemon juice until thick and fluffy. Meanwhile melt the gelatine in a small saucepan with the rest of the lemon juice and heat gently until dissolved. Add to mixture whilst still beating. Beat egg whites and fold in with a metal spoon — pour into prepared soufflé dish. Tie a band of oiled silver foil round the soufflé dish so that it stands up above the top of dish like a collar. Leave to set, decorate by peeling off silver foil and press chopped walnuts round the edges.

HOT LEMON SOUFFLÉ

Valerie Ross

Serve 4-6   Preparation 20 mins.   Gas No 5 (375°)   Cook 30 mins   Advance

4 eggs
8 oz. castor sugar (225 grms)

6 tablespoons lemon juice
½ teaspoon salt

Separate eggs. Beat egg yolks until thick and fluffy. Gradually beat in half the sugar. Carefully fold in lemon juice. Beat egg whites and salt until stiff. Gradually fold in the remaining sugar. Fold egg whites into yolk mixture. Lightly oil a big soufflé dish. Pour in the lemon soufflé and place the dish in a larger pan of boiling water. Bake in oven. Serve immediately.

ORANGE MOUSSE

Renata Hausler

Serves 6   Preparation 20 mins.

4 eggs
4 oz. castor sugar (100 grms)
2 large juicey oranges

1 teaspoon lemon juice
Pinch of salt
½ oz. gelatine (15 grms)
2 tablespoons water

Beat yolks with sugar for 10 minutes, add orange and lemon juice and pinch of salt and stir well. Beat whites to stiff froth. Melt gelatine in warm water, add quickly to mixture and continue stirring. When it begins to thicken fold in whites and pour quickly into glasses for serving.

ORANGE SURPRISE

Barbara Green

Serves 6   Preparation 45 mins   Cook 15 mins.   Refrigeration time 4 hours.   Advance

¾ cup sugar
1 packet orange or lemon jelly
1 cup sweet red wine
4 egg yolks, slightly beaten
1 tablespoon lemon rind

Pinch cinnamon (optional)
4 egg whites
2 teaspoons cream of tartar
6 oranges
1 cup orange juice

Slice off the top third of six medium-sized oranges. Scoop out flesh and juice so that shells are as clean as possible - keep flesh in lids. Blend ¼ cup sugar, jelly orange juice, wine and yolks in top part of double boiler. Cook over hot water stirring constantly until mixture almost boils. Stir in lemon rind and cinnamon, allow to cool. Beat egg whites until stiff with ½ cup of sugar and cream of tartar and fold into mixture. Fill shells with mixture, replace with lids, allow to cool for several hours in refrigerator before serving.

PACIFIC FRUIT SALAD

Faith Duke

Serves 6   Preparation 20 mins.

8 chinese gooseberries
4 fresh peaches

8 dark plums

Peel the chinese gooseberries and slice crossways, stone plums and cut into wedges. Skin and stone peaches, then cut into wedges. Combine all fruits. Add sugar and lemon juice or dressing as for fig salad.

PAREV ICE CREAM

by courtesty of Evelyn Rose

Serves 6   Preparation 5 mins.   Refrigeration time 4 hours.   Freezable   Advance

1 carton Snowcrest Parev cream
6 eggs

3 ozs. castor sugar (80 grms)

Whip yolks with defrosted cream. In a separate bowl beat egg whites and fold in sugar. Fold the whites into the ice cream mixture. Put into 3 pint (1½ litre) souffle' dish and place in deep freeze or freezing cabinet of fridge at maximum setting. For a change split half of the mixture and pour into one half,12 squares of melted plain chocolate, and then freeze. Children love it.

PEACH MELBA

Wendy Max

Serves 8   Preparation 35 mins.   Gas No ¼-½ (250⁰–275⁰)   Cook 3 hours

4 egg whites
9 ozs. icing sugar (250 grms)
¼ teaspoon vanilla essence
8 peaches

8 ozs. granulated sugar (225 grms)
1 pint water (½ litre)
1 block raspberry or lemon sorbet
1 lb. raspberries (450 grms)

Put egg whites, icing sugar and essence into a large bowl and beat over a saucepan of simmering water until very thick and glossy. Pipe out as nests on non-stick paper covered baking tray. Cook for several hours until firm and dry and barely coloured. After 1½-2 hours turn over to allow the base to dry. Poach peaches in skins for 15 minutes in a syrup made from granulated sugar dissolved in water. Leave to cool in skins and slide them off just before assembling.
Melba sauce. Blend raspberries with 1 cup strained hot syrup left from cooked peaches, sweeten with icing sugar to taste. Leave to cool. **To serve.** Put 1 spoonful of sorbet in each meringue nest and press whole skinned peach on top, spoon over sauce.

PINEAPPLE DESSERT

Mrs. A.D. Davis

Serves 6   Preparation 20 mins.   Freezable   Advance

1 medium tin crushed pineapple
1 pineapple jelly
2 eggs

3 ozs. sugar (75 grms)
1 oz. cornflour (30 grms)
Water

Make up jelly with water in normal way, leave to cool. Empty pineapple and juice into saucepan, add cornflour and stir over heat until thick. Remove from heat and add the egg yolks and 1 oz. sugar (30 grms), heat gently for about 1 minute. Pour the jelly over this mixture and stir, do not boil or this will curdle. Transfer into serving dish. Beat the 2 egg whites until stiff, add remaining sugar and fold into pineapple mixture, most will remain on top. Leave in fridge to set overnight.

CHARLOTTE AUX FRAMBOISES-RASPBERRY DESSERT
Eva Schwarcz

Serves 10   Preparation 15 mins.   Setting time 3 hours minimum   Advance

8¾ ozs. Mechaie margarine (250 grms)
   (preferably not tomor)
8¾ ozs. castor sugar (250 grms)
8¾ ozs. ground almonds (250 grms)
2 liqueur glasses Cointreau
3-4 packets sponge fingers
14 ozs. raspberries (400 grms)

Raspberry Sauce
14 ozs. raspberries (400 grms)
5 tablespoons castor sugar
1 glass fruit liqueur or Cointreau

Beat sugar, margarine, almonds and most of cointreau until light and frothy. Lightly grease a mould or pyrex dish, line with sponge fingers and sprinkle with cointreau. Fill dish with alternate layers of almond cream, sponge fingers sprinkled with cointreau, raspberries, finishing with a layer of sponge fingers. Refrigerate for a minimum of 3 hours, or overnight, with a weight on top.
To make sauce Gently heat raspberries, sugar and liqueur for a few minutes, leave to cool. Turn out the Charlotte and serve with sauce. (Mechaie margarine obtainable at kosher shops).

RASPBERRY PARFAIT
Carole Chesterman

Serves 6-8   Preparation 15 mins.

1 lb. frozen raspberries (450 grms)
2 egg whites

4 oz. castor sugar (100 grms)
1 carton snowcrest whip

Allow raspberries to defrost a little, then sieve or liquidise. Beat the egg whites until stiff then add the sugar a little at a time and continue beating until the mixture stands in peaks. Beat the parev whip lightly until a little dropped from the whisk leaves a trail as it falls. Fold the topping and the egg whites together and then fold in the raspberry puree. For good results this should be made just before serving the meal. (½ pint double cream may be used instead of the parev topping for milk meal).

RHUBARB MOUSSE
Susan Stone

Serves 8   Preparation 20 mins.   Advance

2 tins of rhubarb
or 1½ lb. stewed rhubarb (675 grms)
¾ pint water (½ litre) or juice from tins

1 tablespoon lemon juice
1 teaspoon vanilla essence
2 raspberry jellies

Liquidise fruit. Dissolve jellies in water, add vanilla essence and lemon juice. Beat fruit and liquid together. Place in fridge to set. N.B. If stewing rhubarb use 4 tablespoons brown sugar and water to cover.

RUM BOMBE
Ruth Perl

Serves 12   Preparation 1 hour 20 mins.   Freezing time 2 hours   Freezable

3 pieces crystallised fruit
2 tablespoons kirsch
1 packet snowcrest parev chocolate
   ripple ice cream
½ packet snowcrest parev vanilla
   ice cream

1½ ozs. crushed meringue (45 grms)
4 ozs. chocolate rum mousse (page 114)
8 ozs. parev whip
2-3 tablespoons rum
2 tablespoons sugar

Oil bottom and sides of 6" mould, marinate pieces chopped crystallised fruits in kirsch. Semi-defrost the ice creams. Coat bottom and sides of mould with the chocolate ice cream freeze for ½ hour. Add crushed meringues mixed with fruit. On top of this spread vanilla ice cream. Freeze for ½ hour. Place ready prepared chocolate rum mousse on top. Smooth over and freeze for 2 hours. Un-mould and decorate with snowcrest parev whip flavoured with rum and sugar to taste.

HOT SPICED FRUIT
Wendy Webster

Serves 8-10   Preparation 15 mins.   Gas No 6 (400°)   Cook 30 mins

1 large tin white peach halves
1 large tin apricot halves
3 peeled eating apples
2 cups fresh or frozen strawberries
2 bananas
½ cup thin honey

2 teaspoons cinnamon
1 cup walnut halves
½ cup Cointreau or Grand Marnier
½ cup brown sugar
1 teaspoon nutmeg

Peel and slice fruit, place all fruit except bananas in a casserole, pour on liqueur and honey, sprinkle on sugar and spice, cover until ready for baking. Bake uncovered for 20 mins. Put in bananas and nuts and return to oven for further 10 mins. Serve hot.

Puddings & Pies

ALMOND PUDDING OR CAKE
Muriel Rosner

Serves 4   Preparation 10 mins   Gas No 3 (350°)   Cook 40 mins   Advance

6 eggs
6 ozs. ground almonds (175 grms)
4 oz. sugar (100 grms)

Icing
Juice of 2 lemons
Icing sugar

Beat egg whites until stiff. Add yolks and sugar and beat until mixed thoroughly. Stir in almonds and pour into greased cake tin. Cook. When cool add icing sugar to lemon juice and ice top of cake.

APPLE CRUMBLE
Yvonne Clarke

Serves 8-10   Preparation 5 mins.   Gas No 6 (400°)   Cook 1 hour   Freezable   Advance

Crumble
6 ozs. tomor (175 grms)
2 teaspoons cinnamon
6 ozs. semolina (175 grms)
6 ozs. flour (175 grms)
3 ozs. sugar (80 grms)

Apple mixture
4 ozs. sugar (100 grms)
1½ lbs. cooking apples (700 grms)
Little water
6 ozs. raisins (175 grms)

Simmer apples, sugar and water until soft. Melt tomor in saucepan. Stir in sugar, flour, semolina and cinnamon and mix until crumbly. Press half half of mixture in loose bottomed tin. Top with apple mixture. Sprinkle remaining crumble on top. Bake in middle shelf. Do not remove from hot tin.

APPLE SLICE
Eva Schwarz

Serves 6	Preparation 30 mins	Gas No 3 (350°)	Cook 50 mins	Advance

Square tin 11" x 7"
Pastry
½ lb. butter (225 grms)
1 lb. flour (450 grms)
1 teaspoon cinnamon
7 oz. sugar (200 grms)
3 egg yolks
Little water to bind

Filling
8 grated cooking apples
4 ozs. sugar (100 grms)
3 tablespoons ground hazelnuts
3 tablespoons raisins
Lemon juice to taste
1 egg white
Chopped nuts

Rub butter into flour and cinnamon. Beat yolks and sugar and add to flour. Add a little water to bind. Refrigerate. Simmer apples, sugar and lemon juice until lightly cooked. Drain. Add nuts and raisins. Arrange half the pastry in a greased tin. If pastry crumbles just push into shape. Bake for 10 mins. Spread apple mixture onto pastry and cover with remaining pastry. Brush with lightly beaten egg white and sprinkle with chopped nuts. Bake in moderate oven 30-40 mins. Cut into squares or rectangles when cool.

APRICOT OR APPLE SPONGE PUDDING
Mary Fish

Serves 6	Preparation 20 mins	Gas No 4 (360°)	Cook 30-40 mins

3 lbs. Cooking apples or apricots
   (1 k. 350 grms)
4 large eggs
6 ozs. sugar (175 grms)

5 ozs. cake meal or fine matzo meal
   (150 grms)
Castor sugar to taste
Grated rind of small lemon

If using apricots, wash and cut in half if fresh or if dried soak apricots over-night. If using apples, peel and core them and cut into thick slices. Cook in saucepan with a little water and sugar to taste. Bring to boil and remove from heat. Transfer to large deep pyrex dish. Beat yolks of eggs with sugar and lemon rind. Beat whites until stiff. Fold into yolks and add cake meal or matzo meal. Pour over apples and bake. When cooked sprinkle top with castor sugar. Good passover dessert.

APRICOT TART
Sally Bloom

Serves 7-8	Preparation 20 mins	Cook 25 mins	Advance

½ lb. rich shortcrust pastry (225 grms)
1 large tin apricots
1 level teaspoon arrowroot
1 teaspoon of sugar

2 tablespoons water
Little lemon juice
5 tablespoons juice from fruit
3 drops of almond essence

Bake shortcrust pastry blind in large tart tin. Blend arrowroot with water until smooth. Add fruit juice and little lemon juice. Stir well. Put in saucepan and bring slowly to boil. Stir until thick and translucent. Stir in apricots and leave until cold. Pour into case and decorate as desired.

122

DARMSTADT TART
Jeanne Silbert

Serves 6   Preparation 10 mins.   Gas No. 5 (375°)   Cook 55 mins.

4 ozs. shortcrust pastry (100 grms)   1½ tablespoons marmalade
4 ozs. macaroon crumbs (100 grms)   4 eggs
3 ozs. margarine (75 grms)   7″ - 8″ flan dish
     Sugar

Line flan dish with pastry and bake blind. Cream butter or margarine, add macaroon crumbs, egg yolks and marmalade. Pour mixture into case and bake until set, approximately 20-25 minutes. Whip egg whites until stiff, add sugar to taste. Spoon over cooked tart and replace in a slow oven Gas No. 1-2 (275° - 300°) for 30 minutes until crisp.

FRUIT PUDDING
Gertie Millward

Serves 6-8   Preparation 25 mins.   Cook 2-3 hours

½ lb. S.R. flour (225 grms)   2 large grated cooking apples
8 ozs. soft margarine (225 grms)   ¼ lb. raspberry jam (100 grms)
2 tablespoons granulated sugar   6 crushed digestive biscuits
1 tablespoon cinnamon   2 ozs. flaked almonds (50 grms)
3 tablespoons golden syrup   ¼ lb. sultanas (100 grms)

Prepare medium sized pudding basin by greasing it, then coating the sides with golden syrup. Rub margarine into flour mixed with sugar and 1 teaspoon cinnamon. Mix with enough water to make dough that can be rolled out. Roll dugh out (not too thinly), spread with jam, then cover with apples, sultanas, 1 dessertspoon cinnamon, biscuits, almonds and roll up like a swiss roll. Push into prepared basin, cover with paper and a pudding cloth. Place in a saucepan of boiling water and steam for 2-3 hours topping up with water to just below rim of basin during cooking.

GLOUCESTER TARTLETS
Lorraine Coleman

Serves 14   Preparation 30 mins.   Gas No 6 (400°)   Cook 20 mins   Freezable   Advance

Pastry   Filling
8 ozs. flour (225 grms)   2 oz. margarine (50 grms)
1 egg yolk   1 egg
1 teaspoon lemon juice   2 ozs. ground rice (50 grms)
4 ozs. margarine (100 grms)   2 ozs. castor sugar (50 grms)
1 teaspoon castor sugar   Raspberry jam
1 teaspoon cold water   Almond flavouring

Mix pastry ingredients together and roll out $\frac{1}{8}$″ thick. Cut into rounds and line patty tins. Cream fat and sugar, add flavouring and lightly beaten egg. Add ground rice. Put ½ teaspoon jam on bottom of each pastry case and place 1 large teaspoon of mixture on top, making sure mixture covers jam. Cook until just firm and lightly browned.

PORTUGUESE ORANGE ROLL
Barbara Davison

Serves 4-6   Preparation 15 mins.   Gas No ¼ (250°)   Cook 30 mins.   Advance

Juice and rind of 6 oranges
1 scant cup of sugar
2 eggs
1 teaspoon flour

1 fresh orange
Candied peel
Cold orange sauce (see sauces)

Place juice and finely grated rind of orange peel in mixing bowl with eggs and sugar. Beat until thick and white (approx. 10 minutes at top speed). Towards end of beating add teaspoon flour. Oil swiss roll tin, then line with oiled foil smoothly. Pour mixture slowly into tin. Bake for 3 minutes. Raise heat to No 3 (350°) for further 30 minutes until spongy to touch. Wet a tea towel and wring out, spread finely with castor sugar. Carefully invert cake on to castor sugar and remove foil. Allow steam to subside and roll cake up using tea towel to hold in position. Leave for at least 1 hour. Decorate at last moment with finely sliced oranges and shredded candied orange peel if desired. Pour over orange sauce. Slice as for swiss roll.

PECAN PIE
Phyllis Rubin U.S.A.

Serves 8   Preparation 20 mins.   Gas No 6 (400°)   Cook 45-50 mins.   Advance

1 cup syrup
3 eggs lightly beaten
$\frac{1}{8}$ teaspoon salt
1 teaspoon vanilla essence

1 cup sugar
2 tablespoons melted margarine
1 cup pecan nuts-whole or chopped
1 9" pastry shell unbaked

Mix all ingredients together adding nuts last. Pour into pastry shell. Bake for 15 minutes then reduce to No 3 (350°) for further 25-35 minutes. When ready, outer edges should be set and the centre slightly soft.

STRAWBERRY FLAN
Rosemary Fisch

Serves 10   Preparation 30 mins.   Gas No 4 (325°)   Cook 50 mins   Freezable   Advance

Pastry
4 ozs. sugar (100 grms)
8 ozs. margarine (225 grms)
12 ozs. plain flour (350 grms)
1 teaspoon lemon juice
1 egg

Filling
¾ pint water (½ litre)
1 strawberry jelly
1½ lbs. strawberries (700 grms)

Pastry Mix all ingredients together and knead into dough. Roll out on floured board. Place in greased, fluted loose bottomed 12" tin. Bake blind. Remove paper from blind case after 30 minutes and cook for further 20 minutes until brown. When cold fill with strawberries, make jelly with water and allow to cool. Cover strawberries with jelly and remove from tin when cold.

QUICK STRÜDEL

Valerie Halpern

Serves 24   Preparation 30 mins.   Gas No 4 (360°)   Cook 25 mins.   Freezable   Advance

1 lb. S.R. flour (450 grms)
½ lb. tomor (225 grms)
Cinnamon
Little water

Sultanas
Dates
Jam
Sugar for topping

Make pastry by rubbing fat into flour and mix with water to bind. Divide into six portions. Roll out pastry quite thinly and spread with jam. Sprinkle sultanas, chopped dates and cinnamon over jam. Roll each strüdel up and sprinkle top with water and sugar. The amount of fruit and sugar is up to the individual.

SUMMER PUDDING

Naomi Phillips

Serves 8   Preparation 30 mins.   Refrigeration 12 hours   Freezable   Advance

6-8 slices thin white bread
1 lb. blackberries (450 grms)
1 lb. raspberries or strawberries (450 grms)
   (or half of each)

2 pint bowl (1 litre)
6 oz. castor sugar (175 grms)
Margarine

Prepare bread by spreading with margarine on both sides and line pudding basin, taking care to patch with small pieces so that there is a solid lining. Cook all fruits with sugar until soft. Pour in half the fruit. Lay a piece of bread carefully over the fruit, then pour in remainder of fruit. Top the pudding with another full layer of bread and place a plate, or cover tightly, over the top to press down well. The fruit must be very moist and you will need all the juice which the cooking created. Leave in fridge for several hours or overnight. Dip into hot water and turn out. You will get excellent results from fresh or frozen fruits and any varieties may be used i.e. gooseberries, red currants etc. I always make two or three at a time and keep some in the freezer — a real family favourite.

TREACLE PUDDING

Wendy Max

Serves 5-6   Preparation 20 mins.   Cook 2-3 hours   Advance

3 eggs
6 oz. castor sugar (175 grms)
2 tablespoons golden syrup

6 oz. margarine (175 grms)
6 oz. S.R. flour (175 grms)
2 pint ovenproof bowl (1 litre)

Grease basin and put two tablespoons of syrup in bottom. Beat the sugar and margarine until light and fluffy. Add the eggs one at a time and beat until well blended. Lastly add the flour, folding in with a metal spoon. Pour the mixture on top of the syrup and tie a pleated piece of silver foil over the top with string to allow the pudding to rise. Boil in a large saucepan of water (topping up if necessary) with the lid on for two to three hours. To serve, turn upside down and serve with hot treacle sauce.
Sauce Simply stand open treacle tin in jug of hot water or stand in low oven for a few minutes.

NOTES

Milk Desserts

HINTS FOR SERVING ICE CREAM

Fill meringue cases or mango with coffee ice cream and Tia Maria.

Vanilla ice cream with crushed raspberries, kirsch and cream.

Vanilla and coffee ice cream with Tia Maria and Marshmallow sauce.

Vanilla ice cream with Honey and Stem ginger.

Vanilla ice cream with Creme de Cacoa and chocolate chips.

Vanilla ice cream with redcurrant juice (thickened with arrowroot) cream and Kirsch.

Vanilla ice cream with bananas sauted in Grand Marnier and grated chocolate.

Pineapple ring with vanilla ice cream, top with syrup from preserved ginger and chopped pieces of ginger.

Vanilla ice cream with marron puree thinned with cream. Fill a cup with sultanas and pour on some Brandy or Grand Marnier, leave for 24 hours then put on top of ice cream while still in the freezer or when just serving.

Pancakes can be made in advance and frozen with sheets of greaseproof paper between each one.

See cake section for extra ideas.

Light Desserts

BANANA SPLIT
Jill Lieuw

Serves 6   **Preparation 5 mins.**

6 bananas (not too ripe)
Drinking chocolate

1 gill single cream (2 dl.)
1 gill double cream (2 dl.)

Halve bananas in skins lengthwise. Gently take banana halves out of skins. Sprinkle the inside of each skin with a generous teaspoon chocolate powder. Replace banana halves. Pipe whipped cream over each half and sprinkle again lightly with chocolate powder. Put in fridge. The chocolate makes a lovely gooey sauce underneath the bananas.

BAVAROISE AUX POMMES
Ilda Dentith

Serves 10   **Preparation ¾ hour**   **Cook 20 mins.**   **Refrigeration 5 hours**

5 cups purée of cooking apples
2 tablespoons gelatine
Rind ½ lemon, juice of ½ lemon
1½ cups castor sugar
6 eggs

CRÈME CHANTILLY
½ pint double cream (3 dl.)
4 drops vanilla
½ teaspoon lemon juice
½ cup icing sugar

Cook apples as for apple sauce. While hot add melted gelatine, rind and juice of lemon. Beat yolks well and add the mixture to the eggs. Keep hot in a doule saucepan. Beat egg-whites stiffly and fold into apple mixture. Put in mould and chill very hard in fridge. When ready unmould and garnish with the Chantilly.
CHANTILLY: Put cream, vanilla, lemon juice and icing sugar in bowl. Whip until cream has set like normal whipped cream. Decorate middle of Bavoroise with the Chantilly, using a savoy piping bag.

CHOCOLATE PARTY CUPS
Charlotte Davis

Serves 8   **Preparation 30 mins.**   **Setting time 2 hours**   **Advance**

8 oz. plain chocolate
Stem ginger
Paper fairy cake cases

¼ pint double cream (2 dl.)
Glacé cherries

Melt chocolate slowly in bowl over saucepan of hot water. Coat insides of paper cases evenly with the chocolate. Leave in cool place to set. (not fridge). Peel cases off gently. Make one or two extra cases to allow for accidents as these cases are very delicate. Fill with whipped cream and stem ginger to taste. Decorate with glacé cherries.

CHOCOLATE SOUFFLÉ (without eggs)   Valerie Selby

Serves 4   Preparation 20 mins.

1 can chilled Carnation milk
1 oz. gelatine (30 grms)
½ cup water

½ lb. plain chocolate (225 grms)
1 tablespoon instant coffee
1 tablespoon brandy or rum

Whisk milk in large bowl until stiff and frothy. Mix all other ingredients in saucepan. Beat well over very low heat with wooden spoon until dissolved. Fold chocolate mixture into milk until well mixed. Pour into serving bowl and chill at once.
Note This soufflé sometimes separates, but it is still delicious. If it does separate, call it "Frothy Blancmange".

HOT CHOCOLATE SOUFFLÉ   Muriel Rosner

Serves 4   Preparation 10 mins.   Gas No 5 (375°)   Cook ½ hour

1 oz. butter (30 grms)
1 oz. plain flour (30 grms)
½ pint milk (3 dl.)

2-3 oz. chocolate (30-50 grms)
1 oz. castor sugar (30 grms)
3 eggs and 1 extra egg white

Melt chocolate in milk. Stand aside. Melt butter in saucepan and add flour. When smooth add chocolate milk and stir until very thick and leaves sides of pan. Remove from heat and beat in sugar, then egg yolks one at a time. Beat whites stiffly, fold into chocolate mixture and put into buttered soufflé dish. Serve immediately with thick cream or hot chocolate sauce.

CRÈME BRULÉE   Leita Coren

Serves 6 Preparation 20 mins Gas No 1 (250°) Cook 45 mins Refrigeration 6 hours. Advance

4 egg yolks
2 oz. castor sugar (50 grms)
Few drops vanilla essence

½ pint single cream (3 dl.)
½ pint double cream (3 dl.)
Extra castor sugar for caramel

Blend together egg yolks and sugar, pour cream onto eggs and sugar mixture with essence. Strain cream custard into 1½ pint dish that can go into oven and be served at table. Stand dish in a little hot water and bake in oven for about 45 minutes. Leave to get cold (this can be left overnight in fridge).
To make caramel
Heat grill to very hot. Sprinkle castor sugar evenly all over top, put under grill and lightly brown turning the dish round and watching all the time (about 5 minutes). When top is hard cool. This can be made early the same day but does not freeze.

NOT QUITE CRÈME BRULÉE

Valerie Selby
Lynn Lindsey

Serves 6   Preparation 20 mins.   Cook 5 mins.   Refrigeration time 6 hours   Advance

6 peeled and sliced oranges
2 tablespoons Grand Marnier or Cointreau
1 lb. soft brown sugar (450 grms)

½ pint double cream (3 dl.)
2 cartons sour cream (3 dl.)
or 1 pint double cream (½ litre)

Lay oranges in fireproof dish and sprinkle with liqueur. Whip creams together and pour over fruit. Put in fridge until very cold. (Overnight if desired). Just before serving, sprinkle brown sugar over top and grill until it bubbles. N.B. In place of oranges, 2 or 3 packets of strained frozen raspberries or poached fresh peaches can be used.

DATE AND BANANA DESSERT

Joyce Keyes

Serves 6-8   Preparation 5-10 mins.   Refrigeration time 3 hours

4-5 bananas
½ lb. stoned dates (100 grms)

½ pint single cream (¼ litre)

Alternate layers of thinly sliced bananas and halved dates in a serving bowl. Pour cream all over and chill. Cream will soak into fruit and give it a soft slightly sticky texture. Delightful way of serving dates.

ICE CREAM

Stephanie Carson

Serves 6   Preparation 10 mins.   Freezing time 6 hours   Freezable

¼ pint double cream (2 dl.)
¼ pint single cream (2 dl.)

2-3 oz. icing sugar (60-90 grms)
2 eggs

Beat egg yolks with icing sugar until fluffy. Beat double cream, add single cream until just thickened. Fold cream into yolk mixture. Pour into freezing tray until just frozen lightly. Whisk egg whites stiffly and fold in. Refreeze.
Delicious with half a pound frozen blackcurrants, puréed and added with extra spoon icing sugar, or strong coffee essence or frozen strawberries.

GOOSEBERRY ICE CREAM

Mrs Goosegog

Serves 6   Preparation 40 mins   Cook 20 mins   Freezing time 6 hours   Freezable

1 lb. gooseberries (500 grms)
2 oz. sugar approx (50 grms)

½ pint double cream (3 dl.)

Lightly cook gooseberries with sugar to sweeten (no water) in casserole in oven. Cool. Whip cream and add to well sieved gooseberries. Add a little green colouring. Put into ice-trays, having turned freezer to coldest setting an hour before. After half an hour take out and beat with a wooden spoon. If you have time repeat this.

131

STRAWBERRY LIQUEUR ICE CREAM   Lydia Waller

Serves 4-6   Preparation 15 mins   Freezing time 6 hours   Freezable

½ pint half whipped double cream (3 dl.)
A few drops vanilla essence
4 óz. castor sugar (100 grms)

1 lb. fresh strawberries (450 grms)
2 tablespoons rum or maraschino
1 pint ice tray (½ litre)

Put all ingredients in blender and blend (or sieve strawberries and mix with other ingredients). Pour into ice-tray and freeze for ¾ of an hour. Turn out and whiks until smooth. Return to tray and freeze until firm.

VANILLA ICE CREAM   Susan Stone

Serves 10-12   Preparation 15 mins   Freezing time 6 hours   Freezable

4 separated eggs
4 oz. icing sugar (100 grms)
½ pint double or whipping cream (3 dl.)
1 teaspoon vanilla essence

Coffee variation
2 heaped teaspoons instant coffee
1 tablespoon boiling water
1 tablespoon Tia Maria

Whisk whites until stiff. Add spoonfuls of sugar, beating after each addition. Whisk in yolks. In another bowl whip cream until thick. Add vanilla and fold both mixtures together. Freeze in plastic container with lid.
Coffee Variation To basic mixture fold in coffee dissolved in water with liqueur.

JELLY CREAM   Marion Segall

Serves 6   Preparation 20 mins.   Refrigeration time 2 hours

1 orange jelly
4 eggs
3 tablespoons water

4 tablespoons Grand Marnier
½ pint double cream (3 dl.)

Dissolve jelly in boiling water. Cool and add Grand Marnier and beaten egg yolks. Whip whites until stiff and fold in double cream. Fold all into jelly mixture and blend well. Put in mould and refrigerate.

LEMON SOUFFLÉ   Valerie Selby

Serves 6   Preparation 20 mins.   Refrigeration time 3 hours   Advance

Juice of 6 lemons
2 lemon jellies
½ pint water (¼ litre)

Grated rind of 3 lemons
1 pint cream (½ litre)

Dissolve jellies in water, add lemon juice and rind. Transfer into bowl of electric mixer. Put in fridge until just beginning to set. Take out, pour cream over and beat until thick and creamy. Pour into serving bowl and put in fridge at once. Can also be made with oranges and orange jellies.

RASPBERRY MOUSSE
Ann Millett

Serves 8   Preparation 30 mins.   Refrigeration time 3 hours   Advance

1 lb. fresh or frozen raspberries (450 grms)
4 tablespoons water
½ oz. gelatine (15 grms)
2 ozs. castor sugar

¼ pint double cream (2 dl.)
2 egg whites
3 ozs. pkt. full fat soft cheest (80 grms)

Purée fruit in blender and sieve. Put water in saucepan, sprinkle on gelatine, soak five minutes, then stir over low heat until dissolved. Draw off heat. Beat cheese and sugar until light. Stir in raspberry purée very slowly, stirring constantly. Stir in lightly whipped cream. Set aside until mixture begins to thicken. Stiffly beat egg whites and fold in gently and evenly. Pour into serving dish and chill until firm. Serve with cream.

STRAWBERRY ROMANOFF
Pearl Barnett

Serves 8   Preparation 15 mins.

2 lbs. strawberries (900 grms)
½ pint whipping cream (3 dl.)
2½ teaspoons Cointreau

1 pint vanilla ice cream (½ litre)
Juice of ½ lemon
1¼ tablespoons Rum

Whip cream. Combine with softened ice cream. Add lemon juice and liqueurs. Pour over whole chilled sugared strawberries.

STRAWBERRY SYLLABUB
Faith Duke

Serves 4   Preparation 15 mins.

1 lb. strawberries (450 grms)
½ pint double cream (¼ litre)
1 orange
Sugar to taste

2 ozs. chopped almonds (50 grms)
Sponge fingers
½ pint Chablis (¼ litre)
Icing sugar

Hull strawberries. Divide between four glasses and sprinkle with a little icing sugar. Whip cream until thick, add grated rind and juice of orange. Whip in wine and castor sugar to taste and pour over strawberries. Decorate with almonds and serve with sponge fingers.

YOGHURT CREAM
Sigrid Harris, W. Germany

Serves 8   Preparation 20 mins.   Refrigeration 2 hours   Advance

2 eggs, separated
5 ozs. sugar (150 grms)
Juice of 1 lemon
5 tablespoons whipped cream

5 tablespoons water or orange juice
2 cartons natural unsweetened yoghurt
1 pkt. gelatine and a little water

Beat yolks and sugar until fluffy. Add lemon juice, orange juice or water and yoghurt. Beat. Dissolve gelatine in a little water in a basin over pan of hot water. Add to mixture and leave to cool. When beginning to set, fold in stiffly beatedn egg whites. Place in bowl and decorate with whipped cream.

QUICK YOGHURT   Anita Elman

| Serves 4 | Preparation 15 mins. | Culturing time 8 hours | Advance |

1 pint milk (½ litre)   1 teaspoon plain yoghurt

Boil milk, simmer for two minutes and leave to cool to blood heat. Put yoghurt in a cup and beat until smooth. Remove skin from milk and stir in yoghurt. You can then either leave in saucepan covered, or transfer to bowl and cover tightly with foil or plastic film. Place in a warm spot wrapped in a towel for at least 8 hours, but not more than 12 hours. Then place in fridge. This yoghurt can then be added to the next pint of milk to continue the process. Serve plain, as a salad dressing or mixed with fruit.

Puddings & Pies

APPLE PIE   Shirley Byre

| Serves 4-6 | Preparation 30 mins. | Gas No. 4 (350°) | Cook ¾ hour | Advance |

PASTRY
1 egg
6 ozs. margarine (175 grms)
8 ozs. S.R. flour (225 grms)
Pinch of salt
1 tablespoon sugar

FILLING
2 lbs. grated apples (900 grms)
3 tablespoons apricot jam
Sugar
1 tablespoon milk
2 teaspoons sugar

Mix pastry ingredients together with wooden spoon. Knead. Cut in half. Pastry is very soft and may break. Grease pie-dish well. Roll cut pastry on a well floured board. Line dish with pastry using fingers to smooth where pastry has broken. Place jam on pastry and add apples and sugar. Roll out second half of pastry and cover pie. Brush with milk and sugar and bake.

SWISS APPLE PIE   Shiela Rosen

| Serves 6 | Preparation 15 mins. | Gas No. 8 (450°) | Cook 20-30 mins. |

2 large eggs
2-3 tablespoons caster sugar
2 lbs. apples (900 grms)

2 tablespoons plain flour
8 ozs. milk (¼ litre)
Packet puff pastry

Line swiss roll tin with thinly rolled puff pastry, making sure base and four sides are covered Peel and slice apples into eights. Place in overlapping layers on pastry. Whisk eggs, sugar, milk and flour. Pour this custard over apples and bake.
Note: This pie can be made with hard eating apples.

134

AUSTRIAN APPLE SQUARES
Valerie Gee

Serves 16   Preparation 30 mins.   Gas No. 5 (375°)   Cook 45 mins.   Advance

PASTRY
9 ozs. plain flour (250 grms)
1 oz. ground almonds (30 grms)
3 ozs. butter (80 grms)
3 level tablespoons caster sugar
Grated rind ½ lemon
1 egg yolk
3 tablespoons pouring cream or
    top of the milk
Pinch of salt
3 ozs. margarine (80 grms)

FILLING
1½ lbs. baking apples (675 grms)
5 oz. sugar (150 grms)
2 tablespoons sultanas
½ teaspoon cinnamon
1 egg white
Baking tin 12″ x 8″ (30cms by 20cms)

Mix flour, ground almonds, salt, sugar and lemon rind. Cut fat, then gently rub into flour until it looks like fine breadcrumbs. Beat yolk and cream together and stir into mixture, to make a soft dough. Divide in two, wrap in foil and chill for one hour. Roll half the dough to fit tin about 12″ x 8″. Grate apples on top, then smooth until level and sprinkle with sugar, cinnamon and sultanas. Roll out remaining dough to fit top, pressing it well down round sides of tin. Beat egg white until frothy and paint all over the top. Mark lightly into squares and sprinkle thickly with granulated sugar and bake until golden brown. Leave in tin until required. The squares are nice served just warm. Cover them with tin-foil and reheat in moderate oven for fifteen minutes. To be successful there must be a thick juicy apple filling with a very thin layer of cakey pastry top and bottom. Makes about two dozen 2″ squares.
Note: The ground almonds give a melting quality to the pastry, but would make it too soft to hold its shape in a ordinary pie-dish.

APRICOT BOMBE
Cimmie Winton

Serves 6-8   Preparation 20 mins.   Refrigeration time 12 hours   Freezable   Advance

BOMBE
Sponge cakes
½ pint whipped cream (3 dl.)
Shelled almonds
1½ pint basin (1 litre)

FILLING
1 lb. dried apricots (500 grms)
Water
1 tablespoon Curaçao
¼ lb. Demerara sugar (100 grms)
Squeeze of lemon

Soak apricots overnight with sugar in cold water to cover. Adding more water if necessary, cook until soft (about ½ an hour). Line a 1½ pint basin with spongecakes cut into strips. Sprinkle over Curaçao. Place cooked apricots in centre. They should be soft and mushy and some liquid may be needed. Cover with a weighted plate and refrigerate overnight. To serve — turn onto serving plate and decorate with whipped cream — either forked or piped rosettes. Sprinkle with toasted almonds. A good Passover dessert.

CHEESE DESSERT

Nurit Raphael

Serves 8   Preparation 45 mins.   Freezing time 5 hours   Freezable   Advance

2 eggs
17 ozs. curd cheese (500 grms)
3 ozs. pineapple jelly (80 grms)
½ pint whipping cream (3 dl.)

½ cup apricot or orange brandy
½ cup sugar
½ cup cold milk
8 ozs. sponge fingers (225 grms)

Put milk, 2 egg yolks and sugar in saucepan and stir over very low heat until it resembles mayonnaise. Dissolve jelly in one cup boiling water. Cool. Beat egg-whites stiff. Beat cream. Dip each sponge finger quickly in brandy. Line bottom and sides of square buttered pyrex dish with sponge fingers. In the mixer blend cheese with milk mixture and cooled (not set) jelly. Carefully fold in beaten egg-whites. Pour mixture over sponge fingers. Cover carefully with foil and freeze. Unfreeze at room temperature for about forty-five minutes before serving. It may be served topped with apple sauce, canned peaches or fresh strawberries.

CHOCOLATE BROKEN BISCUITS

Gemma Levine

Serves 6-8   Preparation 5 mins.   Refrigeration 12 hours   Freezable   Advance

½ lb. broken biscuits (225 grms)
¼ lb. Petit Beurre (100 grms)
¼ lb. castor sugar (100 grms)
4 ozs. bitter chocolate (100 grms)

1 egg
1 teaspoon black coffee
2 ozs. walnuts (50 grms)
1-2 cartons cream
2 ozs. grated chocolate (50 grms)

Melt chocolate in a double saucepan. Cream butter, sugar and biscuits. Add chocolate and beaten egg, add black coffee and walnuts. Put mixture into a flat buttered dish and leave overnight in fridge. Turn out. Dress with whipped cream and grated chocolate.

CHOCOLATE LAYER TRIFLE

Mirelle Dessau

Serves 8   Preparation 15 mins.   Refrigeration 12 hours   Freezable   Advance

4 ozs. fresh brown breadcrumbs (100 grms)
3 tablespoons drinking chocolate powder
½ pint single cream (3 dl.)

4 ozs. demerara sugar (100 grms)
2 tablespoons Nescafé
½ pint double cream (3 dl.)

Mix all dry ingredients. Whip creams together. Place a layer of chocolate mixture in a bowl. Place a layer of cream on top. Repeat until there are three layers of each. Refrigerate overnight.

CHOCOLATE LOG
Carol Chinn

Serves 8   Preparation 10 mins.   Freezing time 6 hours   Freezable   Advance

4 oz. butter (100 grms)
2 egg yolks
4 oz. plain chocolate (100 grms)
½ pint double cream (3 dl.)

4 ozs. caster sugar (100 grms)
2 egg-whites
1 dozen meringues
Peppermint essence

Cream butter and sugar, add beaten egg-yolk. Melt chocolate in double saucepan and add. Beat egg-whites until stiff and fold into mixture. Line ice-tray or loaf tin with greaseproof, allowing paper to cover sides. Crush maringués, four at a time and place on tin. Cover with chocolate mixture, then meringue, then chocolate mixture, finishing with meringue. Cover with greaseproof and press down. Freeze until needed. Lift out and cover all over with whipped double cream slightly flavoured with peppermint. Refrigerate until required, or refreeze, making sure to defrost well before serving. Serving with fresh fruit or orange salad as this dessert is very rich.

CHOCOLATE ROLL
Muriel Rosner

Serves 6   Preparation 15 mins. Gas No. 6 (425⁰)   Cook 15-20 mins.   Freezable   Advance

3 eggs
6 ozs. plain chocolate (175 grms)
Large cup of black coffee
Icing sugar

2 ozs. flaked almonds (50 grms)
5 ozs. castor sugar (150 grms)
¾ pint double cream (½ litre)

Beat yolks and sugar until creamy. Melt chocolate in coffee and stir until chocolate in melted. Boil until thick and creamy. Pour onto yolks and mix. Whisk whites of eggs stiffly and fold into chocolate mixture. Pour into greaseproof lined and oiled tin and bake until top is firm. Put in a cool place and next day remove paper, spread with whipped cream and roll up in swiss roll. Decorate with icing sugar and flaked almonds.

CRÉPES
Jewels Leader-Cramer

Serves 6-8   Preparation 10 mins.   Refrigeration 1 hour   Cook 30 mins.   Freezable   Advance

5 ozs. plain flour (150 grms)
1 breakfast cup milk
1½ ozs. melted and cooled butter (45 grms)
1 breakfast cup water

3 eggs
½ teaspoon salt
1½ ozs. melted butter (45 grms)
1 tablespoon vegetable oil

Combine flour, eggs, milk, water, salt and 1½ ozs. melted butter in blender and blend at high speed for a few seconds. Turn off. Scrape down sides of jar and blend again for forty seconds. The batter should then be like double cream. Dilute if necessary by beating in cold water – a teaspoon at a time. Refrigerate batter in blender jar for an hour or two before using. Heat 5" crépe pan over a high heat until a drop of water flicks off. With a pastry brush lightly brush the bottom and sides with a little of the melted butter and oil combined. With a small ladle pour about two tablespoons of batter into the pan, tip pan so that batter quickly covers the bottom. Crépes should be paper thin. Cook for a minute then turn over with a spatula.
Note: When freezing stack in airtight container.

DINNER CAKE
Esther Taub

Serves 8   Preparation 30 mins.   Refrigeration 12 hours   Advance

3½ ozs. butter (100 grms)
2½ ozs. castor sugar (65 grms)
3½ ozs. chopped walnuts (100 grms)
1 egg
½ pint double cream (3 dl.)

2 tins drained and stoned cherries
4 pkts. boudoir biscuits
½ teacup rum
½ teacup milk

Line a square tin with foil. Press down and rinse in cold water. Cream butter and sugar. Add egg and beat well. Add nuts, leaving some for decoration. Mix milk and rum. Dip biscuits in, sugar side down. Place in bottom of tin. Spread half butter mixture on top and sprinkle cherries (leaving some for decoration). Repeat finishing with a layer of biscuits. Cover with foil and press down gently. Cover with plate and refrigerate. Whip cream with a little sugar. Turn cake out and coat with cream. Decorate with nuts and cherries.

FRESH FIGS FLAMBÉ
Faith Duke

Serves 6   Preparation 10 mins.   Cook 5-10 mins.

12 ripe purple figs
3 tablespoons brandy

3 tablespoons Curaçao
Serve with double cream

Carefully peel the figs and put into a chafing dish with Curaçao and brandy. Light the alcohol lamp and in a few seconds put a match to the liqueurs. Prick each fig with a silver fork and shake the pan gently until the flare dies. The figs will be warm and a little softened and the liqueur reduced. Serve immediately with a separate jug of cream.

HAZELNUT MERINGUE CAKE
Barbara Sandler
Ruby Pearce
Barbara Stern

Serves 8-10   Preparation 10 mins.   Cook 30-35 mins.   Gas No 5 (375°)   Advance
Refrigeration 3 hours   Freezable

4 egg whites
9 ozs. castor sugar (250 grms)
4 drops vanilla essence
½ teaspoon vinegar
4 ozs. ground hazelnuts (100 grms)
2 x 8" sandwich time (2 x 20¼ cms)

½ pint double cream (¼ litre)
1 lb. raspberries (450 grms)
MELBA SAUCE
Icing sugar 4 tablespoons
8 ozs. raspberries (225 grms)
Bakewell paper

Oil sides and bottom of tin and line with Bakewell paper. Whisk egg whites until stiff and add sugar a tablespoon at a time beating until really stiff. Whisk in vanilla essence and vinegar. Fold in nuts carefully and divide mixture into 2 tins smoothing the tops with a knife. Bake. Watch carefully to see they do not brown. When cool, turn out and remove paper. To serve, sandwich meringues with half the whipped cream and all the raspberries. Pipe remaining cream on top. To make sauce: Sieve the raspberries and gradually add the icing sugar until well mixed and serve in jug with cake.

LEMON FRIDGE CAKE

Mrs. Iris Mattey

Serves 8-10   Preparation 2½ hours   Refrigeration time 3 hours

Large pkt trifle sponges
2 egg yolks and whites
4 ozs. sugar (100 grms)
½ oz. gelatine (15 grms)
2 lemons

3 tablespoons sherry
1 small carton whipped double cream
   (Parev may be used)
¼ pint cold water (2 dl.)
6" loose bottomed cake tin
Flaked almonds

Slice sponge cakes and place on bottom of tin. Spoon over sherry. Heat together juice and grated rinds of lemons, sugar and water. Stir in beaten yolks. Cook for two minutes — but do not allow to boil. Dissolve gelatine in a little water and add to mixture. Leave to refrigerate until nearly set (about two hours). Fold in stiffly beaten egg whites. Pour half onto sponge cakes. Place a further layer of sponge cakes over and finally spoon rest of mixture on top. Place in the fridge to set and decorate with chopped nuts before serving.

LEMON GATEAU

Mirelle Dessau

Serves 8   Preparation 20 mins.   Refrigeration time 12 hours   Freezable   Advance

6 ozs. butter (175 grms)
6 ozs. caster sugar (175 grms)
3 large eggs

Juice and rind of 4 large lemons
12 trifle sponges
½ pint double cream /Parev (3 dl.)

Line a 2 lb. loaf tin with silver foil. Cream fat and sugar until fluffy. Beat in eggs one at a time and add lemon rind. Put half the trifle sponges in bottom of tin and pour half the lemon juice over them. Place half creamed mixture over and press well down. Repeat. Cover with a plate and press well down. Refrigerate overnight. Turn out and cover with cream.

VACHERIN AUX MARRONS

Madame Glacé

Serves 8   Preparation 30 mins.   Gas No. 1 (300⁰)   Cook 50-60 mins.   Freezable   Advance

4 egg whites
8 ozs. sugar (225 grms)
1 tin sweetened chestnut purée
¼ pint whipped double cream (2 dl.)
Or ¼ pint Parev whip with a little brandy

DECORATION
Icing sugar
1 oz. plain grated chocolate (30 grms)

Line two baking sheets with silicone paper. Beat egg-whites stiffly add one tablespoon sugar and beat for one minute. Fold in remaining sugar slowly. Divide mixture and spread evenly into two rounds 8" or 9" in diameter. Bake until lightly browned and dry. Peel off paper and leave to call on rack. Mix chestnut purée and half quantity of whipped cream and sandwich between meringues. Dust top with icing sugar and pipe rosettes of remaining whipped cream around edge. Sprinkle grated chocolate over top in bands or circular pattern.

MOCHA PANCAKES
Ruth Starr

Serves 8   Preparation 15 mins.   Standing time 2 hours   Cook 20 mins.

4 ozs. plain flour (100 grms)
1 tablespoon caster sugar
Pinch of salt
1 tablespoon powdered chocolate
1 tablespoon powdered coffee
2 eggs

¾ pint milk (½ lt.)
2 tablespoons melted butter
½ pint whipped cream (3 dl.)
1 tablespoon rum
Sugar
2-3 poached pears

Sift together flour, sugar, salt, chocolate and coffee. Beat eggs and add to dry ingredients. Mix in milk and melted butter. Strain and allow mixture to stand for two hours. In a small thick bottomed pan melt a little butter for each pancake. Put two tablespoons of batter in pan and cook over medium heat until crisp. (one minute per side). Makes 20-24 pancakes. Fill pancakes with whipped cream flavoured with rum and sugar. Garnish with poached pears.

ORANGE MERINGUES
Valerie Gee

Serves 8   Preparation ½ hour   Gas No. 1 (300°)   Cook ½ hour

4 large oranges
4 heaped teaspoons custard powder
8 bare tablespoons milk
4 teaspoons caster sugar

TOPPING
4 egg whites
4 tablespoons caster sugar
Small bunch of grapes

Cut each orange in half. Squeeze out juice and scoop remaining flesh, being careful to leave stem intact to form a plug and prevent leakage of mixture. Put the custard powder into a saucepan and blend to a smooth paste with the orange juice. Warm over a low heat until the mixture starts to thicken, then add milk and caster sugar. Put this mixture into scooped orange halves. **Topping.** Beat egg whites and caster sugar, folding in sugar gently. Pile on top of oranges. Dust with sugar and put in oven. **To serve:** top each dessert with a grape. Serve from a platter with small bunches of grapes between the orange halves.

PEACHES IN SYRUP
Shelley Stewart

Serves 4   Preparation 10 mins.   Gas No. 5 (375°)   Cook ½ hour

4 peaches
2 dessertspoons sugar
1 egg yolk

2 ozs. Amaratti Macaroons (50 grms)
1 tablespoon soft butter
Squeeze of lemon juice
Pot of cream

Crumble macaroons into bowl. Mix in egg, sugar and butter. Scald and peel peaches and remove stones. Stuff macaroon mixture into cavities. Butter a fireproof dish, arrange peaches in this, squeeze lemon juice over and place in oven. Serve warm with cream.

M.W.M.H.   K

PROFITEROLES WITH CHOCOLATE SAUCE

Wendy Max

Serves 10   **Preparation 30 mins.**   **Gas No. 5 (375⁰)**   **Cook 20 mins.**   **Freezable**

CHOUX PASTRY
15 fl. ozs. water (½ litre)
6 ozs. margarine (175 grms)
7½ ozs. plain flour (210 grms)
6 eggs

SAUCE
1 lb. plain chocolate (450 grms)
¾ pint water (3½ dl.)
8 ozs. granulated sugar (225 grms)

FILLING
1 pint thick custard (½ litre)
½ pint double cream (3 dl.)
Chocolate - optional

Melt margarine in water and when bubbling take off heat. Let bubbles stop and add the flour all together beating hard with a wooden spoon until smooth. Cool for five minutes, then add the eggs, one at a time, beating hard until each egg is blended in well. The mixture should be smooth and glossy when all the eggs have been added. Dampen a baking sheet and put a small teaspoonful of dough about 1½" apart. Bake for ten minutes and then a further ten minutes at No. 6 (400⁰). When done, remove from oven and immediately make a small hole in each one to let out the steam to prevent them becoming soggy. **Filling.** Beat cream until thick but not stiff, and blend with the custard which can have been flavoured with two tablespoons drinking chocolate, if required. Using a forcing bag and plain nozzle, fill the choux with custard mixture and pile up into pyramid shape. Dust with icing sugar. **Sauce.** Gently melt chocolate in water, when smooth add sugar and stir until dissolve. Bring to the boil and simmer until thick and syrupy. Allow to cool and serve in jug separately. **Note.** Choux may be frozen filled or unfilled, but unfilled preferably. When using for meat meals, fill profiteroles with Parev ice-cream instead of custard filling.

STRAWBERRY GATEAU SLICE

Susan Stone

Serves 8   **Preparation 20 mins.**   **Gas No. 5(375⁰)**   **Cook 15 mins.**

Swiss roll tin (10" x 12") (25 x 30cms)
3 eggs
4 ozs. flour (100 grms)
4 ozs. castor sugar (100 grms)
½ teaspoon vanilla essence

FILLING
1½ lb. strawberries (700 grms)
½ pint double cream (3 dl.)
1 dessertspoon vanilla flavoured icing sugar

Oil tin and lining paper. Beat eggs, sugar and vanilla in basin over saucepan of hot water until lemon coloured and fluffy. Remove from heat and fold in sifted flour with metal spoon. Pour into tin and bake. Turn out whilst still hot. When cold cut in half lengthwise. Beat cream and vanilla sugar until stiff. Put half cream on one sponge slice and slice half the strawberries and place on top of cream. Cover with other half of sponge. Spread thinly with cream, and place rest of strawberries on top in straight rows. Decorate with rosettes.

STRAWBERRIES IN RASPBERRY CREAM

Avril Kleeman

Serves 8   **Preparation 30 mins.**   **Refrigeration time 30 mins.**

2 lbs. strawberries (1 kilo 400 grms)   **8 tablespoons icing sugar**
1 lb. raspberries (450 grms)   **1 pint whipping cream**
Caster sugar

Place strawberries in a bowl and cover with sugar. Sieve the raspberries and add the sieved icing sugar. Mix the purée with the whipped cream and pour the mixture over the strawberries. Chill well.

NOTES

Snacks & Supper Dishes

To use left over vol-au-vent cases, heat and place a spoonful of cooked chopped mushrooms or tomatoes in the bottom, top with creamy scrambled eggs. Sprinkle with parsley.

When making toasted cheese sandwiches, make sandwich with dry bread, then Flora top side and place under grill. When crisp and brown, turn over and repeat.

Put a little oil in the water when cooking spaghetti, to prevent boiling over.

The following fillings make very nice toasted sandwiches. Cheddar cheese, chutney and tomato slices, Dutch cheese and anchovies, sardines and tomatoes.

Mushrooms on toast. Fry chopped onion in a little margarine, add chopped mushrooms, sprinkle on a tablespoon of flour, add ½ cup of milk then stir well until thick over a low light.

HOT ASPARAGUS CRISP
Jeanne Silbert

Serves 4   Preparation 20 mins.   Gas No. 6 (400°)   Cook 15-20 mins.

1 large tin of asparagus
3 tablespoons butter
3 tablespoons flour
½ cup asparagus liquid
Small packet potato crisps

½ cup cream
1 large cup grated cheese
Cayenne pepper
Salt
Pepper

Drain asparagus reserving liquid. Place asparagus in a buttered dish. Melt butter in a saucepan. When bubbling add flour. Remove from heat and gradually add asparagus liquid a little at a time. Return to stove and stir continuously until thickened. Add cream and seasonings to taste. Pour mixture over asparagus and sprinkle cheese and crushed potato crisps on top. Bake for 15-20 minutes.

STUFFED CABBAGE
Rusty Sotnick

Serves 4   Preparation 30 mins.   Cook 1-1½ hours   Advance

6-8 large cabbage leaves
3-4 ozs. cooked rice (80-100 grms)
4 ozs. margarine (100 grms)
1 finely chopped onion
4 ozs. finely sliced mushrooms (100 grms)
½ lb. minced beef (225 grms)
Salt and pepper

1 clove garlic
Worcester sauce
2½ cans tomato purée
1 teaspoon sugar
Mixed herbs to taste
1½ pints water (1 litre)
Beef cube or vegetable stock.

Blanche leaves in boiling water for 5 mins. and drain well. Melt margarine and fry onions and garlic until soft, add mushrooms and beef, fry until meat is browned and remove from heat. Stir in the remaining ingredients except the stock. Put spoonfuls of meat mixture on each cabbage leaf and make into separate parcels. Arrange in large saucepan and pour over stock to just cover. Simmer gently. Serve on a flat dish.

CHEESE AND SALMON QUICHE
Shirley Baum

Serves 4   Preparation 20-30 mins.   Gas No. 6 (400°)   Cook 40 mins.   Freezable   Advance

4 ozs. shortcrust pastry (100 grms)
1 egg
¼ pint milk (2 dl.)
Salt and pepper

½ grated medium onion
3 ozs. grated cheddar cheese (80 grms)
7 ozs. can of salmon (200 grms)
Parsley sprigs to garnish

Line greased 7″ flan dish with thinly rolled out pastry. Whisk together egg, milk, salt and pepper, add onion and cheese and mix well. Spread the drained and flaked salmon over the pastry and spoon the cheese mixture over the salmon. Bake in the centre of oven for fifteen minutes. Reduce heat to Gas No. 4 (350°) and bake for a further twenty-five minutes until golden brown and set. Garnish. Serve hot or cold.

CRÔUTON FROMAGE

Faith Duke

Serves 4   Preparation 10 mins.   Cook 10 mins.

4 slices of large sliced white bread   4 slices gruyère cheese
1 thinly sliced spanish onion   Oil for frying

Cut crust off bread. Heat oil and fry bread until crisp and brown. Drain and cover with sliced onion to taste. Place slices of cheese on top and put under grill until cheese melts and bubbles. Serve at once.

CHICKEN RISOTTO

Frederica Harris

Serves 4   Preparation 15 mins.   Cook 45 mins.

½ boiled chicken (from soup)   Tomato paste
1 onion   Beef cube
1 clove garlic   Mixed herbs
1 teaspoon paprika   ½ pint water (¼ litre)
Salt and pepper   Oil for frying

Bone and cut chicken into small cubes. Heat oil and fry onions with garlic. Add all ingredients except chicken and stir. Add chicken and simmer gently. If desired a small packet of frozen mixed vegetables can be added to this. Serve on a bed of cooked rice.

CHILI CON CARNE

Gloria Shaw

Serves 4   Preparation 15 mins.   Cook 1-1½ hours   Freezable   Advance

2 onions chopped   2 cloves garlic
1½ lbs. minced beef (675 grms)   Chili powder to taste
1 15ozs. can red kidney beans (425 grms)   ½ teaspoon cumin
1 large can tomatoes   ½ teaspoon oregano
2 tablespoons tomato paste   1 teaspoon salt
                                                                  Olive oil

Heat oil in large saucepan, brown onions and garlic over medium heat. Add beef and fry until brown stirring occasionally, mix in spices and chili powder, tomato paste, tomatoes and salt and stir. Cover and simmer for about one hour. Add kidney beans and cook for a further half hour. Serve in separate bowls, sprinkled with shredded lettuce, arrange slices of French bread (hot or cold) around bowl.

DIETER'S LUNCH

Diane Krais

Serves 2   Preparation 10 mins.

1 carton sour cream   Diced cucumber
1 tomato   Shredded lettuce
1 spring onion   Salt and black pepper

Mix everything together and serve with melba toast or ryvita.

EGG FLORENTINE

Mrs. Rosaner

Serves 6   Preparation 10 mins.   Cook 30 mins.   Gas No. 4 (350°)   Advance

12 eggs (hard boiled)
8 ozs. frozen spinach (225 grms)
  (or frozen corn)
2 ozs. flour (50 grms)

2 ozs. butter (50 grms)
1 pint milk (½ litre)
Cheddar cheese to taste
1 carton sour cream

Defrost spinach or corn and place in oven dish. Slice hard boiled eggs and put on top. Melt butter in saucepan. Add flour and stir. Add milk to make a thick creamy sauce. Remove from heat. Mix in grated cheese, salt and pepper to taste. When slightly cool beat in sour cream. Pour sauce over prepared eggs and vegetables, top with a little extra grated cheese and a few bread-crumbs and bake.

EGG MOULD

Ann Aubrey

Serves 8   Preparation 30 mins.   Advance

8 hard boiled eggs
½ pint mayonnaise (¼ litre)
½ pint double cream
½ oz. melted gelatine
Anchovy essence
Worcester sauce
Aspic jelly
Stuffed olives

Filling
This may be filled with tuna fish
and tomato, cucumber and sour
cream, etc.

Grease a ring mould with oil. Set sliced olives in aspic in mould base. Sieve egg yolks into mayonnaise and add seasonings. Add cream and chopped egg whites. Mix in gelatine. Pour over set olives. Turn out when firm and fill with chosen filling.

FETTUCCINE À LA PANNA

Diana Marks

Serves 4   Preparation 20 mins.   Cook 20 mins.

1 lb. egg noodles (450 grms)
½ finely chopped spanish onion
4 ozs. butter (100 grms)
½ lb. mushrooms (225 grms)

¼ pint double cream (2 dl.)
2 egg yolks
Grated cheese
Salt and freshly ground black pepper
Pinch nutmeg

Sauté onion in butter until transparent, add mushrooms and cook until tender. Put cream, beaten egg yolks and cheese in top of double saucepan. Cook slowly, stirring constantly with wooden spoon until thickened. Add salt, pepper nutmeg and fried mushroom and onion mixture to sauce, making sure the water in the double saucepan does not boil. Cook noodles in usual way until tender. Drain and mix with sauce. Serve immediately.

GNOCCHI

Gillian Burr

Serves 6   Preparation 20 mins.   Cook 20 mins.   Freezable   Advance

16 ozs. milk (½ litre)
10 ozs. flour (275 grms)
6½ ozs. butter (187½ grms)

5 eggs
Nutmeg to taste
6 ozs. parmesan cheese (175 grms)

Heat milk in saucepan together with 4 ozs. butter (100 grms) and a pinch of salt. Stir until it boils and add the flour, remove saucepan from heat when stirring in flour. Return the pan to heat and continue stirring with a wooden spoon for three to four minutes until it forms a hard paste and makes a frying sound. Allow to cool and mix in each egg separately then add 2 ozs. parmesan cheese (50 grms) and nutmeg. Drop small teaspoons of the paste into a large saucepan of boiling water for two to three minutes. Remove gnocchi with straining spoon and place on a dry tea cloth. Allow to dry and arrange them in a greased heatproof dish, sprinkle with some parmesan cheese. Make a white sauce and pour over adding more parmesan. Place dish in hot oven for fifteen to twenty minutes, until brown.

GNOCCHI NAPOLITANA

Meriel Joseph

Serves 4   Preparation 10 mins.   Cook 10 mins.   Gas No. 6 (400°)   Freezable   Advance

1 pint milk (½ litre)
Bouquet garni
Small sliced onion
4 ozs. semolina (100 grms)
2 eggs

8 ozs. strong grated cheese (225 grms)
1 oz. melted butter
Salt
Pepper
Good tomato sauce

Heat milk in large saucepan until almost boiling. Remove from heat, add bouquet garni and leave for ten minutes to allow herbs to infuse. Strain and return to pan. Beat in semolina and stir over moderate heat, cook until this mixture becomes very thick stirring constantly. Remove from heat and beat in eggs one at a time and add ½ grated cheese and seasonings. Grease a 12" x 8" Swiss roll tin and spread mixture on to tin smoothing as evenly as possible. Leave overnight. Cut into small triangles, place in heatproof dish, brush with melted butter, sprinkle on the remaining grated cheese. This can be cooked in oven or grilled until brown and crisp. Serve with tomato sauce.

GNOCCHI VERDI

Marion Cohen

Serves 4   Preparation 20-30 mins.   Cook 10 mins.   Advance

8 ozs. frozen chopped spinach (225 grms)
8 ozs. ricotta or curd cheese (225 grms)
Salt and pepper
Grated nutmeg
½ oz. butter (15 grms)
2 lightly beaten eggs

1½ ozs. grated parmesan (40 grms)
2 ozs. plain flour (50 grms)
Topping
2 ozs. butter (50 grms)
1 oz. parmesan (25 grms)
Tomato sauce (optional)

Cook spinach over low heat, stirring constantly until all moisture has disappeared. (This is important). Add cheese and season liberally with salt, pepper and nutmeg, add butter. Stir together over low heat for a few minutes. Remove from heat, add eggs, flour and parmesan and mix well. Allow to cool until firm. Shape into balls with well floured hands, using approximately one dessertspoonful of mixture. Place the gnocchi into simmering salted water gently, a few at a time. They are cooked when they rise to the surface. Remove immediately with straining spoon and drain well. Transfer to shallow greased flameproof dish and keep warm. Pour over melted butter and sprinkle with parmesan. This dish can be served with tomato sauce.

147

SMOKED HADDOCK AND COTTAGE CHEESE QUICHE

Ann Moss

Serves 4   **Preparation 25 mins.**   **Cook 50 mins.**   **Gas No 5 (375°)**   **Freezable**   **Advance**

8 ozs. shortcrust pastry (225 grms)
8 ozs. smoked haddock (225 grms)
1 oz. butter (30 grms)
2 ozs. mushrooms (50 grms)
Parsley

Juice of ½ lemon
2 eggs
3 tablespoons cream
4 ozs. cottage cheese (100 grms)
Salt and pepper
1 small onion

Roll shortcrust pastry out thinly and put into 8″ flan ring, leave for half an hour and bake blind for about fifteen minutes. Oven No 6 (400°). Poach haddock in water. Fry finely chopped onion and mushrooms and mix with fish. Place on bottom of baked flan case. Mix together eggs, cream, cheese, lemon juice and seasoning. Pour over fish mixture and bake in oven gas No 5 (350°) for approximately 35 mins., or until brown and set.

LASAGNE

Claire Jacobs

Serves 8   **Preparation 30 mins**   **Gas No 5 (375°)**   **Cook 30 mins.**

1 lb. lasagne (450 grms)
Nutmeg
Mixed herbs
1 large tin tomatoes
1 large tin tomato puree
1 large onion
Pepper
Sugar

¼ lb. grated parmesan (100 grms)
¼ lb. grated bel paese (100 grms)
¼ lb. grated gruyère (100 grms)
1 pint milk (½ litre)
2 ozs. margarine (50 grms)
2 ozs. flour (50 grms)
3″ deep, ovenproof dish
Wine

Boil lasagne in a large saucepan and drain.
Cheese Sauce. Melt margarine in saucepan and add flour, remove from heat and add milk by stirring with a wooden spoon. Mix together with the nutmeg and cheeses, return the saucepan to the heat and keep stirring until this has blended.
Tomato Sauce. Fry thinly chopped onion until soft, add tomatoes and tomato purée, mixed herbs, wine, salt, pepper and sugar to taste. Line base of dish with a layer of tomato sauce, then lasagne and cover with cheese sauce, repeat and sprinkle with a little extra parmesan. Bake.

LEEK AND CHEESE QUICHE

Diane Krais

Serves 4   **Preparation 30 mins.**   **Gas No 4 (350°)**   **Cook 30 mins**   **Freezable**

8 ozs. shortcrust pastry (225 grms)
4-6 ozs. cheese (100-175 grms)
2 leeks
½ pint single cream (3 dls.)
4 eggs

½ teaspoon English mustard
Salt and Black pepper
Garlic salt (to taste)
1 teaspoon dried chives (optional)

Line 10″ quiche dish with pastry. (No need to bake blind.) Blanche leeks for two minutes in boiling water firstly having cut them in half and into two inch strips. Dry thoroughly. Grate cheese on to pastry and arrange leeks on top. Put eggs, cream, mustard and seasonings into blender, blend for thirty seconds. Pour over cheese and leeks. Bake.

GRANDMA'S MACARONI CHEESE   Sandy Prevezer

Serves 8   Preparation 20 mins.   Gas No 4 (350°)   Cook 40 mins.   Freezable   Advance

1 lb. macaroni (450 grms)   ½ pint milk (3 dls.)
2 ozs. butter or margarine (50 grms)   Topping
2 dessertspoons flour   2 ozs. grated cheddar cheese (50 grms)
1 tablespoon tomato ketchup   Golden breadcrumbs
4 ozs. grated cheddar cheese   2 ozs. butter or margarine (50 grms)

Cook pasta in salted boiling water in large saucepan. Strain and rinse in cold water and put to one side. Using same saucepan melt butter, remove from heat and blend in flour, gradually add milk over heat stirring with wooden spoon to make smooth sauce. Add ketchup and cheese and blend together. Stir in pasta until well covered with sauce, place in large greased gratin dish., top with cheese and breadcrumbs and dot with butter. (If freezing this dish, do not bake first.) Bake until brown and crispy. Serve with ketchup.

MANICOTTI   Gloria Brown

Serves 8   Preparation 50 mins   Gas No 4 (350°)   Cook 30 mins.   Freezable

MANICOTTI PANCAKES   SAUCE
6 eggs (room temperature) $\frac{1}{3}$ cup olive or salad oil
1½ cups self rasing flour   1½ cups finely chopped onion
½ teaspoon salt, 1½ cups water   1 clove crushed garlic
FILLING   1 large tin tomatoes
2 lb. ricotta or cooking cheese (900 grms)   6 ozs. tomato puree (175 grms)
8 ozs. diced mozzarella (225 grms)   2 tablespoons chopped parsley
$\frac{1}{3}$ cup grated parmesan   1 tablespoon salt
2 eggs   1 tablespoon sugar
1 teaspoon salt   1 teaspoon dried oregano
¼ teaspoon pepper   1 teaspoon basil
1 tablespoon chopped parsley   ¼ teaspoon pepper
¼ cup grated parmesan

Pancakes: – In medium bowl, combine the eggs, flour and salt with water and beat until smooth. Allow to stand for at least half an hour. Heat 8″ non-stick frying pan, pour in three tablespoons of batter rotating the pan quickly to spread batter evenly over the base. Cook over medium heat until top of pancake is dry, but bottom now brown. Cool on wire rack and stack with waxed paper between. Makes twenty-six.
Filling: – In large bowl mix cream cheese, mozzarella, $\frac{1}{3}$ cup parmesan, eggs, salt, pepper, parsley. Mix with wooden spoon and blend well. Spread about a quarter of this filling in the centre of pancake and roll up tucking in the sides to form parcels. Place in two 12″ x 8″ x 2″ greased ovenproof dishes, put eight filled pancakes, seam side down having poured one and a half cups of sauce into dish first. Place five more on top and cover with one cup of sauce (directions below). Sprinkle with remainder of parmesan and bake uncovered.
Sauce: – Sauté onions and garlic in hot oil for five minutes. Mix in rest of ingredients and 1½ cups water, mashing tomatoes with fork. Bring to the boil reduce heat and simmer for fifty minutes. If cooking for the freezer, line baking dish first with foil and fold foil over entire dish to seal. This enables you to remove frozen contents and use the dish. When baking the frozen manicotti, allow to defrost for one hour, and bake covered for half the baking time, approx. one hour.

MUSHROOM FLAN
Wendy Sheinman

Serves 6   Preparation 20 mins.   Gas No 5 (375°)   Cook 30 mins.   Freezable   Advance

8 ozs. shortcrust pastry (225 grms)
1 medium onion
1½ ozs. butter (45 grms)
1½ ozs. plain flour (45 grms)
½ gill milk (1 dl.)
1 bay leaf

8 ozs. mushrooms (225 grms)
2 tablespoons cream
1 egg yolk
Mace
Salt
Pepper

Line 7" flan case with shortcrust pastry. Chop onions and fry until soft in butter. Remove from heat and add flour and seasoning. Boil milk with bay leaf and mace, strain into onion mixture to make roux, mix well and stir with wooden spoon over low heat until boiling and thickened. Chop mushrooms, Sauté quickly. Add to sauce. Add cream and egg yolk. Mix well. Pour into flan case and bake. This recipe can be made into bite size tartlets for cocktail canapes.

SAVOURY STUFFED MUSHROOMS
A Friendly Chef

Serves 4   Preparation 15 mins.   Cook 10 mins.

16-2" diameter mushrooms (must be even sized)
1 green pepper
1 red pepper
Clarified butter
1 oz. spring onions (30 grms)
Salt and Black pepper
¼ cup dry white wine
Flour
1 egg
Fresh white breadcrumbs

SAUCE
1¼ cups milk
2 tablespoons butter
2 tablespoons flour
Salt
White pepper
Nutmeg
4 ozs. cheddar cheese (100 grms)
Tartare sauce

Preheat oil in deep fryer to 350°. Remove stalks from mushrooms. Finely dice red and green peppers. Finely chop spring onions. Fry the peppers gently and then add onions, season with salt and papper and allow to fry for a few minutes. Add the wine -- cook one minute more and place aside to cool.
Sauce:– Melt butter in saucepan add sifted flour, stir with wooden spoon to form a roux and cook over gentle heat for one minute. Add the milk stirring until smooth. Season with salt, pepper and nutmeg, bring to the boil and cook gently for fifteen minutes. Add grated cheese and stir until melted. Cover with piece of buttered paper to avoid skin forming and allow to cool. Combine sauce with vegetables. Place a large spoonful of mixture on one mushroom, sandwich with another mushroom, flour, egg and breadcrumb the sandwich, place the mushrooms in deep frying basket and deep fry for five minutes. Serve hot.

NOODLE PUDDING

Ilda Dentith

Serves 10   Preparation 20 mins.   Cook 20 mins.   Gas No 7 (425°)

2 large packets egg noodles   Salt
¾ cup melted butter or margarine   Pepper
3 cups plain cottage cheese   Nutmeg
6 eggs

Boil noodles in a very large saucepan with plenty of water and one tablespoon salt. Boil for five minutes. Strain and sprinkle with cold water. Set aside. In large soufflé dish put one layer of noodles, one of cottage cheese and one of beaten egg until the dish is full, finishing with noodles. Pour melted butter over, sprinkle with pepper and bake. Serve immediately.

BAKED STUFFED POTATOES

Valerie Ross

Serves 4   Preparation 10 mins.   Gas No 7 (425°)   Cook 2 hours.

4 very large potatoes   ½ teaspoon dried thyme
Left over minced lamb or beef   1 tablespoon Worcester sauce
1 chopped Spanish onion   Cooking fat
1 crushed clove garlic   Salt, pepper
          Olive oil

Wash and dry unpeeled potatoes, prick and smear skins with a little olive oil. Cook in oven for one and a half hours. Towards end of cooking time fry onions and garlic in fat until soft, add meat and stir well, add thyme and Worcester sauce. Remove potatoes from oven, cut slice from top, scoop cooked potato, put in a bowl with meat mixture. Season and pile back into potato skins, replace tops and cook for a further twenty-five to thirty minutes.

FRESH SALMON MOUSSE

Lynn Leader

Serves 4   Preparation 15 mins.   Advance

8 ozs. fresh cooked salmon (225 grms)   ¼ peeled and chopped cucumber
¼ pint mayonnaise (2 dls.)   ½ oz. gelatine (50 grms)
¼ pint double cream (2 dls.)   3 tablespoons warm water
1 tablespoon lemon juice   Salt and pepper

Dissolve gelatine in warm water in basin over a pan of hot water. Mash the salmon with fork, mix with mayonnaise and fold in the lightly whipped cream. Gradually add the dissolved gelatine, lemon juice, finely chopped cucumber and salt and pepper to taste. When mixture is evenly blended pour into a mould which has been lightly greased or rinsed in cold water. Cover and place in refrigerator to set. Turn out mould by very briefly immersing in a bowl of hot water. Garnish with parsley.

SALMON MOUSSE
Janet Dwek

Serves 5   **Preparation 15 mins.**

7½ ozs. tinned salmon (220 grms)
1 pint lemon jelly (½ litre)
1 cup boiling water
½ cup mayonnaise

Salt
Pepper
6 tablespoons tomato sauce
Worcester sauce

Dissolve jelly in boiling water. When cold add flaked salmon, salt and pepper, Worcester sauce to taste, mayonnaise and tomato sauce. Oil mould and pour in mixture. Refrigerate to set.

SALMON MOUSSE
Jackie Leigh

Serves 6   **Preparation 15 mins.**   **Refrigeration 3 hours.**

1 lb. tinned salmon (450 grms)
½ cup finely chopped celery
¼ cup minced onion
2 tablespoons gelatine

½ cup cold water
½ cup ketchup
¼ cup wine vinegar
1 cup mayonnaise

Drain and flake salmon, reserve liquid. Mix in celery and onion. Soften gelatine in water, combine salmon liquid, ketchup and vinegar bring to boil and add softened gelatine, stir until dissolved. Gently blend hot liquid into salmon mixture. Stir in mayonnaise. Put into ramekins or greased ring or fish mould. Chill for several hours, decorate and serve.

SALMON MOUSSE
Pat Fine

Serves 6-8   **Preparation 30 mins.**   **Freezable**   **Advance**

2 x ½ lb. tins of salmon (452 grms)
½ oz. gelatine (15 grms)
½ cup cold water
2 tablespoons sugar
1 teaspoon salt
1 teaspoon prepared mustard

½ cup white wine vinegar
2 (beaten) egg yolks
1 tablespoon prepared horseradish
1 cup (finely chopped) celery
½ cup (lightly whipped) double cream

Soften gelatine in cold water. Mix together sugar, salt, mustard, vinegar and egg yolks, put in double boiler over hot water, cook for a few minutes whisking until mousse like. Remove from heat, add gelatine. Mix in horseradish, chill until it begins to set then add celery and salmon and fold in cream. Pour into well oiled mould and chill.

SALMON SAVOURY

Mrs. J. Shapiro

Serves 4   Preparation 10 mins.   Cook 10 mins.   Advance

8 ozs. tinned salmon (225 grms)
½ cup mayonnaise
1 chopped gherkin
1 stalk chopped celery

1 medium chopped onion
tabasco sauce (to taste)
¼ lb. grated cheese (100 grms)
salt and pepper

Drain and flake salmon. Mix together with mayonnaise, gherkin, celery onion, salt, pepper and tabasco sauce, top with grated cheese. Place under grill for about ten minutes to allow cheese to melt and the salmon savoury to warm. This recipe can be prepared in vol-au-vents or directly in an ovenproof dish. Serve warm with strips of toast.

SAVOURY SAUSAGE AND BEANS

Janis Brown

Serves 8   Preparation 10 mins.   Cook 10 mins.   Advance

2 large tins baked beans
2 lbs. viennas diced (900 grms)
2 large onions chopped

2 tablespoons brown sugar
Oil for frying

Sauté chopped onions lightly, stir in sugar and add diced viennas. Fry for five minutes. Add beans and mix well. If not served immediately this can be placed in an ovenproof dish and kept warm. This recipe can also be served as a side dish with cold meats.

SLOPPY JOES OR HAMBURGERS

Barbara Pressley

Serves 4-6   Preparation 10 mins.   Cook 60 mins.

2 lbs. minced beef (900 grms)
2 large onions (chopped)
1 green pepper (chopped)
1 tablespoon sugar

2 tablespoons dry mustard
5 fl. oz. vinegar (1¼ dls.)
1 medium jar tomato ketchup

Brown the first three ingredients together, add rest and cook slowly for approximately one hour, stirring occasionally. To serve place tablespoons on a bun or roll.

SPAGHETTI BOLOGNESE

Tina Greenspan

Serves 4   Preparation 10 mins.   Cook 30 mins.   Freezable   Advance

1 large onion
Oil or margarine
1½ lbs. minced meat (700 grms)
Tomato purée
2 beef cubes

Garlic powder
Sugar
White wine
Salt and pepper
Cooked spaghetti

Heat oil, dice and fry onions lightly. Add minced meat, salt and pepper. When meat is cooked add beef cubes, tomato puree, white wine, garlic powder and sugar to taste. Simmer for fifteen minutes.

SPAGHETTI SOUFFLÉ

Mrs. Rossner

| Serves 4 | Preparation 20 mins. | Gas No 5 (375°) | Cook 30 mins |

1 oz. butter (30 grms)
½ oz. flour (15 grms)
1 gill milk (1 dl.)
3 egg yolks
4 egg whites

3 ozs. grated cheese (80 grms)
Salt
Cayenne Pepper
1 oz. spaghetti (30 grms)
3-4 tablespoons tomato purée

Boil spaghetti until tender, drain and rinse in cold water, add tomato purée and a little butter. Prepare soufflé case with greaseproof paper bringing paper about 2" above top of dish. Melt butter in a saucepan add flour, mix with wooden spoon and when smooth gradually add milk, continue stirring over gentle heat until roux thickens. Cool slightly and add egg yolks one at a time. Beat in cheese and salt and pepper to taste. Fold in stiffly beaten egg whites. Turn one third of mixture into prepared dish, add half spaghetti, continue to layer this way and finish with soufflé mixture. Sprinkle with grated cheese and breadcrumbs. Bake.

SPINACH TART

Lesley Bennett

| Serves 6 | Preparation 15 mins. | Gas No 4 (350°) | Cook 30 mins. |

1 shortcrust pastry case
¾ lb. frozen spinach (325 grms)
Salt
Black pepper
8 ozs. cottage cheese (225 grms)

3 eggs (lightly beaten)
1-2 ozs. grated parmesan (30-50 grms)
6 tablespoons double cream
Grated nutmeg
2 tablespoons butter

Line a flan tin with pastry, chill, prick with a fork and bake blind for fifteen minutes. (Oven No 7 425°), allow to cool. Cook spinach with butter, salt and pepper. Drain thoroughly. To cottage cheese add beaten eggs grated parmesan, cream and nutmeg to taste and mix together with spinach. Spread mixture in pastry shell and bake until brown and set.

TOMATO AND CHEESE CRUMBLE

Carole Jay

| Serves 3-4 | Preparation 10 mins. | Cook 12 mins. | Gas No 7 (425°) | Freezable | Advance |

1 oz. butter or margarine (30 grms)
1 large finely chopped onion
2 ozs. grated strong cheese (50 grms)
2 ozs. breadcrumbs (50 grms)
6 medium peeled and sliced tomatoes

Salt
Pepper
1 egg
4 tablespoons milk
Chopped parsley to garnish

Melt butter and fry onions until golden brown. Remove from heat and stir in grated cheese and breadcrumbs. Grease an ovenproof dish and place a thin layer of cheese mixture on the bottom, add a layer of tomatoes and seasoning, continuing layering ending with cheese mixture. Beat eggs with four tablespoons of milk, pour into the dish. Bake on middle shelf. Garnish.

TORTILLA

Gillian Berman

Serves 8   Preparation 20 mins.   Cook 10 mins.

8 eggs
8 medium potatoes
3 Spanish onions

Salt
Pepper

Chop the onions finely and dice potatoes. Use large non-stick frying pan or two medium sized ones. Fry onions slowly until brown. Fry potatoes in the other pan until soft and golden brown. Mix potatoes and onions together. Beat eggs with fork and fold in the fried ingredients. Heat a little oil in both clean non-stick frying pans and pour half the mixture in each pan. Cook for about five minutes. Place a plate on top of the frying pans and turn over on to plate. Slide back into pan and cook the other sides until golden brown and cooked through. Slide onto plates. This will resemble a cake and can be cut into slices and served with salad either hot or cold. Suitable for picnics.

TROUT MOUSSE WITH SMOKED SALMON   Marion Warshaw

Serves 8-10   Preparation 30 mins.   Refrigeration 12 hours   Freezable   Advance

8 medium sized boned and
    skinned smoked trout
½ lb. smoked salmon (225 grms)
Radishes, parsley, slices of
    cucumber to decorate

½ pint single cream (3 dl.)
½ pint double cream (3 dl.)
1 level teaspoon English mustard

Mouli trouts into bowl. Add English mustard and mix. Add double cream slowly. Add sufficient single cream so that the mousse is light and fluffy. Line an 8" baking tin with smoked salmon so that it comes about ½" over sides. Pour in mousse, fold back salmon over mousse. Refrigerate overnight. Turn onto a serving dish and cut into portions with a really HOT knife. Decorate and keep in fridge until needed. Serve with hot toast and chilled white wine.

TUNA AND RICE CASSEROLE   Millie Harris

Serves 6   Preparation 30 mins   Cook 50 mins.   Gas No 5 (375°)   Advance

2½ cups boiled rice
3 ozs. butter (75 grms)
1½ heaped tablespoons flour
¾ pint milk (½ litre)
1 cup grated cheddar cheese
2 x 7 oz. tin tuna (400 grms)

3 tablespoons chopped parsley
Paprika
Fresh ground black pepper
Topping
1 oz. parmesan cheese (25 grms)
1 oz. breadcrumbs (25 grms)
1 oz. melted butter (25 grms)

Melt butter in saucepan over low heat. Add flour. Mix with a wooden spoon and remove from heat. Gradually add milk and return to heat stirring until sauce thickens. Add cheese and continue stirring until cheese melts. Grease a casserole dish, arrange layers of rice, cheese sauce and flaked tuna fish sprinkling a little parsley on each layer. Mix topping ingredients together crumble over and bake.

VEGETABLE SAVOURY

Jackie Bennett

Serves 6-8   **Preparation 30 mins.**   **Gas No 4 (350°)**   **Cook 40 mins**

Cauliflower
Beans
Cabbage
Sprouts
Peas
Green vegetables available
1 large chopped Spanish onion
Carrot
Leek
Aubergine
Celery
Mushrooms

2 ozs. mixed dried vegetables (50 grms)
Tomatoes
Garlic and Salt
Black pepper
Sunflower seed oil
Mixed herbs to taste
Soya sauce to taste
¼ teaspoon cumin powder
½ pint water (3 dls.)
4 ozs. cheddar cheese (100 grms)
2-3 tablespoons ketchup
¼ teaspoon gravy browning

Using equal quantities of vegetables according to taste, steam until barely cooked all green vegetables. Fry onion in oil, add chopped carrots, leaks, aubergine, celery, mushrooms, tomatoes and mixed vegetables, continue cooking for six minutes stirring constantly. Add cumin powder, gravy browning, ketchup soya sauce and mixed herbs. Simmer and stir another three minutes. Add water and bring to boil. Reduce heat and cook gently for a further twenty minutes. Put steamed vegetables through coarse mould and add to fried vegetable mixture. Mix. Add cheese and stir. Place in a greased gratin dish, sprinkle top with grated cheese and bake.

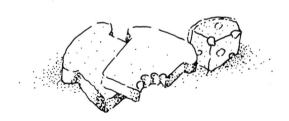

Biscuits, Breads & Cakes

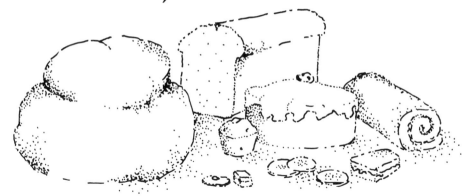

Fresh yeast can be frozen. Freeze in 1 oz. packs. 1 oz. (30 grms) fresh is equal to ½ oz. (15 grms) dried yeast.

If plain biscuits lose their crispness put them on a baking sheet and return them to the oven for about 5 minutes Gas No. 3 (325°).

When making sponge cakes — if recipe tells you to cream butter and sugar together — it is more successful if you cream the butter first and then add the sugar.

For quick greasing of baking tins — impregnate a place of kitchen paper with corn oil and keep it in a plastic bag in the fridge.

To vary cheese cake topping. Cook cake as usual. Beat 1 carton of soured cream with 1 tablespoon sugar and pour onto top of cake. Then put contents of a small can of fruit (i.e. pitted cherries, pineapple) into blender and blend for 10 seconds. Pour onto cream and rebake cake for 10 minutes.

A slice of apple, changed frequently, helps to keep soft cookies moist in their containers.

The mixture for Joe's Kichlach makes a very good base for cheese cake — Roll out surplus mixture, cut into strips then form a lattice pattern with them over top of cake. Bake in the usual way.

To vary texture of cakes and biscuits. Replace 2 tablespoons of flour with equal quantity of cornflour.

Place nuts in plastic bag and roll with a rolling pin — to crush them without mess.

When storing a big cake in a large biscuit tin — use lid as base and bottom as cover.

A tablespoon of thick marmalade improves a fruit cake.

Don't waste broken plain biscuits — crumble them and store in a polythene bag — they will be very useful for cheese cake bases etc.

Cover spare egg yolks with cold water to prevent a skin forming on top.

Egg whites keep for up to 1 year when stored in polythene bags in the freezer.

Use corn oil applied by brush to baking tins and trays instead of other fat or flour.

To remove cake from loose bottomed tin — stand tin on jam jar and allow outer frame to drop down.

A little glycerine added to cakes will make them moist.

To whip fresh double cream successfully have bowl, whisk and cream really cold. Whip quickly at first until it looks matt, then slowly until it stands in smooth light peaks.

Prunes soaked in brandy to cover, for one month — make delicious petit fours.

Biscuits

ALMOND FLAVOURED BISCUITS   Charlotte Benedict

Makes 48 Preparation 30 mins.   Gas No. 5 (375°)   Cook 10 mins.   Refrigeration 20 mins.

1 lb. S.R. flour (450 grms)
½ lb. tomor (225 grms)
2 ozs. cooking fat (50 grms)
2 eggs

Almond essence
1 teaspoon Baking powder
1 cup castor sugar

A biscuit making tool is helpful for these biscuits. Sawa brand is recommended.

Cream fats and sugar. Add eggs and 2 drops of essence. Fold in flour with baking powder to make dough. Chill. Make into biscuits using biscuit tool and bake.

BUTTER BISCUITS   Gertrude Greenspan

Makes 30 approx. Preparation 15 mins. Gas No. 3 (350°) Cook 20 mins. Refrigeration 30 mins.

4 ozs. icing sugar (150 grms)
10 ozs. plain flour (275 grms)
8 ozs. butter (225 grms)

1 egg separated
2 teaspoon vanilla essence
Whole chopped almonds

Rub in flour and butter until coarse crumbs. Add sugar. Mix beaten egg and essence and knead lightly. Cover and place in fridge to chill. Roll very thinly and cut out biscuits. Place on greased tray and brush with white of egg. Sprinkle biscuits with chopped almonds. Bake until golden.

BUTTER NUT BISCUITS   Sheila Cox

Makes 90   Preparation 8-10 mins.   Gas No. 4 (360°)   Cook 10 mins.   Freezable   Advance

6 ozs. unsalted butter (175 grms)
4 ozs. icing sugar (100 grms)
8 ozs. S.R. flour (225 grms)

2 teaspoons vanilla essence
4 ozs. chopped almonds (100 grms)

Cream butter and sugar. Add essence and flour. Knead well. Add nuts. Roll into marble sized balls. Place on an ungreased baking tray, allowing room for biscuits to spread. Flatten slightly. Bake.

DUTCH BUTTER BISCUITS   Judith Wynik

Makes 30 approx.   Preparation 10 mins.   Gas No. 5 (375°)   Cook 25 mins.   Advance

6 ozs. demerra sugar (175 grms)
6 ozs. S.R. flour (175 grms)
6 ozs. salted butter (175 grms)

1 egg yolk
2 ozs. chopped almonds (50 grms)

Place flour and sugar in bowl. Cut in butter until fine crumbs. Bind with egg yolk. Flatten into a Swiss roll tin. Sprinkle with chopped nuts and press gently into dough. Place in oven. When baked leave in tin, cut into squares while still hot. Remove when cold.

JOE'S KICHLACH

Joe Clapman

Makes 50 approx. Preparation 10 mins. Gas No 4 (360°) Cook 20 mins. Freezable Advance

8 ozs. butter (225 grms)
2 eggs
12 ozs. castor sugar (350 grms)

1 lb S.R. flour (450 grms)
½ teaspoon vanilla essence
1 teaspoon almond essence

Beat butter and sugar. Add eggs and remaining ingredients. Roll out and cut into rounds or shapes. Place on greased baking tray and bake for 15 minutes. Remove from oven. Sprinkle with a little castor sugar and return to oven for 5 mins. If desired, cinnamon can be mixed with final sugar coating. 2 tablespoons raisins or chocolate drops can be added to the mixture for variety.

LEMON BISCUITS

Leone Djanogly

Makes 40   Preparation 10 mins.   Gas No. 5 (375°)   Cook 10 mins.   Freezable   Advance

2 eggs
6 fluid ozs. corn oil (1½ dl.)
5 ozs. castor sugar (150 grms)
1 teaspoon vanilla

1 teaspoon grated lemon peel
8 ozs. sifted S.R. flour (225 grms)
1 oz. granulated sugar (30 grms)

Beat eggs well, add oil, vanilla and peel then add sugar and beat hard until thick. Stir in flour. Drop teaspoonfulls, well apart, onto a greased baking sheet. Sprinkle with granulated sugar and bake.
N.B. Using a larger spoon this mixture will make very nice sponge drops, that can be sandwiched with cream and jam.

MARIA'S BISCUITS

Jewels Leader-Cramer

Makes 25 approx. Preparation 10 mins. Gas No. 9 (460°) Cook 15 mins. Freezable   Advance

8 ozs. S.R. flour (225 grms)
3 ozs. sugar (80 grms)
2½ ozs. ground almonds (65 grms)

4 ozs. butter (100 grms)
1 egg
2 ozs. split almonds (50 grms)

Mix by hand in large bowl the flour, sugar, ground almonds and butter. Add egg, knead well. Cover dough with greaseproof paper and roll out. Remove paper, cut with biscuit cutter. Place on a greased baking sheet. Put half an almond on each biscuit. Place in hottest part of oven for 15 minutes. These biscuits should not be too thin.

PAINS DE SEIGNE BISCUITS   Doris Goldbart

Makes 20 approx.   **Preparation 20 mins.**   **Gas No. 3 (350⁰)**   **Cook 15 mins.**

4 ozs. ground almonds (100 grms)   Icing sugar
4 ozs. castor sugar (100 grms)   Praline
1 oz. plain flour (25 grms)   2 ozs. whole almonds (50 grms)
2 egg whites   2 ozs. castor sugar (50 grms)

To make Praline. Place the whole almonds with skins on and sugar over low heat in a heavy saucepan. Allow sugar to dissolve slowly without stirring. At sugar turns to caramel, stir with a metal spoon to make sure the almonds are toasted right through. When rich brown, turn at once onto an oiled plate and allow to cool. When hard crush with heavy rolling pin to a fine powder.

To make Biscuits. Sieve together ground almonds, sugar and flour. Lightly beat egg whites and reserve quarter of them. Mix rest of egg white with other ingredients, pounding well. Add praline to almond mixture. Roll into balls the size of a walnut. Roll in the remaining egg white and icing sugar. Put the balls onto a baking sheet covered with rice paper about 2" apart as they spread. Bake. Allow to cool before removing from rice paper.

SHORTBREAD BISCUITS   Muriel Rosner

Makes 15 approx.   **Preparation 20 mins.**   **Gas No. 2 (325⁰)**   **Cook ½ hour**   **Advance**

6 ozs. plain flour (175 grms)   2 ozs. castor sugar (50 grms)
4 ozs. butter (100 grms)

Grease 2 baking sheets. Place butter and flour in a bowl and mix until crumbly. Add sugar and mix until the mixture sticks together and becomes a dough. Roll out to $\frac{1}{8}$" thick and cut with shaped cutter. Bake until pale golden. Cool. Sprinkle with castor sugar.

SYLVIA'S BISCUITS   Mrs. M. Silverman

Makes 50 approx.   **Preparation 20 mins.**   **Gas No. 6 (400⁰)**   **Cook 20 mins.**   **Advance**

1 lb. Kake Mako flour (450 grms)   2 eggs
½ lb. butter (225 grms)   Split almonds
6 ozs. castor sugar (175 grms)   Halved glacé cherries

Grease two baking sheets. Cream butter and sugar. Add beaten eggs and mix well. Add flour gradually until the mixture becomes a firm pliable dough. Roll into walnut size balls. Press an almond or cherry in the centre of each biscuit. Bake in oven checking after 15 mins.

VANILLA CRESCENTS

Mrs. M. Silverman

Makes 40 approx. Preparation 15 mins. Gas No. 3 (350°) Cook 18 mins. Refrigeration 1 hour
Freezable Advance

8 ozs. plain flour (225 grms)
8 ozs. butter (225 grms)
2 ozs. ground almonds (50 grms)

2 ozs. ground hazelnuts (50 grms)
1 teaspoon vanilla essence
Icing sugar   4 ozs. granulated sugar

Cut fat into small pieces and put into bowl with the sugar and vanilla essence. Work together on slowest speed of mixer. Gradually work in the flour, nuts and pinch of salt until mixture forms a ball. Wrap in film and chill. Roll into walnut size balls. Roll each ball into a pencil shape and form into crescents. Place on a greased baking sheet 1" (24 cms) apart and bake until pale honey coloured. Cool for 5 minutes. Gently roll in icing sugar.

ELISSIAS WALNUT FINGERS

Phyllis Horal

Makes 15   Preparation 15 mins.   Gas No 5 (375°)   Refrigeration 1 hour   Freezable   Advance

8 oz. ground walnuts (225 grms)
8 oz. icing sugar
1 egg yolk

ICING
5½ oz. icing sugar (165 grms)
1 egg white

Combine all biscuit ingredients and knead well. Chill. Roll out ½" thick and cut into fingers with a sharp knife. Place on a greased baking sheet and bake.
ICING Mix egg white with icing sugar and ice biscuits when cool.

Pastry

RICH SHORT CRUST PASTRY

Sally Bloom

Preparation 5 mins.   Freezable   Advance

1 lb. self raising flour (450 grms)
6 oz. sugar (175 grms)

12 oz. butter or Tomor (350 grms)
2 eggs

Rub fat into flour. Add sugar. Knead into dough. Wrap in greaseproof paper and refrigerate. This is sufficient to make 2 large tart cases or 20 small cases.

SAVOURY PASTRY

Valerie Ross

Preparation 5 mins.   Refrigeration 1 hour.   Freezable   Advance

½ lb. plain flour (225 grms)
Good pinch of salt

1 tablespoon icing sugar
5 oz. softened butter or margarine (150 grms)

Sieve flour, salt and sugar in mixing bowl. Mix in softened butter gently until mixture resembles bread crumbs. Roll into a ball and chill. This pastry is suitable for quiches.

Petit Fours

CHOCOLATE BRANDIED CHERRIES

Helen Bloom

Makes 20　　　Preparation 25 mins.　　　Advance

20 maraschine cherries
Brandy
½ lb. almond paste (225 grms)

¼ lb. quick setting cooking chocolate
(100 grms)
20 cocktail sticks

Soak cherries in brandy overnight. Drain. Roll almond paste to ¼" (¾cm) thick. Wrap each cherry individually in almond paste. Insert cocktail sticks and dip in melted chocolate. Stand to dry on greaseproof paper.

CHOCOLATE FUDGE SWEETS

Pauline Going

Preparation 20 mins.

8 oz. jar peanut butter (225 grms)
1 oz. melted butter (30 grms)
4 ozs. seedless raisins (washed
　and dried) (100 grms)

4 oz. icing sugar (100 grms)
6 oz. Cake Brand chocolate (175 grms)

Place peanut butter into warm mixing bowl and mix until soft with melted butter. Add seedless raisins and mix well. Add sifted icing sugar a few spoonsful at a time and mix well. Do not allow mixture to be too dry. Roll into balls and dip into melted chocolate. Place onto foil covered tray or foil containers – they will not stick, and place in fridge until set. Store in boxes or if preferred put in petit four cases for serving.

CHOCOLATE RUM TRUFFLES

Jane Bennett

Preparation 20 mins.　　　Advance

4 oz. plain chocolate (100 grms)
2 oz. unsalted butter (60 grms)
2 tablespoons cream
2 oz. digestive biscuits (60 grms)

Rum or sherry to taste
Icing sugar
Chocolate vermicelli

Chop up the chocolate and melt with the butter in a double saucepan. Remove from heat and stir in cream, rum and biscuit crumbs. Chill. Mix again. Stir in enough icing sugar to make a soft paste and leave the mixture to cool until firm. Form into small balls and coat with chocolate vermicelli. Place in small paper sweet cases and refrigerate overnight.

COLLETTE'S PETITS FOURS
Helen Bloom

Preparation 1 hour   Advance

1 pkt. Kake Brand chocolate
5 oz. plain chocolate (150 grms)
½ gill of cream (1 dl.)
A few chopped nuts

2 oz. butter (50 grms)
3 teasp. rum or brandy
2 egg yolks
1 pkt. Petit Four paper cases.

Melt ½ pkt. of Kake brand on a plate over hot water. Place cream in a saucepan. Add plain chocolate and cook slowly until thick. Cool. Cut butter into small pieces and add gradually into chocolate mixture. Add 2 egg yolks and brandy. Refrigerate to harden.
Coat petit four cases on inside with melted Kake Brand. When dry, coat again. Cool. Pipe cream mixture into cases. Decorate with chopped nuts. Peel off paper cases.

Breads

HERB BREAD
Hilary Brass

Preparation 10 mins.   **Gas No 4 (350°)**   **Cook 25 mins**

1 French bread
Mixed herbs
Salt and black pepper

Butter
Crushed garlic if desired
Lemon juice to taste

Cut bread into 1" (2½ cms) thick slices to within half an inch of bottom crust. Mix softened butter with herbs, lemon juice, salt and pepper and garlic on both sides of each slice. Put together, wrap in foil and bake.

FRUIT AND MALT LOAF
Pat Julius

Preparation 10 mins.   Resting time 1 hour   Gas No 4 (350°)Cook 1½ hrs.   Freezable   Advance

Heaped cup castor sugar
Heaped cup All Bran
Heaped cup milk
Greased and lined loaf tin

Heaped cup S.R. flour
Heaped cup mixed dried fruit
1 egg

Put all ingredients except milk and flour in a bowl with beaten egg. Pour milk over and leave for one hour. Add flour and mix. Place in loaf tin and bake. Should be baked day before it is required and sliced and buttered.

SCONE SPLIT
Jane Halperin

Makes 4   Preparation 10 mins.   Gas No 6 (400°)   Cook 20 mins   Freezable   Advance

2 cups flour
2 oz. butter or margarine (50 grms)
¾ cup approx. milk

Pinch salt
Chocolate or sultanas

Put flour, salt and butter into a bowl and mix with fingertips. Add milk and make into a dough. Chip chocolate and press this or sultanas into the dough. Make dough into round shape, flatten a bit and make a cross. Bake until ready. Cut into four quarters. Butter and jam as required.

TEA BREAD PATRICIA

Joy Walker

Preparation 10 mins   Gas No 3 (350°)   Cook 2 hours   Advance

1 cup tea
1 cup brown sugar
1 beaten egg

1 lb. mixed dried fruit (450 grms)
2 cups S.R. flour
Pinch of salt

Soak fruit and sugar over night in tea. Next morning add flour, salt and egg and mix well. Pour into small well-greased loaf tin and place in oven, middle shelf. Leave until following day. Serve sliced and buttered.

Small Cakes

BAKLAVA

Gill Caplan

Makes 48   Preparation 12 mins   Gas No 8 (450°)   Cook 30 mins   Freezable   Advance

3 oz. butter (80 grms)
2 tablespoons water
3 teaspoons cinnamon
4 oz. castor sugar (100 grms)
6 oz. chopped walnuts (175 grms)
13 oz. frozen puff pastry (375 grms)

OPTIONAL TOPPING
1 oz. sugar (30 grms)
Juice of 1 lemon
2 tablespoons honey

Heat together 2 oz. butter (50 grms), the sugar and water until the sugar is dissolved. Remove from heat, add nuts and spice. Mix well and leave to cool. Cut pastry into four pieces and roll out each pastry to 11″ x 7″ (28cms x 17¾ cms). Brush tin liberally with melted butter. Place on oblong of pastry in tin and spread over it one-third of filling. Place second piece of pastry on top, brush with melted butter and cover with another third of filling. Repeat process, finishing with fourth layer of pastry. Brush top with butter and carefully mark into diamonds, this makes cutting easier when cold. Brush top liberally with honey mixture. If nut filling seems dry, add some of the honey topping to it. Bake on Gas No 8 (450°) for 20 mins then reduce heat to Gas No 3 (325°) for further 10 mins.

CHOCOLATE CHEESE CAKES

Phyllis Rubin U.S.A.

Makes 20   Preparation 20 mins   Gas No 3 (350°)   Cook 15 mins

CRUMBLE
8 oz. packet chocolate wafers (225 grms)
2 tablespoons granulated sugar
$\frac{1}{3}$ cup melted butter
¼ teaspoon nutmeg
TO DECORATE
Carton of double cream
Small tin of fruit

FILLING
3 eggs
1 cup granulated sugar
8 oz. semi-sweet melted chocolate (225 grms)
Pinch salt
1½ lb. softened cream cheese (675 grms)
1 teaspoon vanilla essence
Carton sour cream

Make crumble crust. Blend wafers until fine. Add butter, sugar and nutmeg and mix well. Line bun tins with paper foil cases. Press crumble in evenly. Beat eggs and sugar in large mixing bowl until light. Beat in cream cheese until smooth. Add melted chocolate, vanilla, salt and sour cream and beat until smooth. Spoon into cups and bake about 13 mins until just firm. Decorate when cold with fresh cream roses and desired fruit.

164

CHOCOLATE SQUARES

Lillian Ressler

Makes 16-18   Preparation 20 mins.   Gas No 4 (350°)   Cook 35 mins

BASE
4 oz. butter (100 grms)
2 egg yolks
1 teaspoon baking powder
3 oz. grated or chopped unsweetened
   chocolate (80 grms)
12 oz. plain flour (350 grms)
½ teaspoon salt
6 oz. granulated sugar (175 grms)

MERINGUE
2 egg whites
½ teaspoon vanilla essence
6 oz. brown sugar (175 grms)

Grease 8" square cake tin. Beat together butter, sugar and yolks. Add flour, salt and baking powder sifted together. Press into tin and sprinkle with grated chocolate. Beat whites until stiff, gradually add brown sugar and vanilla and bake. Cool in tin on rack and cut in 16-18 squares when cool.

DANISH PASTRIES

Phyllis Kilstock

Preparation 15 mins   Gas No 6 (400°)   Cook 30 mins

4 oz. plain flour (100 grms)
4 oz. butter (100 grms)
Apricot jam

Small amount of glacé icing
4 oz. cooking cheese (100 grms)
Raisins

Rub butter and flour together. Add cheese. Roll out and spread with jam. Sprinkle with raisins and roll over — cut into 2" (5 cms) pieces. Press centre of each piece and bake on non-greased baking sheet. Cool and ice.

DATE AND NUT COOKIES

Eva Schwarcz

Makes 24   Preparation 10 mins   Gas No 3 (350°)Cook 30-35 mins   Freezable

2 eggs
1 cup icing sugar
Pinch of salt
1 teaspoon baking powder

2 tablespoons S.R. flour
1 cup stoned chopped dates
1 cup roughly chopped walnuts

Beat eggs until light and fluffy. Gradually add sugar beating all the time. Sift together dry ingredients and mix with dates and nuts. Fold into egg mixture. Spread on greased tin approximately 9" square. Bake. Cool slightly before cutting into squares. Sprinkle with icing sugar.

FAIRY CAKES

Karen Segall

Makes 20   Preparation 5 mins   Gas No 5 (375°)   Cook 15 mins

4 oz. S.R. flour (100 grms)
2 eggs
4 oz. castor sugar (100 grms)
4 oz. margarine (100 grms)

2 oz. sultanas (50 grms)
2 drops vanilla essence
Paper cases

Cream fat and sugar until light and fluffy. Beat in eggs one at a time. Mix in other ingredients, fold in flour. Bake.

GINGER SQUARES

Gillian Garden

Makes 15 Preparation 20 mins Refrigeration time 1 hour Gas No 3 (350°) Freezable Advance

8 oz. S.R. flour (225 grms)
2 oz. ground almonds (50 grms)
6 oz. butter (175 grms)
3 oz. soft brown sugar (80 grms)
1 egg

Squeeze of lemon
1 lb. ginger marmalade (450 grms)
1 oz. slivered almonds (30 grms)
Pinch ginger
Greased Swiss roll tin

Mix flour, sugar and almonds. Rub in butter. Beat in egg and lemon juice (keeping a little for glazing). Mix into dry ingredients to form a dough and divide into two. Knead each half until smooth and chill for 1 hour. Roll each half to fit Swiss roll tin. Put one half in and spread with marmalade, cover with other half. Glaze and scatter with almonds. Bake.

POLKA DOT CAKES

Muriel Rossner

Makes 12   Preparation 5 mins   Gas No 6 (400°)   Cook 10 mins

2 large eggs
¼ lb. sugar (100 grms)
¼ lb. polka dots (100 grms)

¼ lb. butter (100 grms)
¼ lb. S.R. flour (100 grms)

Beat butter and sugar until creamy. Beat in eggs. Stir in polka dots and flour. Put in fairy cake cases and bake.

Large Cakes

ALMOND CAKE

Suzanne Rose

Preparation 10 mins.   Gas No 4 (360°)   Cook 30 mins   Freezable

8 oz. butter (225 grms)
8 oz. sugar (225 grms)
8 oz. ground almonds (225 grms)

4 eggs
4 oz. S.R. flour (100 grms)

Grease a large shallow flan tin. Cream butter and sugar, add lightly beaten eggs alternately with flour. Fold in ground almonds. Place in tin, and smooth top of mixture. Bake.

APPLE SPICE CAKE

Marion Segal

Preparation 15 mins   Gas No 3 (350°)   Cook 1½ hours   Advance

5 oz. margarine (150 grms)
9 oz. plain flour (250 grms)
8 oz. castor sugar (225 grms)
1 oz. chopped walnuts or raisins (30 grms)
1 beaten egg
1½ teaspoons cinnamon

1 teaspoon nutmeg
1 teaspoon bicarbonate of soda
1 teaspoon mixed spice
½ pint apple puree (unsweetened)
Pinch of salt

Place all ingredients in bowl and beat together until well mixed. Put into 7″ (17¾cms) square cake tin. Bake in oven. When cool wrap in foil and keep in fridge.

TRADITIONAL APPLE STRÜDEL

Claire Jacobs

Preparation 40 mins.   Gas No 8 (450°)   Cook 1½ hours   Freezable   Advance

3 large grated cooking apples
3 large grated carrots
½ lb. sultanas (225 grms)
½ packet crushed plain biscuits
2 packets puff pastry

2 tablespoons flaked almonds
Cinnamon
Brown sugar
Oil
Raspberry jam

Add crushed biscuits to grated apples and carrots to absorb juice. Do not let apple stand. Line a baking tray with Bakewell paper and brush with oil. Roll pastry paper thin spread with oil. Cover pastry with a layer of jam. apple and carrot mixture leaving a 1″ (2½ cms) margin all round. Scatter with nuts and sprinkle all over with cinnamon and brown sugar. Roll up, shaping as you roll. Cut into 3 pieces to fit tray. Knife mark portions and brush with oil. Sprinkle with brown sugar. Place in oven on high shelf. Bake until very brown for about 20-30 minutes. Turn oven down to No 3 (350°) and cook for 1 hour. Delicious served hot with cream as a desert.

APPLE CAKE

Audrey Stone

Preparation 20 mins.   Gas No 6 (400°)   Cook ½ hour

4 oz. margarine (100 grms)
4 oz. brown sugar (100 grms)
4 oz. S.R. flour (100 grms)
A little lemon juice

3 apples
Grated rind of 1 lemon
2 eggs
Extra brown sugar

Mix margarine, brown sugar, flour, eggs and lemon juice and then pour into a greased 7″ (17¾cms) square tin. Slice apples on top. Grate on lemon rind. Cover with brown sugar. Bake.

Large Cakes

BELGIAN APPLE CAKE

Charlotte Benedikt

Preparation 30 mins.   Gas No. 4 (360^{0})   Cook 45 mins.

½ lb. S.R. flour (225 grms)   3 egg whites
½ lb. margarine (225 grms)   2 egg yolks
1½ lbs. cooking apples (675 grms)   3 ozs. sugar (80 grms)

PASTRY Rub flour and margarine and 2½ ozs. sugar (65 grms), mix in egg yolks, leave mixture at room temperature overnight. Grease a 2″ (5 cms) deep dish 10″ (25½ cms) diameter. Put in pastry mixture and bake for 20 mins.
APPLE MIXTURE Peel and core apples. Add sugar to taste and cook until soft. Put through sieve and spread over pastry. Re-bake for 15 minutes.
MERINGUE Beat egg whites until stiff. Add sugar. Spread on top of cake and re-bake for further 10 minutes until lightly browned.

CONTINENTAL APPLE CAKE

Eleonore Levin

Preparation 20 mins.   Gas No. 6 (400^{0})   Cook ½ hour   Refrigeration 1-2 hours

PASTRY   FILLING
10 ozs. S.R. flour (275 grms)   4 large cooking apples
8 ozs. margarine (225 grms)   2-3 tablespoons sugar
1 egg   Cinnamon
3 tablespoons sugar

Make pastry and place in fridge. Roll our. Line a loose-bottomed pie tin, leaving a little pastry over for use later. Slightly cook apples with the sugar and cinnamon and place on pastry. Arrange pastry strips over apples. Glaze with egg. Bake in oven.

EGGLESS CARROT CAKE

Lauren Brown

Preparation 20 mins.   Gas No. ½ (275^{0})   Cook 80 mins.   Advance

1 cup melted butter   ½ teaspoon nutmeg
1 cup honey   1 teaspoon mixed spice
1½ cups finely grated carrots   2 tablespoons baking powder
1 lb. fine whole wheat flour   1½ cups brown sugar
1 teaspoon salt   2 tablespoons cinnamon

Grease 2 loaf tins. Mix together melted butter, honey, sugar and grated carrots. Sift together dry ingredients and combine all ingredients. Bake in oven.

AUNTIE BESSIE'S CHEESE CAKE
Suzanne Barnett

Preparation 10 mins.   **Gas No. 4 (360⁰)**   **Cook 35 mins.**   **Freezable**   **Advance**

1 lb. curd cheese (450 grms)
2 eggs
1 teacup castor sugar

2-3 cartons sour cream
6-8 digestive biscuits

Crush biscuits in liquidiser. Line greased cake tin with crushed biscuits. Beat cheese, sugar and eggs very well and pour on top of biscuits in tin. Bake for half an hour and withdraw gently. Pour over sour cream to which 1 tablespoon sugar has been added. Replace in oven for 5 minutes only and leave in tin until cold.

For a change drain a tin of mandarins and put some on top of biscuit base. Add cheese mixture and arrange rest of mandarins on top and decorate with walnuts and bake.

CHEESE CAKE 1
Marion Warshaw

Preparation 10 mins.   **Gas No. 3 (350⁰) for 30 mins.**   **Freezable**   **Advance**

3 x ½ lb. packets philadelphia cheese
½ lb. crushed digestive biscuits (225 grms)
Juice of ½ lemon

4 ozs. sugar (100 grms)
2 eggs

Beat cheese with egg and sugar until creamy — add lemon juice and beat again. Melt butter add biscuit crumbs and line greased loose bottomed tin with them. Pour on cheese mixture. Bake, then allow to cool in oven.

CHEESE CAKE 2
Muriel Rosner

Preparation 10 mins.   **Gas No. 4 (360⁰)**   **Cook ¾ hour**   **Freezable**   **Advance**

1 packet digestive biscuits
1 oz. butter (30 grms)
12 ozs. cooking cheese (350 grms)
4 ozs. best cream cheese (100 grms)
½ lb. castor sugar (225 grms)

1 teaspoon almond essence
2 tablespoons lemon juice
4 cartons sour cream mixed with
½ lb. castor sugar (225 grms)
1 teaspoon vanilla essence

Put cheese and sugar in mixer, beat well and add essence to taste. Crush biscuits and mix with butter and press in loose-bottomed tin. Put in cheese mixture and bake for half-an-hour. When cold pour sour cream mixed with sugar on top. Replace in oven for 15 minutes. Wrap in foil and store.

CHEESE CAKE 3
Shelley Stewart

Preparation 20 mins.   **Gas No. 5 (375⁰)**   **Cook 20 mins.**   **Refrigeration 12 hours**

4 ozs. crushed digestive biscuits (100 grms)
2 ozs. butter (50 grms)
Pinch cinnamon
Round tablespoon cornflour
¼ pint sour cream (2 dl.)

1 lb. smooth cooking cheese (450 grms)
½ teaspoon vanilla essence
2 eggs separated
2 ozs. castor sugar (50 grms)
2 ozs. melted butter (50 grms)

Blend together biscuits, butter and cinnamon and press into 8″ (20¼ cms) loose-bottomed cake tin. Beat egg yolks, butter, sugar, vanilla and cornflour with cheese in mixing bowl. Beat whites until stiff. Fold sour cream into cheese mixture, followed by egg whites. Spoon into tin and bake until brown round the edges. Leave to cool and refrigerate.

STRAWBERRY CHEESE CAKE
Gill Caplan

Preparation 15 mins.   **Uncooked**   **Refrigeration 3 hours**   **Freezable**   **Advance**

1 lb. single cream cheese (450 grms)
4 ozs. carton sour cream (100 grms) or
8 ozs. tin Nestle's cream (200 grms)

1 tin strawberries (350 grms)
1 strawberry jelly
8″ (20¼ cms) round loose-bottomed tin

Dissolve jelly in juice from strawberries. Cool. Mix cheese with sour cream OR tinned cream. Mash strawberries. Add cooled jelly mixture to cheese gradually, beating constantly. Add crushed strawberries. Pour mixture into greased cake tins and set in fridge.

To Freeze: Leave in cake tin. Cover top with foil and place in freezer sealed. Do not freeze until set firmly.

CREAM CHEESE AND RAISIN POUND CAKE
Phyllis Rubin U.S.A.

Preparation 30 mins   **Gas No. 2 (300⁰)**   **Cook 1½ hours**   **Advance**

6 tablespoons chopped pecan nuts
4 tablespoons sugar
8 ozs. cream cheese (225 grms)
2 teaspoons vanilla
2¼ cups sifted flour
¼ teaspoon salt

1 cup butter
1½ cups sugar
4 eggs
2 teaspoons baking powder
1½ cups chopped raisins

Grease 8″ (20¼ cms) tin well. Sprinkle with nuts then lightly with 4 tablespoons sugar. Turn out excess. Beat butter and cheese together until soft and add gradually 1½ cups sugar beating until smooth. Add vanilla. Beat in eggs one at a time, (batter may look curdled). Blend in flour sifted with salt and baking powder. Mix in raisins and turn into nut-coated pan. Bake and let stand 10 minutes before turning out.

COTTAGE CHEESE CAKE
Janet Dwek

Preparation 20 mins.   Gas No. 3 (350°)   Cook 45 mins.

5 separated eggs
1 tablespoon flour
1 lb. cottage cheese (450 grms)
6 tablespoons sultanas (optional)
Grated rind of 1 lemon

7 ozs. sugar (200 grms)
1 tablespoon semolina
½ cup milk
1 teaspoon vanilla
6 tablespoons biscuit crumbs

Cream yolks and sugar until light. Add flour, semolina, sieved cheese and milk. Mix well and add lemon rind, vanilla and raisins. Beat egg whites until stiff and fold in. Butter 8" (20¼ cms) baking tin and sprinkle on crumbs. Spoon over mixture and bake. Turn off oven and leave cake to cool for another 15 minutes.

CHESTNUT GATEAU
Hilda Dean

Preparation 20 mins.   Gas No. 3 (350°)   Cook 1-1½ hours

2 ozs. grated hazelnuts (50 grms)
¾ tin chestnut purée (unsweetened)
6 eggs separated
Marron glacé and pistachio nuts
    for decoration

11 ozs. sugar (300 grms)
Little vanilla essence
½ pint whipped cream (3 dl.)

Whisk egg yolks and sugar until light and fluffy. Add chestnut purée, grated hazelnuts and vanilla essence. Whisk whites until stiff and fold into mixture. Put into one large cake tin or three small ones, greased and lined with bakewell paper. Bake for about 1½ hours. When cool sandwich with whipped cream. Decorate top and sides with marron and nuts.

CHOCOLATE CAKE   1
Hilda Dean

Preparation 30 mins.   Gas No. 4 (360°)   Cooking 40 mins.

4 ozs. castor sugar (100 grms)
4 ozs. butter (100 grms)
5 ozs. S.R. flour (150 grms)
2 ozs. ground almonds (50 grms)
3 ozs. drinking chocolate (80 grms)
2 eggs
2 tablespoons hot water

2 tablespoons cold milk
½ teaspoon vanilla essence
Icing:
4 ozs. butter (100 grms)
12 ozs. icing sugar (350 grms)
3 tablespoons cocoa

Cream butter and sugar. Beat in eggs with a little flour and add hot water. Gradually add remaining flour with ground almonds and drinking chocolate, alternately with cold milk and vanilla essence. Bake in 8" (20¼ cms) loose-bottomed tin lined with greased paper. **Icing:** Soften butter, add icing sugar alternately with cocoa that has been mixed with a little boiling water to form a paste. When cake is cold, out in half and sandwich together with some of the chocolate cream, using remainder for decorating top. If liked add glacé cherries on top of chocolate coating.

M.W.M.H.—M

CHOCOLATE CAKE 2

Colette Levy

Preparation 35 mins.   Gas No. 3 (350⁰)   Cook 50 mins.

8 ozs. S.R. flour (225 grms)
9 ozs. white or brown sugar (250 grms)
3½ ozs. cocoa (100 grms
3 eggs

½ teaspoon bicarbonate of soda
2 drops vanilla essence
9 ozs. milk (250 grms)
4 ozs. Trex (100 grms)

Mix all ingredients together except eggs. Add these last. Bake in 8″ (20¼ cms) lined tin.

RICH CHOCOLATE SPONGE BIRTHDAY CAKE

Judith Cohen

Preparation 40 mins.   Gas No. 4 (360⁰)   Cook ½ hour

6 ozs. butter (175 grms
2 ozs. plain chocolate (50 grms)
2 tablespoons milk
6 ozs. castor sugar (175 grms)
3 eggs
8 ozs. S.R. flour (225 grms)
1 tablespoon cocoa powder
Pinch of salt
1 tablespoon apricot jam
1 teaspoon water

Butter cream:
4 ozs. butter (100 grms)
½ lb. icing sugar (225 grms)
Few drops vanilla essence
Chocolate glacé icing:
4 tablespoons warm water
3 ozs. plain chocolate (80 grms)
½ teaspoon oil
¼ pint double cream (2 dl.)
Few drops vanilla essence

Grease two 7″ (17¾ cms) sandwich tins. Dissolve chocolate in milk over gentle heat. Cool. Cream fat and sugar, beat in melted chocolate. Add lightly beaten eggs. Fold in flour sifted with salt and cocoa. Put mixture in the two tins and bake. Cool. Sandwich cakes together with butter cream.
Butter cream Cream fat, add sifted icing sugar, beat until smooth and add vanilla. Melt apricot jam with teaspoon of water and strain. Brush top and sides of cake with warm jam.
Glacé icing Mix sifted icing sugar with warm water and vanilla. Melt chocolate in double saucepan with oil. Combine with sugar and beat well. Pour icing over cake and allow to run down sides to coat evenly. Leave until set. Pipe whipped cream round top and write name and greetings in cream.

CHOCOLATE CAKE 3

Muriel Rosner

Preparation 15 mins.   Gas No. 4 (360⁰)   Cook 45 mins.

8 ozs. bitter chocolate (225 grms)
4 ozs. butter (100 grms)
1½ ozs. cornflour (45 grms)
4 tablespoons water
4 ozs. sugar (100 grms)
4 eggs

4 ozs. crushed hazelnuts (100 grms)
1 teaspoon Baking powder
Icing:
4 ozs. chocolate (100 grms)
2 ozs. butter (50 grms)
8″ (20¼ cms) greased loose bottomed
    cake tin

Melt chocolate in double saucepan. Cool. Make a paste of the cornflour and water. Beat in to chocolate, the butter, cornflour paste and sugar. Add yolks one at a time, hazelnuts and baking powder. Fold in stiffly beaten whites. Bake and leave to cool. **Icing.** Melt chocolate in double saucepan, add softened butter.

172

CHOCOLATE CAKE WITHOUT FLOUR   Marion Warshaw

Preparation 20 mins.   Gas No. 4 (360⁰) for 15 mins.   Advance

5 eggs
2½ ozs. sugar (65 grms)
2 ozs. drinking chocolate or cocoa (50 grms)

¾ pint whipped cream (½ litre)
Small tin of pitted sour cherries

Separate eggs. Beat yolks with chocolate mixture and sugar until creamy. Fold in stiffly beaten egg whites. Pour into two 7″ (17¾ cms) sandwich tins. Bake 15 minutes and allow to cool in oven for 10 minutes. This cake will drop but tastes delicious. Fill with double cream and sour cherries. Sandwich top, cover whole with cream and decorate with flakes of chocolate.

CHOCOLATE LOG   Carole Chinn

Preparation 20 mins.   Uncooked   Freezable   Advance

4 ozs. butter (100 grms)
4 ozs. castor sugar (100 grms)
4 ozs. plain chocolate (100 grms)

½ pint double cream (3 dl.)
2 eggs
12 meringues
Peppermint essence

Cream butter and sugar. Separate eggs and add beaten yolks to butter mixture. Add melted chocolate. Beat whites until stiff and fold in. Line an old-fashioned ice-tray or loaf tin with greaseproof paper, allowing it to come up above sides. Crush meringues four at a time. Make a sandwich with layer meringue, layer chocolate mixture, then meringue, finishing meringue. Cover with greaseproof paper and press tightly down. Freeze until required. Lift out and cover all over with whipped double cream, slightly flavoured with peppermint essence. Serve quickly. Suitable as a rich dessert for milk meal with fresh fruit salad.

COFFEE WALNUT CAKE   Helene Littlestone

Preparation 10 mins.   Gas No. 4 (360⁰)   Cook 45-50 mins.   Freezable

6 ozs. butter or tomor (175 grms)
6 ozs. castor sugar (175 grms)
6 ozs. S.R. flour (175 grms)
3 eggs

2 ozs. chopped walnuts (50 grms)
3 teaspoons instant coffee
1 tablespoon water
1 teaspoon baking powder

Cream fat and sugar. Add eggs and flour (mixed with baking powder) alternately. Dissolve coffee with boiling water and add to mixture. Finally add chopped nuts. Put in greased tin and bake. Can be served plain or with glacé coffee icing decorated with walnuts.

DATE AND WALNUT CAKE
Pearl Barnett

Preparation 30 mins.   Gas No. 4 (360⁰)   Cook 40 mins.

2 tablespoons butter
1 cup sugar
1 egg
¾ lb stones dates (350 grms)
1 teaspoon bicarbonate of soda

1½ cups S.R. flour
½ lb. walnuts (225 grms)
¼ teaspoon salt
1 cup hot water
2 x 9″ (22¾ cms) greased and lined
    sandwich tins

Cut dates into small pieces. Soak them in hot water and cool. Cream butter and sugar, add egg, salt, dates and mix well, add walnuts. Sift flour with bicarbonate of soda and mix all together. Bake and serve with sweetened cream.

DUTCH APPLE CAKE
Rachelle Stewart

Preparation 20 mins.   Gas No. 4 (360⁰)   Cook ½ hour   Advance

3 ozs. Dutch butter (80 grms)
3 ozs. castor sugar (80 grms)
1 large egg
3 ozs. S.R. flour (80 grms)
2 tablespoons milk
Greased 8″ (20¼ cms) loose bottomed tin

Topping:
2 ozs. Demerera sugar (50 grms)
1 large cooking apple
1 oz. Dutch butter (30 grms)
1 teaspoon cinnamon

Cream butter and sugar until light and fluffy. Beat in egg. Fold in flour in two parts, alternating with milk, using a metal spoon. Place in tin. Mix demerera sugar and cinnamon and sprinkle half on top of mixture. Peel, core and slice apple and place in circle on top. Sprinkle with remaining sugar mixture. Melt 1 oz. (25 grms) butter and dribble over top. Serve hot or cold with double cream.

5 MINUTES CAKE
Anita Elman

Preparation 5 mins.   Gas No. 5 (375⁰)   Cook 35 mins.

3 eggs
4 ozs. butter (100 grms)
3½ ozs. castor sugar (90 grms)
4 ozs. plain flour (100 grms)
½ level teaspoon cream of tartar (S.R. flour may
be used thus omitting cream of tartar and
bicarbonate of soda)

2 tablespoons milk
¼ level teaspoon bicarbonate of soda
Pinch salt
Almond essence

Put eggs, sugar, melted butter, flavouring, flour and salt into basin and mix well for five minutes. (if using plain flour add cream of tartar and bicarbonate of soda and beat for further ½ minute) Bake in greased 6″ x 3″ (15¼ cms x 7½ cms) loaf tin.

FRENCH FRUIT BRAID

Ilde Dentith

Preparation 2 hours   **Gas No. 6 (400°)**   **Cook 35-40 mins.**   **Rising time 1 hour 50 mins.**

1 lb. plain flour (450 grms)
Large pinch salt
7 fl. ozs. milk (0.2 litres)
1 oz. yeast (30 grms)
4 ozs. butter (100 grms)
4 ozs. castor sugar (100 grms)
2 eggs

Filling:
1 large cooking apple
½ lb. raisins (225 grms)
4 ozs. sugar (100 grms)
½ teaspoon cinnamon
1 oz. butter (30 grms)
Icing:
6 tablespoons sugar mixed with
1 tablespoon water

Sift flour with salt into mixing bowl. Warm milk carefully to blood heat, add to yeast and butter, stir until dissolved, then mix in sugar and beaten eggs. Make well in centre of flour, pour in liquid ingredients and mix until smooth, first with wooden spoon, then with your hand. When dough comes away cleanly from sides of bowl, turn onto floured board and knead until it becomes elastic in consistancy. Place dough in a greased bowl, turn it around until greased all over, cover with damp cloth and leave to rise in warm place for 45-50 minutes or until it has doubled in bulk. Knock down the dough, pull the sides to the centre, turn it over, cover and let rise again for 30 minutes before shaping and baking. This is a 1 lb. (450 grms) quantity of foundation dough for "coffee" breads.

Well grease a baking sheet and set oven at No. 6. While dough is rising the second time prepare filling. Peel and core the apple, chop roughly and put in pan with raisins, sugar, cinnamon and butter. Cook until apple is soft and pulpy and allow to cool. Turn dough onto floured board, roll out to an oblong about 8" x 14" (20¼ cms x 35½ cms). Spread the fruit mixture down the middle, covering a space about 3" (7½ cms) wide. At each side of the filling make cuts 2" (5 cms) long at 1" (2½ cms) intervals. Take a strip from each side and cross to form a plait. Tuck the last two strips underneath the end of the braid. Lift the plait onto the prepared baking sheet, cover with a damp cloth. Leave it to rise in a warm place for about 30 minutes until double the size. Bake in pre-set oven. Whilst still warm brush braid with icing.

BOIL AND BAKE FRUIT CAKE

Devorah Freeman

Preparation 10 mins.   **Gas No. 4 (360°)**   **Cook 1¼-1½ hours**

1 cup water
½ lb. luxury margarine (225 grms)
1 level teaspoon mixed spice
2 large eggs
2 cups S.R. flour

1 cup sugar
¾ lb. dried fruit (350 grms)
1 level teaspoon bicarbonate of soda
8" (20¼ cms) greased and lined tin

Put sugar, water, margarine, dried fruit, mixed spice, bicarbonate of soda in a saucepan and bring slowly to boil. Simmer for ten minutes. Remove from heat and allow to cool. Add two well beaten eggs and the flour, stir well. Put in cake tin on middle shelf. A little sherry may be added and cake could be decorated with cherries and nuts.

CANDIED FRUIT CAKE

Elisa Bennett

Preparation ¾ hour   **Gas No. 3 (325°)**   **Cook 2½ hours**   **Maturing time 10 days**

Grated rinds of ½ lemon and 1 orange
8 ozs. unsalted butter (225 grms)
8 ozs. castor sugar (225 grms)
8 ozs. plain flour (225 grms)
Good pinch salt
1 level teaspoon baking powder
4 large eggs

4 ozs. glacé pineapple (100 grms)
4 ozs. crystallised ginger (100 grms)
4 ozs. glacé cherries (100 grms)
2 ozs. angelica (50 grms)
8 ozs. sultanas (225 grms)
2 ozs. ground almonds (50 grms)
8″ (20¼ cms) loose bottomed tin, greased
     and lined

Cut pineapple, ginger, angelica and cherries into small pieces. Combine with sultanas, grated rinds and almonds. Beat butter until creamy, add castor sugar and beat well. Beat eggs and add gradually to butter/sugar mixture. Add prepared fruit alternately with flour, salt and baking powder. Turn into prepared tin and smooth top, hollowing centre slightly. Bake on Gas No. 3 (325°) for 1 hour, then turn down to Gas No. 1 (300°) for 1-1½ hours, until a warm knife comes out clean. Leave in tin for 15 minutes, then cool on rack. Foil wrap closely when quite cold and leave to mature.

FRUIT CAKE

Valerie Joels

Preparation 30 mins.   **Gas No. 4 (350°)**   **Cook 1½-2 hours**   **Advance**

1 lb. S.R. flour (450 grms)
½ level teaspoon salt
8 ozs. margarine (225 grms)
6 ozs. sultanas (175 grms)
3 large eggs
7 ozs. granulated sugar (200 grms)

¼ pint milk (2 dl.)
6 ozs. currants or raisins (175 grms)
1-2 teaspoons marmalade
Split or chopped almonds
Finely grated rind of orange
8″ (20¼cms) or 9″ (22¾cms) greased
     and lined tin

Sift flour and salt into mixjng bowl. Add margarine cut in pieces and beat until it resembles fine breadcrumbs. Stir in sugar and sultanas, currants or raisins. Beat the eggs with the milk and add to dry ingredients. Mix with wooden spoon until smooth. Add rind and marmalade; mixture should be soft enough to just drop from a spoon. Transfer mixture to tin, sprinkle almonds on top of mixture and place just below centre of oven.

GINGER CAKE

Jeanne Yudolph

Preparation 10 mins.   **Gas No. 4-5 (360°-375°)**   **Cook 1-1¼ hours**   **Freezable**   **Advance**

2 eggs
6 ozs. sugar (175 grms)
8 ozs. S.R. flour (225 grms)
2 teaspoons cinnamon
2 dessertspoons ginger marmalade (optional)

1 teacup oil
3 tablespoons golden syrup
2½ teaspoons powdered ginger
¼ teaspoon bicarbonate of soda dissolved
     in a cup of warm water

Grease and line 8″ (20¼ cms) or two loaf tins. Mix all ingredients except bicarbonate of soda which you add when the rest is well blended. Two dessertspoons of ginger marmalade improves the cake but it is optional. Oven MUST NOT be opened under 1 hour.

GINGER SPONGE

Preparation 10 mins.   Gas No. 4 (360°)   Cook 1 hour   Freezable   Advance

2 eggs   6 oz. sugar   4 tablespoons golden syrup
$\frac{7}{8}$ cup oil   ginger   9 ozs. S.R. flour (250 grms)
Cup of warm water   ½ teaspoon bicarbonate of soda

Mix sugar and syrup together. Add eggs and mix slowly. Add oil and bicarbonate of soda, then add flour and water slowly.

GUINESS CAKE
Olive Hanks

Preparation 20 mins.   Gas No. 1-2 (300°-325°)   Cook 2½ hours   Maturing time 1 hour

8 ozs. butter (225 grms)   8 ozs. seedless raisins (225 grms)
8 ozs. soft brown sugar (225 grms)   8 ozs. sultanas (225 grms)
4 eggs   4 ozs. mixed peel (100 grms)
10 ozs. plain flour (275 grms)   4 ozs. chopped nuts (100 grms)
2 level teaspoons mixed spice   8-12 tablespoons Guiness
                                   Greased 10" (25½ cms) tin

Cream butter and sugar until creamy. Gradually add lightly beaten eggs. Fold in flour and mixed spice. Add fruit and mixed nuts and mix well. Stir in 4 tablespoons Guiness and mix to dropping consistency. Bake in centre shelf of oven for 1 hour on Gas No. 2 (300°). Reduce to Gas No. ½ (275°) for further 1½ hours. Remove from oven and leave in tin on wire rack to cool before removing. Turn cake upside down. Prick with skewer and spoon over remaining 4-8 tablespoons Guiness. Leave to mature.

HAZELNUT CAKE
Trish Beecham

Preparation 20 mins.   Gas No. 4-5 (360°-375°)   Cook 45 mins.   Freezable   Advance

½ lb. castor sugar (225 grms)   6 eggs
½ lb. ground hazelnuts (225 grms)   Sherry glass of brandy or rum
A few whole hazelnuts   10" (25½ cms) loose bottomed cake tin

Cream sugar and yolks until light and fluffy. Add ground hazelnuts and liqueur. Beat whites stiffly and fold in. Pour into greased tin and bake. Remove cake from tin, leaving it on metal base. Place on rack to cool. Dust with icing sugar. Press on whole hazelnuts to garnish. Ideal to make at Pesach.

HONEY CAKE
Terry Goodman

Preparation 15 mins.   Gas No. 2½ (335⁰)   Cook 1½ hours

1 lb. plain flour (450 grms)
8 ozs. sugar (225 grms)
¼ teaspoon ginger
2 teaspoons cinnamon
2 teaspoons mixed spice
½ teaspoon baking powder
1 teaspoon bicarbonate of soda

1 lb. tin golden syrup (450 grms)
½ syrup tin of warm water (225 grms)
5 ozs. oil (1½ dl.)
3 beaten eggs
3-4 tablespoons kiddush wine or sweet
    red wine
12" x 9" (30½cms x 22¾cms) tin

Put dry ingredients in bowl, Add liquid ingredients gradually and beat well. Line cake tin with foil, pour in mixture and bake.

KUGELHOPH
Ilde Dentith

Preparation 45 mins.   Gas No. 5 (375⁰)   Cook 1 hour   Resting time 30 mins.   Advance

7 fl. ozs. milk (2½ dl.)
1 oz. yeast (30 grms)
12 ozs. flour (350 grms)
Pinch salt
1 oz. castor sugar (30 grms)
2 large well beaten eggs

4 ozs. melted butter (100 grms)
2 ozs. currants (50 grms)
2 ozs. raisins or sultanas (50 grms)
24 blanched almonds
Icing sugar
7" x 8" (17¾cms x 20¼cms) Kugelhoph
    tin, which is fluted with a tube in centre

Warm milk to blood heat, pour onto yeast and stir until dissolved. Sift flour and salt into warm bowl, make well in centre, pour in warm milk and yeast, add the sugar and eggs and the melted (not hot) butter. Mix thoroughly, then add dried fruit. Press blanched almonds round sides and bottom of tin which has been well buttered. Turn dough in, which should be three-quarters full, then stand in warm place for 20-30 minutes, until mixture is about 1" (2½ cms) below top of tin. Stand tin on thick baking sheet and put in centre of oven for 50-60 minutes. If top tends to colour too much, lower heat until kugelhopf is done. Leave for a few minutes before turning out and dust with icing sugar.

KÜCHEN
Jeanne Yudolph

Preparation 10 mins.   Gas No. 3 (350⁰)   Cook 1-1¼ hours   Freezable   Advance

1 egg
½ cup oil
¾ cup milk
1 cup sugar

2½ cups S.R. flour
Handful fruit
Greased and lined loaf tin

Do NOT preheat oven. Mix sugar and egg, add oil, mix in flour, milk and fruit and bake. This kuchen should be sliced and buttered and keeps very well.

MADEIRA CAKE

Mary Fish

Preparation 15 mins.   **Gas No. 4 (350⁰)**   **Cook 1 hour**

Grated rind of lemon
8 ozs. sugar (225 grms)
4 eggs
8 ozs. S.R. flour (225 grms)

8 ozs. butter (225 grms)
2 ozs. dried fruit (50 grms if desired
Greased 3 pt Kugelhoph tin (1½ litre)

Cream butter and sugar. Add eggs alternately with flour, then lemon and fruit. Bake.

MARBLE CAKE

Lilly Kerr

Preparation 30 mins.   **Gas No. 3½ (355⁰)**   **Cook 1¼ hours**

8 ozs. castor sugar (225 grms)
8 ozs. butter (225 grms)
1 level teaspoon baking powder
4 eggs
Pinch salt
8 ozs. S.R. flour (225 grms)

¼ cup milk (approx)
2 ozs. glacé cherries (50 grms)
2 ozs. walnuts (50 grms)
1-2 tablespoons Cadbury's drinking chocolate
8" (20¼cms) tin

Cream butter and sugar. Add eggs one at a time. Beat until creamy. Add sifted flour and baking powder. Add warm milk slowly beating well. Add chopped cherries and nuts. Put three quarters of mixture into well greased tin. Add drinking chocolate to remaining mixture and mix well. Add into mixture in tin and stir gently.

ENGADINE NUSSTORTE

Devorah Freeman

Preparation 30 mins. Gas No. 4 (360⁰) Cook 35 mins. Refrigeration 1 hour Freezable Advance

Pastry:
12 ozs. sifted flour (350 grms)
5 ozs. butter (140 grms)
$\frac{5}{8}$ cup sugar
3 ozs. cooking fat (80 grms)
1 egg and 1 egg white

Filling:
Cup castor sugar
8 ozs. roughly chopped walnuts (225 grms)
1 cup slightly heated cream

Mix pastry together in bowl and chill. **Filling** Stir sugar in bottom of hot frying pan, add slightly heated cream and stir in walnuts. Take pastry from fridge and roll out ¼" (¾ cms) thick and and cut in circle to fit base of a flan tin. Pour in filling and put remaining pastry on top. Bake and sprinkle with sugar for last few minutes of cooking.

ORANGE GINGER GATEAU

Rusty Sotnick

Preparation 20 mins.   **Uncooked**   **Chilling time 8 hours**   **Freezable**   **Advance**

½ pint double cream (3 dl.)
3 level tablespoons orange juice
15-16 ginger biscuits (1 packet)

2 level tablespoons icing sugar
3 teaspoons orange rind
Orange slices and angelica

Whip cream until thick, fold in sugar, orange juice and rind to make dropping consistency. Sandwich biscuits together with half the mixture and place in a roll on a dish. Cover roll with remaining cream mixture. Cover with foil and leave in fridge overnight. Decorate with orange and angelica.

PLAVA

Anne Kartoon

Preparation 20 mins.   **Gas No. 2 (325⁰)**   **Cook about 1 hour**

6 ozs. castor sugar (175 grms)
3 ozs. fine matzo meal (80 grms)
1 teaspoon almond essence

6 eggs
3 ozs. ground almonds (80 grms)
Squeeze lemon juice
9" x 9" x 2¼" (22¾ x 22¾ x 6½cms)
    square tin

Beat yolks and sugar until creamy. Add meal and ground almonds slowly. Beat whites stiffly and fold in. Bake in greased tin.

ALL-PURPOSE SPONGE

Barbara Tobias

Preparation 20 mins.   **Gas No. 5 (375⁰)**   **Cook 40 mins. approx.**   **Advance**

4 eggs
8 ozs. sugar (225 grms)

4 ozs. flour (100 grms)
Dash hot water

Put eggs and sugar into mixer and beat for at least 15 minutes until mixture is vastly risen in bowl. Add sieved flour, gently folding in with metal spoon. Add dash of very hot water to make mixture smooth. Put into prepared tin – either 9" (22¾ cms) round or 8" (20¼ cms) square. Bake about 40 minutes until resilient to the touch and light golden brown. Eat plain or split and fill and cover with whipped cream and fruit.
NOTE: Use as basis for sponge puddings. Vary by replacing 1 oz. (25 grms) of flour with 1 oz. (25 grms) of cocoa and split and fill with cream.

STRÜDEL

Sophie Parker

Preparation 30 mins.   Gas No. 4 (360°)   Cook 25 mins.   Freezable   Advance

PASTRY
¾ lb. S.R. flour (350 grms)
2 tablespoons sugar
½ lb. margarine (225 grms)
1 egg mixed with a little cold water

FILLING
1 lb. apricot jam (450 grms)
2 ozs. chopped walnuts (50 grms)
4 ozs. candied peel (100 grms)
1 lb. raisins or sultanas (450 grms)
1 lb. cooking apples (450 grms)
4 ozs. glacé cherries (100 grms)
2 ozs. ground almonds (50 grms)

Make pastry and divide into five pieces. Peel apples and grate coarsely. Mix with remaining filling ingredients. Roll each piece of pastry to 11" x 7" (28 x 17¾ cms). Spread one-fifth of filling on first piece of pastry, leaving 1½" (4 cms) border. Fold edges in and roll up on strüdel shape. Repeat with rest of filling and pastry. If desired brush with beaten egg and scatter with flaked almonds before baking.

STRÜDEL WITH TURKISH DELIGHT

Sheila Finer

Preparation 30 mins.   Gas No. 4 (360°)   Cook 30 mins.   Freezable   Advance

6 ozs. S.R. flour (175 grms)
6 ozs. margarine (175 grms)
Soda water to mix
2 large cooking apples

Mixed spices
Turkish delight (any flavour, not mint)
8 ozs. dried fruit (225 grms)
Plum or raspberry jam

Make pastry with flour, margarine and soda water. Roll into suitable oblong shapes. The amount should make three pieces each enough for 4-5 portions. Grate apples over each portion, sprinkle with spices. Dot with teaspoons of jam, spread dried fruit on top and cut and place small pieces of Turkish delight all over. Roll and seal the ends. **Note:** Use all sweet spices including ginger and coriander.

STRAWBERRY SHORTCAKE

Shortan Sweet

Preparation ½ hour approx.   Gas No. 2-3 (325°-350°)   Cook 30-35 mins.   Freezable   Advance

'3 eggs
3 ozs. plain flour (80 grms)
¾ lb. strawberries (350 grms)
4 ozs. sugar (100 grms)

Grated rind of 2 oranges
Small quantity of lightly whipped cream
3" x 7" (7½ x 17¾ cms) cake tin

Beat eggs and sugar until white. Fold in sifted flour half at a time. Add rind of oranges gently. Tip mixture into greased and floured tin and bake. When cold cut in half and spread centre with generous amount of mashed strawberries. Sprinkle lightly with sugar. Put halves together and cover with lightly whipped cream. Decorate with halved strawberries. If freezing do not add cream and fruit until defrosted.

WICKELTORTE

Daniele Harris, Germany

Preparation 45 mins.   Gas No. 6 (400°)   Cook 10-15 mins.

BISCUIT
4 tablespoons cold water
4 separated eggs
2½ ozs. flour (75 grms)
2 teaspoons baking powder
7 ozs. sugar (200 grms)
1 oz. cocoa (30 grms)

FILLING
2 tablespoons rum
½ glass cranberry or bilberry jelly
¾ pint whipped cream (½ litre)
Icing sugar
Grated chocolate
Greasproof pepper

Whisk yolks and water to a foam. Gradually add two-thirds of the sugar. Beat until creamy. Beat egg whites stiffly and fold in remaining sugar. Blend the two mixtures together. Sieve flour. cocoa and baking powder and fold in gently with a metal spoon. Line a Swiss roll tin with greaseproof which has been cut 1″ - 2″ (2½ - 5 cms) larger than tin all round. Place mixture in tin and fold greaseproof up to form collar, bake. Place a tea towel on to a tray and sprinkle with sieved icing sugar. Turn biscuit mixture on to tea towel so that the greaseproof paper is uppermost. Moisten the paper with cold water to remove carefully. Leave to cool. Splash biscuit all over with a few drops of rum to taste. Cut into 2″ (5 cms) strips lengthways. Whip cream and combine with jelly. Cover each strip with the cream mixture. Roll up the first strip and stand it upright on a serving plate, then roll the other strips round the first one, building up into a dome shape. Cover top and sides of cake with the rest of the cream mixture and decorate with grated chocolate.

Dinner Guests

GUEST LIST

DATE ....

MENU

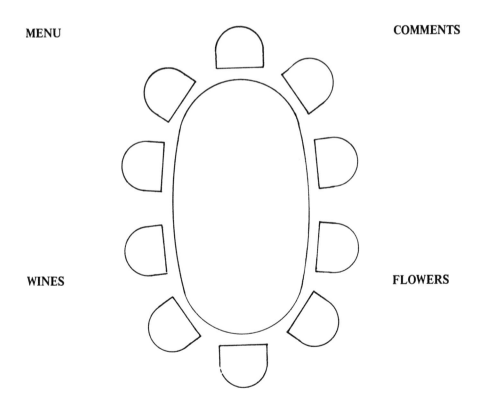

COMMENTS

WINES

FLOWERS

GUEST LIST

MENU

COMMENTS

WINES

FLOWERS

GUEST LIST

DATE ....

MENU

COMMENTS

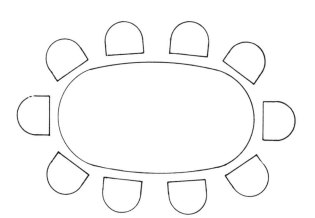

WINES

FLOWERS

184

GUEST LIST

MENU

COMMENTS

WINES

FLOWERS

GUEST LIST

DATE ....

MENU

COMMENTS

WINES

FLOWERS

185

GUEST LIST

DATE ....

MENU

COMMENTS

WINES

FLOWERS

GUEST LIST

DATE ....

MENU

COMMENTS

WINES

FLOWERS

186

GUEST LIST

DATE ....

MENU

COMMENTS

WINES

FLOWERS

GUEST LIST

DATE ....

MENU

COMMENTS

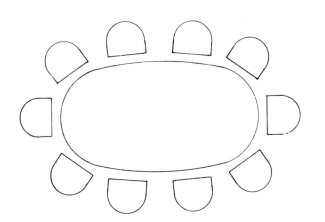

WINES

FLOWERS

M.W.M.H.—N

GUEST LIST

DATE ....

MENU

COMMENTS

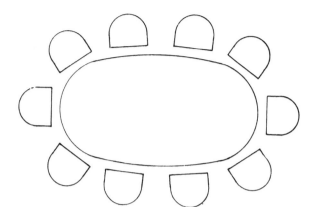

WINES

FLOWERS

GUEST LIST

DATE ....

MENU

COMMENTS

WINES

FLOWERS

GUEST LIST

DATE ....

MENU

COMMENTS

WINES

FLOWERS

GUEST LIST

DATE ....

MENU

COMMENTS

WINES

FLOWERS

GUEST LIST

DATE ....

MENU

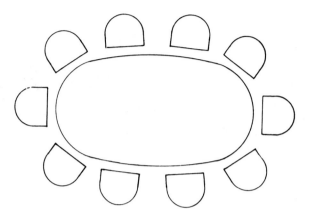

COMMENTS

WINES

FLOWERS

GUEST LIST

DATE ....

MENU

COMMENTS

WINES

FLOWERS

Parties

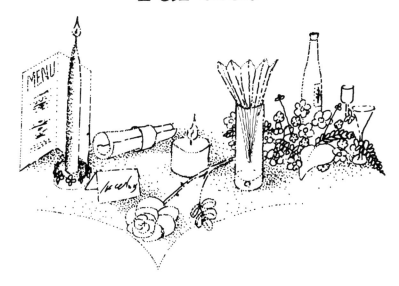

Entertaining should always be an enjoyable event, both for the guests and the hosts, it is easy to say this but harder to achieve! We suggest that the following ideas may be useful:—

Choose a menu that needs little last minute attention.

Do not try to make too many hot courses.

Do not experiment with new recipes when entertaining.

Work out a time table for the preparation of the food and it's cooking — and sellotape a copy on your kitchen wall.

Think of ways to make the meal look as attractive as possible.

Plan to do all the shopping the day before.

Have the telephone numbers of the plumber, electrician etc. handy in case of emergencies.

Ensure that you have the wines required available.

We hope that our guest lists will save you time when wondering what you gave your guests last time they visited you.

The menus in this book are intended to give ideas rather than to be adhered to implicity, "one man's meat is another man's poison." But if they help you plan a successful party they will have achieved their purpose.

When planning a large party the first thing to do is to organise the date, time and any extra help that may be required. Secondly, plan your guest list and suitable menu for the amount of people involved. Next arrange the hiring of any entertaining equipment remembering to refer to our check list (page 192). At this stage you should be able to relax a little and plan with great enjoyment your decor, i.e. candles, tablecloths, etc. When choosing your colours bear in mind which flowers will be in season.

The intention of this section is that it should make interesting reading and will help you to arrange any party that may arise from a tea party to a Sabbath luncheon after your son's Barmitzvah.

PARTY CHECK LIST

Bar	Kitchen	Dining Room/Lounge	Miscellaneous
Ashtrays	Tea	Hot Plate	Plasters
Matches	Coffee	Trays	Comb
Lighters	Lemon	Tray Cloths	Tissues
Cocktail Napkins	Milk	Tablecloths	Guest Towels
Cocktail Cherries	Salt	Table Mats	Guest Soaps
Cocktails Sticks	Pepper	Napkins	Tampax
Lemon Slices	Mustard	Place Cards	Toilet Paper
Orange Slices	Parsley	Ashtrays	Hangers
Cocktail Onions	Herbs	Cigarette Containers	Coat Rails
Cucumbers	Spices	Wine Glasses	Coat Tickets
Olives	Cream	Tumblers	Needles
Nuts	Lump Sugar	Liqueur Glasses	Cottons
Crisps	Coffee Sugar	Ice Bucket	Safety Pins
Dips	Petits Fours	Ice	Clothes Brush
Bottle/Tin Opener	Mints	Sugar Sifters	Pain Killers
Corkscrew	Rolls/Bread	Sugar Bowls and tongs	Air Freshener
Tea Towels	Kitchen Roll	Condiment Sets	Hair Laqueur
"J" Cloths	Silver Foil	Finger Bowls	Cologne
Cigarettes	Cling Film	Tables	Emery Boards
Cigars	Doylees	Chairs	Stain Remover
Ice Bucket	Paper Knapkins	Butter Dishes	Light Bulbs
Ice Tongs	Greaseproof Paper	Serving Dishes	Fuse Wire
Ice	Menu Ingredients	Serving Bowls	Screwdriver
Jugs	Artificial Sweetener	Serving Platters	Flower Containers
Glasses	Cooking Utensils	Sauce/Gravy Boats	Flowers
Drinks	Cooking Pans	Bread Baskets	Florapak
Wines	Sharp Knives	China	Fruit
Liqueurs	Tin Opener	Coffee/Tea Spoons	Candles
Tomato/Fruit Juices	Scissors	Dessert Spoons	Chocolates
Squashes	Chopper	Soup Spoons	Burn Creams
Tonic Water	Egg Slicer	Serving Spoons	Emergency numbers
Ginger Ale etc.	Parsley Grater	Ladles	of Plumber
Soda Water	Water Urn	Fish Knives/Forks	Electrician
Worcester Sauce	Coffee/Tea Pots	Meat Knives/Forks	Suppliers of food
Straws	Silver Cleaner	Small Knives/Forks	
	Washing Up Liquid	Fruit Knives/Forks	
	Tea Towels	Butter Knives	
	Oven Cloth	Pastry Forks	
	Mopping up Cloths	Cake Slices	
	Time Table		

HELP! ! !

192

PARTY QUANTITIES

BREAD	1 large loaf	20 slices
BRIDGE ROLLS	30	20 people
BUTTER	1 lb. (450 grms)	40 slices of bread
CHAMPAGNE	1 bottle	8 glasses
CHICKEN	3 x 5½ lbs. (3 x 2k 475 grms)	20 portions
CHICKEN SLICED	5 lbs. (2k 250 grms)	20 portions
CHOCOLATES etc.	1½ lbs. (675 grms)	20 people
COFFEE INSTANT	2 oz. (4tbls.) + 1 gallon water (4½ litres)	20 cups
COFFEE GROUND	6 oz. (12tbls.) + 1 gallon water (4½ litres)	20 cups
COLE SLAW	4 lbs. (1k 800 grms)	20 portions
CREAM POURING	2 pints (1¼ litres)	20 portions
CRISPS	3 large boxes	20 portions
CUCUMBER SALAD	4 large cucumbers	20 portions
FISH	6 oz (175 grms)	1 portion
FRUIT SALAD	4 pints (2½ litres)	20 portions
ICE CREAM	1 gallon (4½ litres)	20 portions
MAYONNAISE	1½ pints (1 litre)	20 portions
MEAT for ROASTING	½ lb. (225 grms)	1 portion
MEAT for BRAISING	6 oz. (175 grms)	1 portion
MILK for TEA	1 pint (½ litre)	20 cups
NUTS	1 lb. (450 grms)	20 portions
ORANGE SQUASH	1 pint (½ litre)	20 glasses
POTATO SALAD	5 lbs. (2k 250 grms)	20 portions
RASPBERRIES	¼ lb. (100 grms)	1 portion
SALAD DRESSING	2 pints (1 litre)	20 portions
SHERRY	1 bottle	14 glasses
SOUP	1 gallon (4½ litres)	20 portions
STRAWBERRIES	¼ lb. (100 grms)	1 portion
SUGAR for TEA	1 lb. (450 grms)	20 portions
TEA	¼ lb. (100 grms) + 1 gallon water (4½ litres)	20 cups
TOMATO SALAD	5 lbs. (2k. 250 grms)	20 portions
VEGETABLES	¼ lb. (100 grms)	1 portion
VIENNAS	1 lb. (450 grms)	14 viennas approx
VIENNAS COCKTAIL	1 lb. (450 grms)	32 viennas approx
WHISKY	1 bottle	30 tots
WINE	1 bottle	8 glasses
WINE	1 litre	10 glasses

PARTY IDEAS

AMERICAN
Wild West

Western bar type decor. Check cotton or denim tablecloths. Flags with stars and stripes. Jive music. Serve hamburgers. Baked beans. Tomato Ketchup, Pepsi Cola with straws. Ice Cream Sodas. Fruit Pies, Chewing Gum, Beer, Doughnuts, Toy guns. Hurrican lamps on tables.

BARBEQUE

Casual clothes. Big Chef's apron and hat. If in the evening, place candles in bottles round the garden or use fairy lights. Steaks, chops, kebabs, hamburgers, sausages, chicken portions. Jacket potatoes wrapped in foil. Lots of sauces. Salads, French Bread. Bananas in their skins.

BREAKFAST/
BRUNCH

Pillows to sit on. Pyjamas will be worn. Newspapers to read. Kippers, scrambled eggs and waffles, with Maple Syrup. Griddle cakes, Coffee, tea, orange juice, toast and marmalade.

CHINESE

Hanging latterns. Chopsticks and bowls. Saki wine. Use some of the many Chinese recipes in this book. Plenty of rice. Lychees, Stem ginger and Kumquats. Serve food on low tables made by using folded card tables on low brick pillars. Cover with red or black cloths and let guests sit on scatter cushions.

CHANUKAH

Menorah and correct amount of coloured candles. Games with the Dreigel (spinning top). Traditional food with latkas.

CORONATION
(children)

Hire a film of the Queen's Coronation. Decorate the room with flags. Make crowns and tiaras for the children. Make or buy a Doll Birthday Cake (using a pudding basin to make the skirt shape and then put the top half of a small doll on it. Put a crown on its head and a cape of net on the shoulders. Give a Royal Family booklet as a going home present. Stick sequins and gold and silver stars on plates.

DICKENSIAN

Fancy dress – guests to come as Dickensian characters. Simple English fare. Mulled wine. Candlelight.

ELECTION

Hire or borrow extra television sets. Hang a large scoreboard of the "State of the Parties" Have chalk or felt-tip pens ready. Decorate table with coloured rosettes and hang portraits of main contenders on walls.

FANCY HATS or
MASKS

This is less trouble than full fancy dress and just as much fun. Have prizes for the most original ones.

FOOTBALL

Cover the table with green baize or paper to resemble a pitch. Stick or paint on white lines. Serviettes and rosettes in team colours. Football cake and casual type food.

GOLFING

The above idea could be adapted to golf by making the table look like a course. Small flags, trees, etc.

GUY FAWKES

A large Guy. Bonfire Fireworks under supervision. Jacket potatoes Hot Dogs. Soup in Cups. Hot chocolate to drink with a marsh-mallow on the top or cold drinks. Hot chestnuts.

194

HALLOWE'EN	Scoop out a Pumpkin and cut out eyes, nose and mouth. Place nightlights inside. Have dim lighting perhaps with red or green bulbs. Hang skeletons and spiders in dark corners. Make a table-cloth from black material or crepe paper and stick on silver moons or stars. Decorate table with witches and white balloons painted with white faces to look like ghosts. Hot roast chestnuts. Sausage rolls. Goulash in a cauldron. Hot Punch. Toffee apples and apple snow.
HAWAIIAN	Aloha sign on the front door. Flowers for the girls to wear in their hair. South Seas Posters for the walls. Hide lamps with real or paper palm trees. Garlands of paper flowers (Leis). Food or drink served in coconuts. Palm Hearts with Thousand Island dressing. Chicken with Hawaiian rice or Pineapple Duck. Fresh fig salad or Pacific fruit salad. Spiced hot fruit. Pineapples filled with rum or coffee ice cream.
HIPPY	Jeans and cheese cloth gear. No chairs. Loud music. Plenty of canned drinks. Finger Health food. Buckwheat cakes, wholemeal bread, brown rice. Hippy art on walls. Dim lighting.
1920's	Flapper clothes essential. Music of the time. Art Deco posters on the walls. Long cigarette holders. Punch and Champagne cocktails. Swizzle sticks for drinks. Canapes.
NEWSPAPER	Have newspapers on the walls and a giant crossword puzzle that everyone can help with. Have blown up comic strips with empty balloons. Copies of cartoons with a prize for the funniest caption. Games to play:– Races to find a specific piece of information in a newspaper (Have sufficient copies). Quiz. See who can make the most interesting object out of a newspaper. Use recipes from newspaper articles on cookery and stick a copy of the recipes on the wall above finished dishes. Fish and chips served in newspapers. Big cake or desserts decorated with headlines.
OUT OF THIS WORLD	Silver or white tablecloths, etc. Rockets and planets and martians to decorate.
PICNIC	If an afternoon party borrow cake boxes and make an assortment of sandwiches, biscuits and a bag of crisps per person. Cold drinks with straws and rugs to sit on. For a lunch party, roast chicken legs, sticks of celery and carrots, hard boiled eggs, meat balls, wide necked thermos flask with Viennas in it. Cold quiches. Chopped and fried fish balls. Salmon fish cakes. Chicken croquettes. Wrap small pieces of cooked lean meat or chicken in lettuce leaves and secure with an olive on cocktail stick. Cold Borsht. Thermos with cold drinks or canned drinks and straws. Cold bottles of wine and wedges of Water Melon. Halva. Assortment of salads. Cheeses.
PURIM	Fancy dress with prizes for the most topical Biblical character. Hamantachan to eat.

ROMAN

Grass matting rugs as used by the greengrocers. A foil Cornucopia filled with nuts and raisins. A cascading fruit decoration arranged on a tall tiered cake stand. Scatter cushions on the floor. Roman busts on pedestals or Photographs of them. Palm leaves to be sprayed with silver to be used as fans or decoration. Mask children's paddling pool with greenery. Fill it with water and place goldfish and waterlilly candles in it. Guests to wear Roman togas. Cold finger food, ie. chicken legs, cold lamb cutlets, raw vegetables, salads and fresh fruit. Finger bowls recommended. Drinks in goblets.

SANDWICH FILLINGS

Mashed bananas
Grated cheese and chutney
Grated cheese and tomato
Sliced cheese with cucumber
Cream cheese with lettuce
Cream cheese with gherkin
Cream cheese with tomato and
    mustard and cress
Cream cheese with chopped walnuts
Cucumber and tomato
Chopped egg with cucumber
Chopped egg with anchovy
Sliced egg and tomato
Cream cheese with paprika

Lemon Curd
Marmite
Peanut Butter
Mashed Smoked Roe with Black
    Olives and unsalted Butter
Mashed sardine with vinegar and tomato
Salad Sandwich
Sandwich Spread
Tuna Fish with lettuce
Tuna Fish with gherkin
Tinned salmon with cucumber
Smoked salmon with lemon
Honey
Jam

BRIDGE ROLLS

Any of the above fillings plus:--
Cream cheese with asparagus tips. Cold scrambled eggs with pimento.
Chopped herring on lettuce, or strips of Roll Mops. Asparagus with a strip of tomato on top.
Tinned salmon with cucumber butterflies on top.

MENUS FOR SEDER NIGHT DINNERS

MILK MEAL

Borscht
(page 27)

—oOo—

Gefilte Fish Fried and Boiled
(page 41)   *(page 48)*
Fried Fish
Halibut in Egg and Lemon Sauce
(page 43)
Various Salads
New Boiled Potatoes

—oOo—

Hazelnut Cake   Fruit Salad   Parev Ice Cream
(page 177)   *(page 115)*   *(page 118)*

MEAT MEAL

Gefilte Fish Boiled and Fried
(page 42)

—oOo—

Chicken Soup with Matzo Balls
(page 30)   *(page 30)*

—oOo—

Roast Chicken, Duck or Turkey
Brussel Sprouts, Roast Potato Balls or French Potatoes, Carrots
Apple Sauce

—oOo—

Apricot Sponge Compote de Fruit Almond Pudding
(page 122)   *(page 121)*

MILK DINNER PARTIES

SPRING

Cucumber Vichysoisse
(page 31)

—oOo—

Sole en croûte
(page 48)
Webb Lettuce and Avocado Salad
(page 96)
New Potatoes

—oOo—

Hazelnut Meringue Cake
(page 138)
Gooseberry Ice Cream
(page 131)

—oOo—

AUTUMN

Gnocci Verdi
(page 147)

—oOo—

Crispy Baked Halibut
(page 42)
Potatoes with Mushrooms
(page 87)
Fresh Broccoli

—oOo—

Swiss Apple Pie
(page 134)
Pears poached with Grenadine
Raspberry Mousse
(page 133)

—oOo—

SUMMER

Cold Asparagus Vinaigrette
(page 102)

—oOo—

Quennelles au Fromage
(page 47)
Celery with Almonds
(page 83)
Spinach
Boulangerie Potatoes
(page 87)

—oOo—

Not Quite Crème Brulée
(page 131)
Strawberries

—oOo—

WINTER

Mozzarella in Carozza
(page 22)

—oOo—

Fish Fillets with cream and Mushrooms
(page 40)
Potatoes Almandine
(page 86)
Carrots
Green Salad

—oOo—

Fruits Refraichais
(page 115)
Vanilla Ice Cream with Fudge Sauce
(page 132)   *(page 109)*
Meringues

MEAT DINNER PARTIES

SPRING

Stuffed Tomatoes (2)
(page 24)

—oOo—

Shoulder of Lamb
(page 60)
Rosti Potatoes
(page 87)
Mange Tous
Ratatouille
(page 88)

—oOo—

Crepes Suzettes
(page 124)
Honeyed Oranges
(page 116)
Pacific Fruit Salad
(page 118)

—oOo—

AUTUMN

Asparagus Paté
(page 12)

—oOo—

Duck with Apricots
(page 75)
Greek Beans and Spinach
(page 80)
Potatoes Almondine
(page 86)
Peas

—oOo—

Cherry Meringue
(page 123)
Lemon Mousse
(page 117)

—oOo—

SUMMER

Avocado Syvala
(page 14)

—oOo—

Chicken a L'orange
(page 71)
Roast Potato Balls
Courgettes
French Beans

—oOo—

Chocolate Rum Mousse
(Page 114)
Summer Pudding
(page 127)
Grapefruit Sorbet
(page 116)

—oOo—

WINTER

Bean and Barley Soup
(page 27)

—oOo—

Veal Chops en Papillote
(page 61)
Aubergine Provençal
(page 80)
Rice with Braised Leeks
(page 85)

—oOo—

Charlotte aux Framboise
(page 119)
Pineapple with Kirch
Citrus Sorbet
(page 115)

—oOo—

MILK BUFFET PARTIES

SPRING

Carrot and Orange Soup or Melon Cocktail
(page 28)

—oOo—

Sole en Croûte — Halibut in Green Mayonnaise
(page 48)   *(page 43)*

Aubergine a La Provençal — Tomato and Cucumber Salad
(page 80)
Green Salad with Hard Boiled Eggs — Potato and Carrot Ring
(page 93)
Brown Bread and Butter

—oOo—

Bing Cherries with Liqueur — Creme Brulée — Chocolate Log
(page 130)   *(page 137)*
Fresh Fruit — Cheese Board

Coffee

—oOo—

SUMMER

Hot Spinach Tart — Mushroom Flan
(page 154)   *(page 150)*

—oOo—

Whole Salmon — Fried Fillets of Plaice

Green Salad — Rice Salad — Celeriac Salad — Eggs in Red Dresses
(page 98)   *(page 93)*   *(page 17)*
Garlic Bread
Palm Hearts with Thousand Island Dressing
(page 98)

—oOo—

Fresh Strawberries and Cream — Peaches in Syrup — Hazelnut Meringue Cake
(page 140)   *(page 138)*

Coffee

—oOo—

AUTUMN

Tarasamalta — Aubergine Paté
(page 23)   *(apge 12)*

—oOo—

Fish Pie — Stuffed Carp
(page 41) – (page 40)

Mixed Green Salad — Beetroot and Onion Salad — Mushroom and Olive Salad
(page 92)   *(page 97)*

Six Day Salad
(page 99)

—oOo—

Raspberry Mousse — Apricot Bombe — Orange and Grape Salad
(page 133)   *(page 135)*
Cheese Dessert
(page 136)

Coffee

—oOo—

WINTER

Avocado Mousse — Stuffed Tomatoes (1)
(page 13) – (page 24)

—oOo—

Manicotti — Halibut in Egg and Lemon Sauce
(page 149)   *(page 43)*

Cucumber Salad — Bean Salad — Cole Slaw — Tomato Salad
(page 94)   *(page 92)*   *(page 94)*   *(page 100)*

—oOo—

Grapefruit Sorbet — Lemon Fridge Cake — Coffee Ice Cream — Chocolate Roll
(page 116)   *(page 139)*   *(page 132)*   *(page 137)*

Coffee

—oOo—

MEAT BUFFET PARTIES

SPRING

Basket of Crudites with accompaniments
(page 16)

—oOo—

Lamb Curry on bed of Rice — Cold Beef — Cold Tongue
(page 57)

Minted New Potatoes — Manges Touts — Six Day Salad — Israeli Mixed Salad
(page 99)   *(page 95)*

Pickled Cucumber — Chutney — Poppadums

—oOo—

Glazed Fruit Slices — Austrian Fruit Salad — Rum Bombe
(page 113)   *(page 114)*   *(page 120)*

—oOo—

SUMMER

Melon or Chicken Liver Paté
(page 20)

—oOo—

Stuffed Marrow — Geflugelsalet
(page 56)   *(page 93)*

—oOo—

Baked Pea Savoury — Tossed Mixed Salad — Red Cabbage Salad
(page 86)   *(page 92)*

—oOo—

Orange Mousse — Strawberry Flan — Raspberry Parfait
(page 117)   *(page 126)*   *(page 120)*

—oOo—

AUTUMN

Egg Mousse or Avocado, Onion and Tomato Appetizer
(page 17)   *(page 14)*

—oOo—

Oven Fried Chicken-in-the-Basket with Pineapple Rings and Corn Fritters
(page 65)   *(page 84)*

Jacket Potatoes or Chips

-oOo—

Vacherin aux Marrons — Rhubarb Mousse — Lemon Mousse — Hot Apple Slice
(page 139)   *(page 120)*   *(page 117)*   *(page 122)*

Fresh Fruit Salad
(page 115)

—oOo—

WINTER

Chicken Soup with Lemon or Melon
(page 29)

—oOo—

Beef Chow Mein — Sweet and Sour Chicken — Cold Turkey with Cocktail Viennas
(page 52)   *(page 73)*

Spring Rolls — Rice with Almonds — Bean Salad — Taboue
(page 89)   *(page 89)*   *(page 92)*   *(page 100)*

—oOo—

Tinned Lichees — Orange Surprise — Cherry Tart
(page 118)   *(page 124)*

—oOo—

CELEBRATION LUNCHEONS

MILK

SPRING

Gaspachio or Vichsoisse (Hot or Cold)
(page 32)   (page 38)

—oOo—

Cold Fried Fish/Halibut in Egg and Lemon Sauce
(page 43)

Horseradish Sauce — Pickled Cucumber — Mayonnaise
(page 102)

Webb Lettuce and Avocado Salad — Tomato Salad
(page 96)   (page 100)
Sillisalatti Salad — Potato Salad
(page 101)

—oOo—

Profiteroles
(page 141)

Dinner Cake — Raspberry Mousse — Lemon Soufflé
(page 138)   (page 133)   (page 132)

Fresh Pineapple

—oOo—

SUMMER

Spinach Tarts — Avocado Mousse — Cream Camembert
(page 154)   (page 13)   (page 15)

—oOo—

Cold Salmon/Smoked Trout

Horseradish Sauce — Mayonnaise
(page 102)
Cucumber Yogurt Salad — Israeli Mixed Salad
(page 94)   (page 95)
Red Cabbage Salad — Cole Slaw
(page 92)   (page 94)

—oOo—

Peach Melba — Creme Brulée — Strawberry Romanoff
(page 119)   (page 130)   (page 133)
Red Currants

AUTUMN

Artichoke Vinaigrette/Soup St. Tropez
(page 102)   (page 35)

—oOo—

Gefilte Fish boiled and fried/Carp — Horseradish Sa
(page 41)   (page 40)

Salad with Spinach and Dill —
(page 99)
Beetroot and Onion Salad — Carrot and Potato Mou
(page 92)   (page 93)

Cucumber Salad
(page 94)

—oOo—

Gooseberry Ice Cream — Vacherin Aux Marrons —
(page 131)   (page 139)
Wickeltorte
(page 182)

Fresh Orange Salad

—oOo—

WINTER

Borscht/Cauliflower Soup
(page 27) — (page 29)

—oOo—

Sole Goujons/Maquereux Mariner
(page 48)   — (page 45)

Tartare Sauce
(page 106)
Bean Salad — Fresh Mushroom Salad —
(page 92)   (page 96)
Avocado, Melon and Tomato Salad — Green Salad
(page 92)

—oOo—

Orange Meringues — Dinner Cake —
(page 140)   (page 138)
Bavaroise aux Pommes
(page 129)

CELEBRATION LUNCHEONS

MEAT

SPRING

Golden Soup/Gravlax
(page 32) – (page 18)

—oOo—

Vitello Tonnato – Roast Beef – Coarse Paté
(page 63) *(page 21)*

—oOo—

Celariac Salad – Rice Salad – Green Salad
(page 93) *(page 98)*

Tomato Salad

—oOo—

Portuguese Orange Roll – Chocolate Rum Mousse
(page 126) *(page 114)*

Apricot Tart – Austrian Fruit Salad
(page 122) *(page 114)*

—oOo—

SUMMER

Chicken Soup/Avocado à la Japonaise
(page 30) *(page 13)*

Cold Galantine Duck/Stuffed Veal – Salt Beef
(page 75) *(page 63)*

—oOo—

Rice Salad – Green and Red Pepper Salad
(page 98) *(page 102)*

Cucumber Vinaigrette
(page 102)

—oOo—

Summer Pudding – Fresh Fig Salad – Lemon Sorbet
(page 127) *(page 115)* *(page 115)*
Strawberry Flan
(page 126)

AUTUMN

Minestrone Soup/Russian Cabbage Borscht
(page 33) *(page 28)*

—oOo—

Apricot Tongue – Cold Roast Beef – Cold Chicken
(page 64)

—oOo—

Cole Slaw – Egg, Tomato and Anchovy –
(page 94) *(page 95)*
Carrot and Potato Mould
(page 93)
Pickled Cucumber
(page 93)

—oOo—

Jelly Fruit Wonder – Lemon Mousse
(page 116) *(page 117)*
Pecan Pie – Apple Strudel
(page 126) *(page 167 and 127)*

—oOo—

WINTER

Courgette and Tomato Soup/Barley Soup
(page 30) *(page 27)*

—oOo—

Cholent/Cold Turkey – Viennas Cranberry Sauce
(page 52)

—oOo—

Pasta Bowl Salad – Celariac Salad –
(page 98) *(page 93)*
Red Cabbage – Chicory Salad
(page 92)

—oOo—

Almond Pudding – Chocolate Pear Flan –
(page 121) *(page 124)*
Orange Mousse – Hot Spiced Fruit
(page 117) *(page 121)*

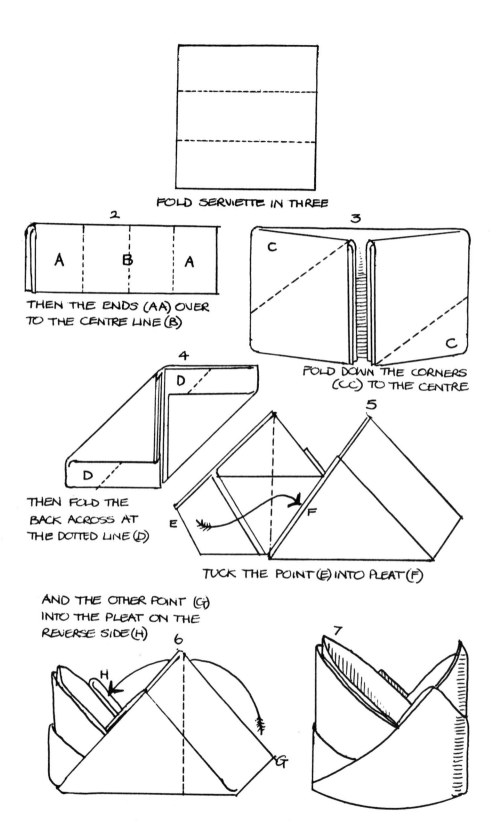

FOLD SERVIETTE IN THREE

2

A   B   A

THEN THE ENDS (AA) OVER
TO THE CENTRE LINE (B)

3

C

C

FOLD DOWN THE CORNERS
(CC) TO THE CENTRE

4

D

D

THEN FOLD THE
BACK ACROSS AT
THE DOTTED LINE (D)

5

E

F

TUCK THE POINT (E) INTO PLEAT (F)

AND THE OTHER POINT (G)
INTO THE PLEAT ON THE
REVERSE SIDE (H)

6

H

G

7

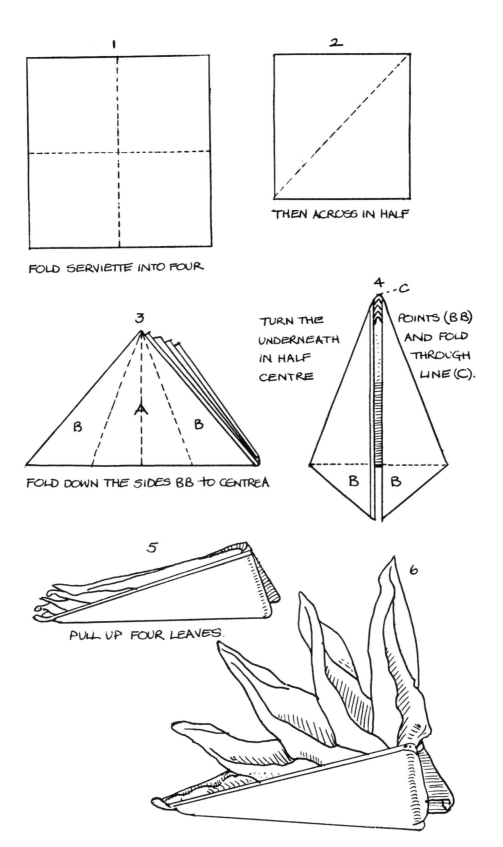

1

FOLD SERVIETTE INTO FOUR

2

THEN ACROSS IN HALF

3

A

B   B

FOLD DOWN THE SIDES BB TO CENTRE A

TURN THE
UNDERNEATH
IN HALF
CENTRE

4   C

POINTS (BB)
AND FOLD
THROUGH
LINE (C).

B   B

5

PULL UP FOUR LEAVES.

6

207

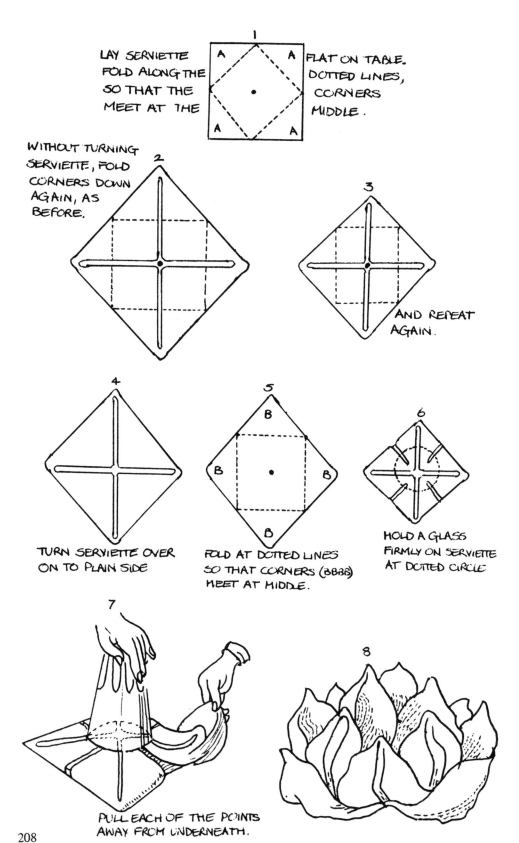

1 LAY SERVIETTE FOLD ALONG THE SO THAT THE MEET AT THE FLAT ON TABLE. DOTTED LINES, CORNERS MEET MIDDLE.

A A

A A

2 WITHOUT TURNING SERVIETTE, FOLD CORNERS DOWN AGAIN, AS BEFORE.

3 AND REPEAT AGAIN.

4 TURN SERVIETTE OVER ON TO PLAIN SIDE

5 FOLD AT DOTTED LINES SO THAT CORNERS (BBBB) MEET AT MIDDLE.

B

B B

B

6 HOLD A GLASS FIRMLY ON SERVIETTE AT DOTTED CIRCLE

7 PULL EACH OF THE POINTS AWAY FROM UNDERNEATH.

8

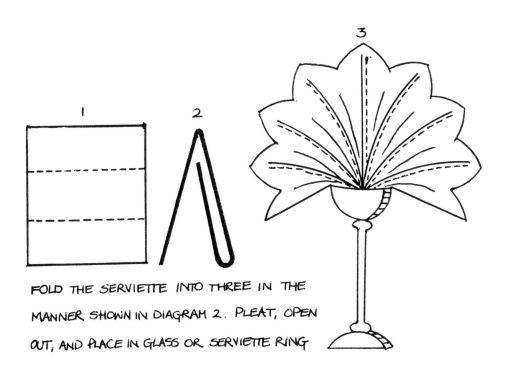

FOLD THE SERVIETTE INTO THREE IN THE
MANNER SHOWN IN DIAGRAM 2. PLEAT, OPEN
OUT, AND PLACE IN GLASS OR SERVIETTE RING

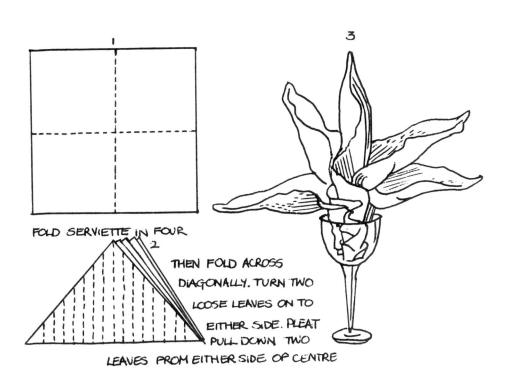

FOLD SERVIETTE IN FOUR

THEN FOLD ACROSS
DIAGONALLY. TURN TWO
LOOSE LEAVES ON TO
EITHER SIDE. PLEAT
PULL DOWN TWO
LEAVES FROM EITHER SIDE OF CENTRE

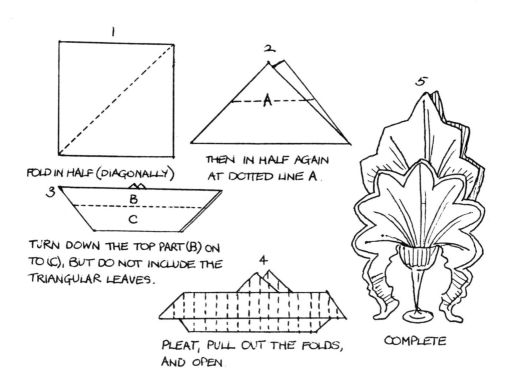

1

FOLD IN HALF (DIAGONALLY)

2

A

THEN IN HALF AGAIN
AT DOTTED LINE A.

3

B
C

TURN DOWN THE TOP PART (B) ON
TO (C), BUT DO NOT INCLUDE THE
TRIANGULAR LEAVES.

4

PLEAT, PULL OUT THE FOLDS,
AND OPEN.

5

COMPLETE

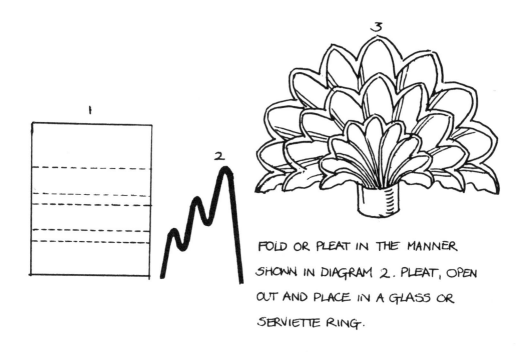

1

2

3

FOLD OR PLEAT IN THE MANNER
SHOWN IN DIAGRAM 2. PLEAT, OPEN
OUT AND PLACE IN A GLASS OR
SERVIETTE RING.

Index

DIPS AND STARTERS

M.W.M.H.— P

SOUPS

FISH

MEAT

213

VEGETABLES

SALADS

DRESSINGS

MILK DESSERTS

BISCUITS, BREAD & CAKES

PARTY SECTION

NOTES